SOJOURNS
of the SOUL

SOJOURNS
of the SOUL

One Woman's Journey around the World and into Her Truth

DANA MICUCCI

QUEST
BOOKS

Theosophical Publishing House
Wheaton, Illinois * Chennai, India

First Quest Edition 2011

Quest Books
Theosophical Publishing House
P. O. Box 270
Wheaton, IL 60187-0270

www.questbooks.net

Cover Photo: Thomas Brown/Digital Vision/Getty Images
Cover design by Kirsten Hansen Pott

Passages in this book were previously published as part of the author's articles in *Art & Antiques* magazine, *Architectural Digest*, and *House Beautiful*.

Library of Congress Cataloging-in-Publication Data

Micucci, Dana.
Sojourns of the soul: one woman's journey around the world and into her truth / Dana Micucci.
   p.   cm.
Includes bibliographical references and index.
ISBN 978-0-8356-0898-5
1. Micucci, Dana—Travel. 2. Women travelers—Biography. 3. Women travelers—Religious life. 4. Sacred space. I. Title.
G226.M53A3 2011
910.4'1—dc22   2011012784

5   4   3   2   1   *   11   12   13   14   15

Printed in the United States of America

To my beloved mother and father,
Mary Jo and Joseph,
my first and best teachers

and there was a new voice
which you slowly
recognized as your own,
that kept you company
as you strode deeper and deeper
into the world,
determined to do
the only thing you could do—
determined to save
the only life you could save.

—Mary Oliver, "The Journey"

CONTENTS

Contents

INTRODUCTION

T he whole world is medicine," says an old Zen koan. In a society shaken by uncertain times, the search for meaning has become increasingly urgent and necessary. Travel is one of the most powerful ways to deepen that search. It broadens our understanding of other cultures, beliefs, and wisdom traditions and teaches us ultimately about ourselves—what attracts and repels us, what we want, who we are. When approached with an open heart and mind, travel at its best can be a creative act, challenging us to redefine ourselves. "Go confidently in the direction of your dreams. Live the life you have imagined," as Henry David Thoreau said.

As a journalist, I've had the privilege of traveling to many of the world's most exotic, sacred places, exploring Aboriginal art in the Australian Outback, the ancient ruins of Angkor in Cambodia, and a newly discovered Egyptian tomb with a well-known archaeologist, among other adventures. I have written mostly about the diverse artistic and cultural traditions of these destinations. But something else happened along the way. I became more intrigued by my inner journey, and the profound connection between art and spirit grew ever more palpable.

For example, while documenting efforts to preserve the exquisite Khmer temples and sculpture at Angkor, one of the world's greatest spiritual monuments inspired by both Hindu and Buddhist beliefs, I walked the "killing fields" amid a new generation of impoverished Cambodians struggling to rebuild their collapsed country. Here, I learned to face my doubts and fears about the future and surrender to a guiding presence. In the Outback, I discovered that the Aboriginal wisdom conveyed through ancient rock paintings is rooted in the integrative dance of spirit and matter—a dance that I must resolve within myself. Each journey offered its own particular thrills, challenges, and teachings. Traveling alone allowed me to focus more intensely inward than I might have in the company of a cherished companion. I immersed myself in the spiritual traditions of these cultures and began applying their wisdom to my life.

The soul journeys I have chosen to write about are those that have had the most powerful impact on my mind, heart, and soul, inspiring me to transform my thoughts, perceptions, feelings, and very way of being. These seven journeys span a fourteen-year period of my life, from ages thirty-four to forty-eight, when I embarked on an outer search for timeless truths and wisdom, only to find that my real destination was myself. The endless quest for self-knowledge, which continues for me, does not come without internal tests and trials. Yet the rewards are great. It is not a path for an exclusive few but one that we all can and must follow if we are to become fully actualized human beings.

Ultimately, we are all on a single journey—a journey beyond the fears, doubts, and judgments that keep us needlessly separated from each other and our own highest selves. Through the ages, the world's great mystics, artists, and truth seekers made the same journey, setting an example for us to follow, and their wisdom inspires these pages.

Whether I was on a specific writing assignment or a more personal mission, the single theme that connects these seven journeys—from the Outback to Cambodia, Egypt, Tibet, the Yucatan, New Mexico, and Peru—is transformation. By that I mean a transformation of the self, in which I was challenged to strip away all previously limiting beliefs and step into my true essence and power. This came about through a series of metaphorical deaths and rebirths. As each journey propelled me into higher dimensions of awareness and consciousness, I realized that such initiations were necessary for spiritual growth and required active engagement, through my intention to realize my fullest potential and surrender to the process, come what may.

The doors of esoteric wisdom opened in what felt like a pre-ordained sequence of seven stages—awakening, surrender, remembering, faith, initiation, healing, and activation—that I experienced through my seven main chakras, or spiritual energy centers of the body. (*Chakra* is the Sanskrit word for "wheel" or "turning.") According to the yogic wisdom tradition, the consistent activation of these spinning energetic vortices—which extend from the base of the spinal column to the top of the skull and serve as transmitters and receivers of life-force energy—greatly assists the soul's infinite journey to enlightenment.

For example, while absorbing the ancient wisdom of the Aborigines in the Outback, I was given the opportunity to connect deeply with the grounding energy of Mother Earth and my sexuality and to learn the true meaning of relationship, which helped to open my first and second chakras. At Angkor in Cambodia, I was forced to confront my shadow side through the second-chakra emotions of grief and despair. In Egypt, my third chakra, the energetic seat of personal power, will, and manifestation was recharged. My journey to Tibet helped me to activate the love and compassion of my fourth, or heart, chakra, along with truthful self-expression, which emanates from the fifth, or throat, chakra. The sacred Mayan sites of the Yucatan and my stay in New Mexico took me deeper into the fourth and fifth chakras, as well as the sixth chakra at the third-eye center, wherein lies our intuition. Peru led me through each of these three chakras to the seventh chakra at the crown of the head, through which we are able to access spiritual knowledge.

Though my experiences were as varied as the landscapes I traveled, many lessons kept revisiting me, demonstrating the inherent similarities of the world's wisdom traditions. Intimate whisperings of the Divine reminded me of the sacred web of connection between all life forms, Mother Earth, and the cosmos, and I learned that I must integrate within myself the many dualities of this Earth plane so that I can fully realize and align with my own divinity. As time seemed to disappear in momentary glimpses of eternity, I learned to be more present in the moment and let go of desired outcomes. And my heart expanded in the ecstatic embrace of unconditional love.

Spiritual lessons on impermanence, ritual and ceremony, sacred art and architecture, synchronicity, trust, prayer, meditation, solitude, and community and service overlapped and interwove, creating an ever-expanding tapestry of truth and beauty that inspires my further exploration, for which I am truly grateful. The French poet Charles Baudelaire wrote of his "horror of home." Given my passion for traveling, I have often wondered whether

I suffer from that same condition. But these soul journeys have shown me that my home is always with me, in my own heart and soul, wherever I go.

I hope my travels will encourage you to reexamine your beliefs and perceptions and open you to new ways of seeing, thinking, and feeling as you undertake your own inner journey. Now, more than ever, world crises demand that we develop a deeper understanding of diverse cultures and wisdom traditions and, therefore, of ourselves. For understanding heightens awareness. Awareness nurtures respect. And respect ultimately breeds love.

The Aboriginals had an earthbound philosophy. The earth gave life to a man; gave him his food, language and intelligence; and the earth took him back when he died. A man's "own country," even an empty stretch of spinifex, was itself a sacred ikon that must remain unscarred . . . as it was in the Dreamtime when the Ancestors sang the world into existence . . . had been poets in the original sense of poesis, meaning "creation."

—Bruce Chatwin, *The Songlines*

1

Into the Outback

Awakening

Under a vast starry sky, deep in the wild bush of Arnhem Land in northern Australia, a region known as the Outback, I am squirming in my tent, unable to fall asleep. Despite the late night chill, I'm on fire; it's as though I'm walking across an endless bed of hot coals. I am exhausted and sweating profusely, and my desperate hope for rest is further compromised by the fact that my ankle is badly sprained, thanks to the clumsy fall I took while boarding the plane in New York days ago—not good considering that two weeks of rigorous hiking lie ahead. My body remains on heightened alert amidst a cacophony of screeching owls, chattering crickets, and howling dingoes. However, hanging thick behind this enchanting night music—laced with the clean, fresh scent of eucalyptus from the eponymous trees so common to the Australian bush—is an unfathomable silence that both delights and disarms me.

It is only because of the silence that there can be noise, so I must be aware of my body being so hot because I know what it feels like to be cold. This is how it is with all pairs of opposites that define our existence—between which we often swing from one extreme to the other without any true contentment or satisfaction. In my early thirties, I'm trying to reconcile the seemingly contradictory poles of my own life—love and work, being and doing, high ideals and humble necessities—while staying balanced and centered without expectations. Easier said than done.

I'm here in the Outback on an assignment to write about Aboriginal art, and I suspect that the Aborigines, the oldest known human culture dating back more than one hundred thousand years, will have much to teach me.

When I began to feel called to delve deeply within, to search for truth and wisdom that has consumed legions of idealists for eons, I thought I could trim a few years off the arduous effort by reading H. H. the Dalai Lama's *The Meaning of Life from a Buddhist Perspective*; surely His Holiness would sum it all up! In my twenties, I passionately adopted Virginia Woolf's dictum to view one's life as a creative act, as though it were a work of art. I took to heart Janet Flanner's belief that "to burn always with this hard gem-like flame, to maintain this ecstasy, is life's greatest challenge." And, of course, there was Joseph Campbell's inspiring imperative to "follow your bliss" whatever the consequences, as well as his conclusion in *The Hero with a Thousand Faces*: "Where we had thought to travel outward, we will have come to the center of our existence. And where we had thought to be alone, we will be with all the world."

So, opting for adventurous uncertainty over routine security, I decided that I would travel the world as a journalist, choosing first my destinations, then my stories. And art, with its many layers of inspiration, would be my vehicle. If I was going to walk the precarious financial edge of freelancing for a living, I might as well be as free as possible. To my delight (and propelled by a lot of hair-raising hard work), my plan succeeded. But, as usual, there were the opposites: my innate optimism is chronically tempered by my self-manufactured discomfort.

A loud thumping calls me back to the Outback.

"What is that?!" I shout. The earth is so alive I can feel it pulsating in my body.

"Kangaroo!" my tent-mate Trish, a native Australian, announces gleefully. "Have you never heard a kangaroo?" She fixes her bright blue eyes on me with such intensity that I feel as though she can see directly into my soul. Beyond her worldliness and aesthetic inclinations—Trish has been a *Vogue* editor and now works as an interior designer—she is possessed of a deep inner knowing that I have rarely encountered. This, combined with her earthy good humor, generosity, and ebullient personality, makes her a magnetic force.

"Of course not! Are they dangerous? How close do they come to humans?!" The fact that I am frozen with fear does not faze Trish, who begins laughing with abandon. "Oh, great! And now, I have to go to the bathroom," I yell and race from the tent to the outhouse, swearing as I trip through the tall bush in the dense darkness, hoping desperately to avoid the kangaroo.

When I crawl back into my sleeping bag, I hear Trish's muffled giggles. We are staying many miles away from civilization at a remote camp owned by bush legend Percy Trezise. It is our home base for excursions to the sprawling sandstone plateau of western Arnhem Land and its thousands of galleries of spectacular, millennia-old Aboriginal paintings, which are among the oldest and richest concentrations of rock art in the world. Our delightful Australian guide, Kate, a tall, elegant blonde with a natural grace and the gentlest of hearts, peeps into our tent.

"You two!" She smiles, shaking her head. "Get some sleep now. We have a big day tomorrow!" A longtime expert in Aboriginal art, Kate has organized a tour of the continent's major Aboriginal art centers for our small group of four. My participation is the result of an unexpected twist of fate. I happened to walk into Kate's gallery in Manhattan one summer afternoon and, captivated by her charm and extensive knowledge, decided that I needed to investigate this incredibly rich artistic tradition, which first expressed itself as early as sixty thousand years ago in numerous rock engravings and paintings throughout Australia.

In the morning we awake to the plangent calls of cockatoos and scramble to get ready for the long day's trek. Hardly a haven of comfort, the camp has crude outdoor shower stalls and a tiny cracked mirror hanging above a tin sink, before which I struggle to apply my red lipstick.

"Hey, isn't there an outlet somewhere around here?!" I scan the premises with frustration, blow dryer in hand.

"We *are* in the Outback," Trish howls. "You're just like that journalist in the film *Crocodile Dundee*! She shakes her head. "Those designer jeans won't last long either."

After a bacon-and-egg breakfast at the long picnic table under the dining tent—during which Trezise, a hearty, charismatic character, recounts his colorful wilderness adventures—Trish and I collect our backpacks and water bottles and venture into the bush with Kate and our other travel companions, Michael and Susan, a kindly, reserved professorial couple from North Carolina. I pick up a fallen eucalyptus branch to use as a walking stick. Though I have wrapped my ankle with a gauze support bandage from Kate's first-aid kit, I'm still limping, and I brace myself for what will likely be an ongoing physical challenge. "Of all times," I mutter, displeased at having to lag behind as Kate, who is beaming and brimming with energy, guides us with the swift, surefooted dexterity of someone who knows this land intimately. Trish's brown leather cowboy hat bobs as a marker in the distance.

The golden sunlight warms the earth and our bodies as we traipse through grassy hills and valleys and dense eucalyptus forests toward the rocky cliff ledges that are our destination. My typically high-octane energy is noticeably drained, and I'm careful to keep myself hydrated. Conscious of my condition, Kate makes an effort to stop and rest now and then. By the time we reach a massive rock face several hours later, my T-shirt and bandana are soaked and my ankle is throbbing. I sit on a boulder, my head between my knees, breathing heavily.

"You okay?" Trish asks.

"Don't worry, I'll be fine."

She reaches into her backpack and offers me some crackers and Vegemite, a salty black yeast paste in a jar to which Australians, who spread it on everything from toast to vegetables, are apparently addicted.

"No, thanks." I grimace.

We proceed further into the sandstone escarpments, stepping precariously along cliff edges, beyond which stretches a magnificent vista of arid, rocky plateau, sinuous rivers, and sweeping grasslands. I try to stay focused on our immediate surroundings, terrified of the abyss below. Even a glimpse downward makes me dizzy. The trek is more arduous than I had imagined. I rarely take physical risks, but I must admit to a secret thrill from the adrenaline rush of imminent danger. Kate leads us into a huge cave, where a stunning gallery of rock art displays simple, elegant, X-ray-like images of animal, human, and spirit forms from Aboriginal mythology. Here are creator-ancestors such as the Rainbow Serpent and Namarrkon the Lightning Man, as well as animals like the kangaroo, long-necked turtle, and barramundi fish that have long functioned both as totems and food sources for the Aborigines. (A totem is usually an animal or other nature-based figure that spiritually represents a group of related people.) I inspect the images more closely, awed that the bold red, black, and white earth pigments have survived for so long. The delicate figures appear to be floating, emanating a curious power. There are concentric circles, too.

The coiling Rainbow Serpent, in particular, captures my attention. It symbolizes the underlying creative energy of the Dreamtime—a period in the distant past when the Aborigines' ancestor gods dreamt, sang, named, and created the Earth and all living things from a void of limitless potential. On an energetic level, the androgynous Rainbow Serpent manifests as a wave-like (or serpentine) rainbow of visible light, comprising both the active masculine and receptive female principles from which all earthly forms arise. The Aborigines believe that this life-giving force also brings the rainy season and thus fertility to the land.

"The hunter-gatherer Australian Aborigines see the body of the nourishing spirit as a serpent energy that connects the earth with the celestial realms," Robert Lawlor wrote in *Voices of the First Day*. The activities of the mythic ancestors "still resonate in the shapes and energies that bathe the earth and all life processes. These energies are often referred to symbolically as the Rainbow Serpent, which . . . exists as a spectrum of various colors, frequencies, or powers. . . . The electromagnetic spectrum, like the Rainbow Serpent, is a profound metaphor for the unity that exists between the tangible and the invisible worlds."

Aboriginal art, too, forms a link between the earthly and spiritual worlds, as well as the present and past and the people and their land. Because the Aborigines have no written language, they have always used art to tell stories that would educate future generations about their culture, Kate explains, shining a flashlight on the rock art images. Most of these stories are based on Dreamtime myths, which for millennia have inspired ceremonial rock, body, and ground paintings as well as more contemporary art forms like the eucalyptus bark paintings that Aboriginal artists from Arnhem Land are making today. The Dreamtime myths describe the origins of the land, whose flora, fauna, and topographical features were laid down as dreaming tracks, or "songlines," by the spiritual ancestors, who sang their way across Australia in a dreaming state.

"Each totemic ancestor, while traveling through the country, was thought to have scattered a trail of words and musical notes along the line of his footprints," Bruce Chatwin wrote in *The Songlines*. "There was hardly a rock or creek in the country that could not or had not been sung." Each feature of the landscape, therefore, has its own story about how it came into existence, depending on which ancestor, whether Kangaroo, Lizard, or Rainbow Serpent, for example, walked that way.

The Aborigines have always believed that the earth is both sacred and perfect, and should therefore be left untouched, as it was in the Dreamtime. Their spiritual connection to it and the gods stretches back to the time of creation, for each Aborigine belongs to a clan associated with a particular totemic species and its related metaphysical ancestor. "The man who went 'Walkabout' was making a ritual journey," Chatwin wrote. "He trod in the footprints of his Ancestor. He sang the Ancestor's stanzas without changing a word or note—and so recreated the Creation." In this sense, Aboriginal songs contain within them a "moral universe . . . in which the structures of kinship reach out to all living men, to all his fellow creatures, and to the rivers, the rocks and the trees."

As an expression of this intricate web of connection, Aboriginal art likewise opens a door to a numinous, moral universe. Kate tells us that the word *painting* in many Aboriginal languages translates to "my country." As in ritual ceremonies, where Dreamtime myths are sung, enacted, and danced in heightened, hallucinatory states of awareness, Aboriginal artists often enter a trance-like state to "sing" their paintings into being, singing the dreaming stories that describe the creation of the land as they paint.

I think about how artistic endeavors in our culture can originate as much from an impulse to reveal and inspire as from one's own personal needs and ambitions. Our emphasis on individual achievement over communal continuity often breeds more isolation than connection, seducing us into a cultural trance of separation from each other, nature, and a higher spiritual order. By associating themselves with their ancestor gods, Aboriginal artists acknowledge and honor their own divinity. How often I have forgotten to do the same.

"One of the main purposes of an image still lies in the act of creation, which regenerates the powers of the ancestral beings and sacred totems," Kate says, explaining that much of the iconography of Aboriginal art is sacred, involving multiple layers of meaning associated with initiation and ceremony. I quickly jot notes. When I look up, I notice that Trish is pacing at a distance from the cave paintings. She appears nervous and distracted. What's going on?

"Secular themes such as female fertility, food gathering, and love magic are also depicted," Kate continues. She points to images on the rocks of a couple engaged in sexual intercourse and two women carrying dilly bags (sacks woven of vines or dried grasses that are worn around the neck) filled with grubs (small white worms that are a basic ingredient of the Aboriginal diet). Dilly bags and digging sticks are the implements used in food gathering, a primarily female activity in Aboriginal culture, which holds its women in great esteem.

"Traditional Aboriginal society is founded on the preeminence of the characteristics of the Universal Feminine, epitomized by its unwavering respect for Earth, which Aborigines refer to as 'the mother,'" K. Langloh Parker and Johanna Lambert wrote in *Wise Women of the Dreamtime*. "Their social order encourages, from infancy, empathetic concern and compassion toward all creatures of nature, as well as deep loyalties and responsibilities to their kin and the group as a whole. . . . Within the Universal Feminine qualities such as receptivity, mutability, inter-relatedness, and diffusion that are predominant in Aboriginal society, the creative Universal Masculine characteristics such as limitation, order, structure, and definition also find balanced expression."

The Aborigines, like other indigenous cultures, recognize that the dualities inherent in the natural world—such as male and female, light and darkness, life and death—are also forces within the human psyche that must be merged in order to experience a state of oneness with all that is. The longing for and painstaking cultivation of this mystical union is a major theme of Aboriginal myths, rituals, and art. So there is more to images like the intercourse couple and the Rainbow Serpent than first meets the eye. Because the Aborigines view "every creature and aspect of nature as a spiritual reflection of the great Ancestral Beings that brought the earth into existence," according to Lambert, all human relationships and interactions must also integrate both the physical and metaphysical dimensions.

I want very much to be able to live in this exquisite state of balance and wholeness and wonder whether I will be up to the task, which is obviously a lifetime undertaking.

I continue taking notes, as Kate explains the intricacies of Aboriginal art. Michael and Susan listen with rapt attention. I am thankful for their easygoing nature, particularly because we are such a small group. They and Kate, with their quiet, peaceful presence, are the perfect foil to Trish's passionate intensity and our garrulous, laugh-infected interchanges. With that thought, I turn to look for Trish. But she has mysteriously disappeared. As the others chat, I slip away and walk farther into the cave, which splinters into a series of small, dark chambers with a dense, musty smell. I feel suffocated and slightly nauseated, so I quickly leave. Outside in the welcoming sunlight, I notice Trish sitting on a boulder.

"Woooooooaaaaa!" she exclaims, as I approach her. "I am not going back in *there*!"

"What do you mean?" I sit down next to her.

"Crazy, strong energy." She scowls. "Felt like I was going to explode, couldn't get my bearings." She looks as though she hadn't slept for days. Then she erupts about the Aborigines, the land, and spirits, speaking at such a breathless pace that I have trouble keeping up. The sentences come in fragments, in a circular pattern that seems to lead nowhere and everywhere at the same time.

"Trish," I whisper nervously. "Trish!" I grab her by the shoulders. She stares at me blankly for a few moments and then calms down.

"I'm all right, don't worry," she says. I breathe a sigh of relief. "There's a powerful spiritual presence inside that cave; the art only magnifies it," she continues. "It was like getting an instantaneous download of all the energy and information in the universe—past, present, and future—nearly blew my circuits!"

I'm not sure how to respond. "It felt strange to me, too."

I was clearly not affected to the same degree as Trish, and I wonder if she somehow connected with the energy of a songline running through the cave. Some anthropologists and scientists believe that the songlines are magnetic force flows emanating from the earth to which the Aborigines possess an acute sensitivity.

"The magnetic songlines guided the physical, ceremonial journeys of the tribes," Lawlor wrote in *Voices of the First Day.* "Initiated men and women learned to travel these subtle and invisible energy veins using their psychic or spirit body. Thus they were able to exchange songs, dances and mythic visions of the ever-unfolding Dreamtime reality over great distances." And each land formation and living creature on the earth carries its own vibration as an "imprint of the metaphysical or ancestral consciousness that created it, as well as the universal energies that brought about its material manifestation."

For the Aborigines, then, the physical and the metaphysical, the visible and the invisible worlds, are not separate (as they are often viewed by Western civilization). I am beginning to understand the depth of this truth. I sense that Trish tapped into the universal consciousness to which the Aborigines have always been attuned, and the immense power of the experience unhinged her.

"Let me explain," Trish continues, her eyes filled with sadness. "I . . . well . . . if you're manic, this is not necessarily a good thing."

"Manic?"

"You know, mania. Have suffered from it for years, took pills, spent time in hospital, against my wishes, I might add! Thanks to my family and friends, I was often yanked right out of my house by the men in the white coats."

"I'm sorry." My heart sinks. "That must be so . . . so painful for you."

"Hell, some people would call me mad!" She laughs, then leans in close as if to reveal a secret. "But I'm not," she lowers her voice. "It's really just a heightened state of awareness, a complete opening of heart, mind, and soul. No barriers, if you know what I mean. It is like soaring out into the stratosphere. Euphoric. Sometimes it just gets the best of me." She gazes into my eyes, waiting for a reaction. "You have some of that, too, but you're grounded, you can handle it."

"Do you get depressed?" I want to comfort her, but I have no experience with mental health issues.

"No, just the mania," she says. "I'm sorry I laid all this on you. But I thought if we were going to spend all this time together, you might as well know. I don't mind talking it about it. Besides, I feel comfortable with you."

"Thanks." My eyes moisten as I reach for her hand. "I feel the same."

"Do you know what you want?" she asks.

Her question takes me by surprise. "Well . . . yes, I think I do." I have never had to verbalize it. "Okay. I want to be a successful writer, of course. Treat people as I would like to be treated. Lead an adventurous, honorable, and conscious life filled with love, joy, and wisdom. And spend it with a wonderful man . . . whom I have yet to find."

"Is that all?" Her eyes widen with expectation.

"I suppose."

"What if it's not that simple?" She smiles knowingly. "Just wait, you may get more than you bargained for."

I suddenly feel challenged and agitated. What if I have no idea what I really want? I have come up with a list of platitudes, after all. It occurs to me that I know very little about myself. I think about all that Trish has endured, yet she is still so spirited and upbeat. Her youthful glow belies the fact that she is eleven years my senior. Though I do not envy her struggles—she is divorced, having reared two children on her own—I admire her inner strength and huge, wide-open consciousness, which, with its unfortunate repercussions, seems both a curse and a rare gift. And while I know I possess my own share of sensitivity and awareness, I wonder what it would be like to see and feel even broader and deeper and more intensely, like Trish does. To me, she is only "mad" in the best sense of the word. She reminds me of a line from the Beat poet Jack Kerouac's *On The Road*: "The only people for me are the mad ones, the ones who are mad to live, mad to talk, mad to be saved, desirous of everything at the same time, the ones who never yawn."

"Let's go, ladies!" Kate shouts, stepping outside the cave and waving us forward. "We need to visit a few more sites before sundown!"

We spend the next few hours hiking and exploring more galleries of spectacular rock art, whose primeval magic seems to work its way through my eyes to a place deep inside where words become inadequate to describe its visceral power. Am I beginning to see as the Aborigines have always seen, think as they have always thought? Even time feels different, and I lose track of it often. It seems to stretch backward and forward ever so slowly without beginning or end—like the circles in the rock art—and I feel cradled, full, and present. "The Aborigines have no concept or word for two things that most torment modern man: the passage of time and the accumulation of possessions," Lawlor wrote in *Voices of the First Day*. During the bumpy jeep ride on our way back to camp, I notice with delight that my watch has stopped.

I recall the hypnotic, circle-saturated paintings that we saw at several galleries in Alice Springs, in the red desert of central Australia, before we headed out to Arnhem Land. Here, contemporary artists from the community of Papunya, such as Clifford Possum Tjapaltjarri and Turkey Tolson Tijupurrula, create abstract, earth-toned acrylic paintings that translate ancestral myths into land maps of concentric circles and dots representing sacred sites, waterholes, clumps of desert scrub, and variations in the local topography and vegetation. Interconnecting lines, or tracks, in the paintings trace the routes of such Dreamtime ancestors as Honey Ant and Wallaby, who journeyed across the land creating its features and infusing them with spiritual power—conveyed through the shimmer of densely packed dots. So even for Aboriginal artists today, there is no separation between life, spirit, and art. All earthly forms and processes belong to and reflect the perpetual dance of creation that originates in an undifferentiated state of unity or absolute oneness.

I think about my own art. Does my writing have to exist apart from me as an objective witness to events? Or, like the circles in Aboriginal paintings, can it connect the substance of my soul with my perceptions of the external world in a cycle of ever-deepening understanding and appreciation?

At Ayers Rock, the sacred Aboriginal monolith that towers flame-orange against the cobalt skies of the central desert, Trish said that she believes the word *understanding* means "standing under"—a humble recognition of our connection at all times to a divine presence both within and outside us. When we hiked around the massive rock (known as Uluru to the Aborigines), with its mysterious caves, eroded sculptural features, and primitive paintings, I felt a power surge in my belly and chest. Later, we watched the sun dip slowly behind the rock, its color shifting to darker shades of orange and red in the evanescent play of light and shadow. There was an insubstantial, surreal quality to the scene which sent a tingle, then alternating waves of heat and chills through me—a sensation that revisits me as we continue exploring rock art sites in Arnhem Land, and I synchronize more deeply with the magical rhythm of this ancient continent—timeless, fluid, serene, and dynamic.

Though I am still limping, my pain seems to have disappeared. Being a city dweller, I am woefully disconnected from nature on a daily basis, which I realize compromises my well-being. Is my Outback initiation heightening my spiritual awareness enough for me to be able to transcend my sprained ankle? One thing is certain: I feel incredibly free and exhilarated, so engaged with my senses, so *alive*.

Hiking through the dense bush scrub, I'm thrilled by the sight of wild horses galloping on a vast open range, a swooping flock of pink-crested cockatoos, fast-dashing kangaroos and wallabies (small squirrel-like creatures), laughing kookaburras, and the ostrich-like flightless emus strutting surreptitiously behind the crackling tall grasses. Even the trees and flowers seem animated with a vibrant life force, as an occasional breeze rustles the leaves of the eucalyptus and paperbark trees and the gold-flowering acacias.

On our return to camp in the late afternoon, we plunge into a billabong—a deep pond carpeted with water lilies. Its icy waters are a welcome relief from the simmering heat. Our nights are filled with laughter and campfire stories, sometimes accompanied by the haunting bass tones of the didgeridoo (an Aborginal ritualistic woodwind instrument made of eucalyptus logs that have been hollowed out by termites.)

This city dweller is growing intimate with nature. It is a nature that caresses my body, leaving me feeling deliciously feminine. At times, the energetic stimulation is overwhelming. When I took kundalini yoga classes in New York, I had little success raising kundalini through my body. (The Sanskrit word *kundalini* means "coiled up." It refers to the latent spiritual potential or cosmic energy that lies coiled at the base of the spine when dormant.) Yet I sense that I may now be getting a taste of what this feels like.

In their initiations, Aboriginal girls must spend time alone in the Outback to experience the interconnection between all living things. "During her isolation she is instructed to listen to the first note that any bird sings throughout the day, to which she must respond with a particular ringing sound," Lambert wrote in *Wise Women of the Dreamtime*. "Likewise, she is to focus her attention so that she is aware of every sound made by members of her tribe in their distant camp. This practice of turning full attention to and filling herself with the sounds, smells, and sights of her natural and social surroundings is believed to increase the life force and animation of her body."

Is this what I'm doing?

"The Dreamtime stories arose from listening to the innate intelligence within all things," wrote Lambert. "In many Aboriginal languages the word for *listen* and the word for *understand* are the same."

Not surprisingly, the freedom with which Aborigines experience their sexuality is an integral component of this holistic vision and is rooted, like all of their earthly preoccupations, in a deep connection with the metaphysical realm. Premarital and extramarital sexual liaisons are encouraged for both sexes, and Aboriginal women, in particular, embrace their sexuality with lusty, joyful abandon. It is considered undesirable, even dangerous, for a woman to be sexually frustrated, according to *Voices of the First Day.*

Given that my own sexual appetite has been aroused, I lament the fact that I'm not traveling with a male companion, though with a kind of strange intuition before leaving New York I have arranged to see Chris in Sydney, where I'll return after the Outback. Chris and I met at the Raffles Hotel in Singapore last year during one of my assignments, and there was enough of an attraction to stay in touch. A native Australian based in Singapore, he generously agreed to fly in for a long weekend. I'm excited by our upcoming reunion, but for the moment my attention is immersed in my adventure.

I long to meet some Aborigines, but they rarely make themselves accessible to outside visitors. This is understandable, for, as it is with many indigenous peoples, their rich culture and refined consciousness have long been severely misunderstood and unappreciated by Western society. For most of their recent history, they have suffered dislocation, land dispossession, and forced cultural assimilation, beginning with the British colonization of Australia in 1788. By the early twentieth century, most Aborigines were confined to Christian missions, government reserves, or cattle stations, where they worked for poor wages. Despite legislation passed in recent years that has given the Aborigines rights to their own land, a wide cultural gap remains between them and the non-Aboriginal population. Many Aborigines still live on the margins of society, and their unemployment rate is several times that of the entire country.

Their plight becomes painfully apparent one day, when we visit the Injalak Arts and Crafts center in the Arnhem Land town of Gunbalanya (formerly Oenpelli), where the Aborigines live in soulless, dilapidated tin shacks with few modern conveniences, many of them suffering from the debilitating effects of alcoholism and diabetes. A fortunate few have been able to make their living as artists. At the art center, we view a host of paintings in natural earth pigments on eucalyptus bark by such well-known artists as Lofty Nadjamerrek and the late Bobby Nganjmira and his sons. Their work is similar in style and subject matter to the ancient rock art we have seen. Among the crocodile, kangaroo, and emu images are ancestral figures in varied states of physical transformation (one of the hallmarks of these spiritual beings was their ability to metamorphose into a variety of other entities, including plants, animals, and humans). My favorites are the paintings of mimi spirits—thin, stick-like figures who are believed to have taught the Aborigines about sexuality and how to paint. Kate explains that the abstract, cross-hatched patterns in these artworks identify Aboriginal clans, while producing a visually vibrating surface or shimmer that invokes spiritual power. I cannot resist buying one.

From Arnhem Land we fly on a small propeller plane to the remote Kimberly region in western Australia in search of more Aboriginal art. The view from this height is spectacular. The red desert cliffs and gorges, waterholes, and clumps of bush scrub make a design of dots, lines, and concentric circles that take on the appearance of a massive Aboriginal earth painting. The plane loops, then swoops down on a tiny airstrip on the outskirts of Broome . . . in the middle of nowhere.

Over the next several days, we drive a jeep in searing heat through the immense, uninhabited desert, leaving clouds of red dust in our wake. It takes my eyes a while to adjust to the brilliant sunlight. We barely make it across the muddy riverbeds, which are just beginning to drain from the recent rainy season.

Unlike in Arnhem Land, where I felt embraced and protected by the fecundity of the earth, here I feel completely exposed. The desert whispers of death. Nevertheless, I'm entranced by its beauty and soon begin to feel more at home. I'm drying up, peeling away—it's like shedding layers of dead skin. And along with the layers go perceptions and beliefs that no longer nourish me. And with each part that peels off, I feel my awareness expand, which is both exciting and a bit unsteadying. But the dusty red film on my hiking boots and clothing keeps me grounded, reminding me of my more pedestrian mission here: I have an article to write!

By day, we view the ancient rock art preserved among the Kimberly's towering cliffs and massive caves; by night we settle at the charming El Questro ranch, outfitted with platform tents; long verandas; rustic, antique bush furniture; and art by the local Aborigines. One afternoon, I receive an unexpected gift while visiting the Waringarri AboriginalArts center in Kununurra. The elderly Aboriginal artist Queenie McKenzie has happened by; her works are for sale here. One of the center's employees translates for me as I excitedly try to engage Queenie, a generously proportioned woman with a warm, toothy smile and deep, dark eyes that seem to hold within them the wisdom of ages.

"What inspires your work?" I ask, hoping to learn something new for my article.

She regards me with a curious grin. "All my paintings tell stories about my land and my people," she says in a melodious voice. "I paint all the time, from morning till the sun goes down."

I pose another question, but Queenie has already lost interest, having struck up a conversation with someone else. The translator shrugs. Despite my further prompting, she has nothing more to say. I understand her reticence. It is difficult to attach words to the inner workings of the heart and soul. Queenie and other well-known Kimberly artists, such as Rover Thomas and Paddy Carlton, depict local topography, animal totems, and the mythical Wandjina cloud spirits found in the region's rock art, working in an abstract style in prints and with earth pigments on canvas.

The following day, my attention is happily diverted from my assignment when Kate takes us to some thermal springs with a spectacular waterfall nestled deep within one of the Kimberly's many inland gorges. It is a remarkably lush oasis. Michael and Susan take off on a hike, while Trish and Kate and I strip down for a refreshing swim. The late afternoon sun filters through a canopy of vines and bottle-shaped boab trees with gnarly branches, creating a golden origami light pattern on the red rocks, while a host of local birds and insects deliver a symphony of sounds. Boab nuts, which look like tiny coconuts, lie scattered about. The waterfall glimmers like a liquid diamond, cascading with great force onto a narrow cliff ledge just above the springs. The Garden of Eden flashes through my mind. Trish and I hoist ourselves onto the ledge so that we are sitting directly under the falls. Ahhhhhhh. Invigorating and soothing at the same time, and suddenly I'm back in that no-time place where there's only dazzling beauty and infinite joy. Trish and I lock eyes; we are on the same wavelength.

"How does this feel?!" she exclaims.

"Like . . . like I'm being baptized," I blurt.

"Good on you!" she shouts back. "Yes, you are!"

After having "died" in the heat of the desert these past days, I'm being "reborn," sitting here naked under the wild, cleansing waters. I've inadvertently participated in my own healing ritual.

"Stories often depict the temporary disintegration of body-spirit relatedness, which is provoked in initiatic procedures and which allows for the possibility of rebirth of an individual within his or her lifetime," Lambert wrote in *Wise Women of the Dreamtime*. "Initiation can be explained as the ritualization of death and rebirth, an experience that is essential to a full embracing of life and one that we seek either consciously or unconsciously in order to prepare for our inevitable final transition. Throughout history, in all religions, these ritual practices have been deemed necessary to unlock a crucial transformative dimension of the human psyche."

Another hallmark of all "initiatic" societies, according to Lambert, is the practice of "ceremonially marking life's major transitions as symbolic death and rebirth experiences and conferring on each stage of life a specific body of secret knowledge." For women, such transitions include the natural processes of menstruation, childbirth, and menopause. Transformation in its myriad forms is thus a necessary, evolutionary aspect of life. The process of transformation also implies a sacred interconnection with all living things. Aboriginal myths often portray humans dying and being reborn into animals, plants, or landforms and vice versa, just as the Dreamtime ancestors themselves frequently shapeshift, or change their physical appearance.

We leave the Kimberly and touch down on the tropical Cape York Peninsula in northern Queensland. On this last leg of our journey across the continent, I am more captivated by our exhilarating side trip to the Great Barrier Reef than by the Aboriginal art, despite its great beauty and interest. We hire a sailboat, with a handsome blond-haired, blue-eyed skipper, and spend the most glorious, sun-drenched afternoon plying the crystalline aquamarine waters of the Pacific, skirting the reef's parched white coral protrusions. I cannot remember ever feeling so tranquil and contented.

Later, we anchor on a small, uninhabited island to snorkel and view the reef close-up. Though I have snorkeled before, I have some difficulty with the mouthpiece, coughing and choking as the water makes its way up my nose, much to Trish's amusement. Being more skilled at this water sport than I, she helps me regain my composure and, in a sweet sisterly way, leads me by the hand through the waters. The exotic undersea vista explodes in a profusion of colors and forms, with many different species of coral, fish, huge clams, and other sea life vying for my attention. I keep blinking, stunned to be able to see with such clarity. The water is soft and warm against my skin as I glide along weightlessly, losing track of where my boundaries end and Trish's hand and the reef begin. I'm floating in the womb of creation, and I don't want to leave.

Afterward, Trish and I relax on the beach and dry off in the sun. She comments on how blue my eyes look. Her eyes, too, are sparkling, filled with light. The sea, the sand, the palm trees, our beach towels—everything around me appears so clear and well-defined, as though it has been newly created, vibrating with an intense energy. I don't feel much like talking, but Trish turns to me expectantly.

"I'm so grateful," I whisper.

"You're learning to see in a new way," she says lovingly.

"Thank you for helping me out there."

"Everything is so much more meaningful, when you share it. I don't just mean sharing experiences and insights. You have to share your light, too." She pauses, as if anticipating a question. "Remember, you're never alone. You're always connected to the universal consciousness. We are multi-dimensional."

I gaze past the reef, across the infinite expanse of sea, its wavelets glimmering with sparks of white light. I've crossed a barrier. And there's no turning back.

This memorable day in paradise ends at the coastal resort of Port Douglas with a curious dinner of emu paté, kangaroo steak, and barramundi fish, followed by a deep, satisfying sleep. The next day I tell Trish that I will be meeting Chris in Sydney, where I've planned to spend a few extra days researching an article on the art scene.

"I cannot believe you!" she shouts. "Afterward you must bring him to my house for dinner!"

In Sydney the following day, we all say good-bye. I know I'll miss everyone, but at least I'll have more time with Trish. My second article feels like a burden, for my main interest now is Chris. He's kind, smart, and very handsome with clean-cut, sandy brown hair. He's also a successful businessman. Check, check, check, all systems go. I wonder whether he could be the *one*?!

I arrive at my hotel to find a huge vase of red roses from him in my room, another good sign. Our reunion is sweet and tender. He is as attractive and attentive as I remember him to be. I spend my days interviewing dealers and artists at the galleries, while Chris meets with clients. Afterward, we take sunset walks along the beach and dine at elegant restaurants.

It is December, which is summertime in Australia. The sunlight is consistently bright, and the magnolias, jacarandas, and flame trees are in full bloom. Sailboats drift gracefully around the white, conch-shaped Opera House overlooking the shimmering harbor. Tile-roofed bungalows stud the surrounding hillsides. The city is gorgeous, so curvy and feminine, fringed with intimate beaches and rocky cliffs. The fire continually burning in the fireplace of my hotel lobby seems out of sync with the lushness of the season. Then again, it is almost Christmas.

As time wears on, I begin feeling, to my surprise, less and less connected to Chris. Our conversations feel flat and uninteresting. He is not living up to my fantasy of him. Even my beautiful hotel suite, with its terrace overlooking the city and our lavish breakfasts in bed, seems like a strange illusion, and I feel oddly removed, observing myself like I would a character in a silly romance novel. The Outback seems to have left me in a suspended state. Yet I also feel more connected than I ever have before—to threads of cosmic consciousness weaving everything together.

Though I have minimal interest in the Sydney art market article, each piece of desired information flows to me at just the right time. I barely consult my city map, for I easily find each gallery and shop with a highly attuned inner compass. In one of the art galleries, I'm shocked when the owner casually lifts a pile of books from her desk only to reveal Trish's business card underneath! She and Trish are friends, but Trish never mentioned this gallery to me. With each moment, I'm aware that I am functioning with much greater lucidity, sensitivity, and efficiency, with fewer internal "coulda, woulda, shouldas." Am I being guided by an unseen hand?

My ankle has completely healed and I'm no longer limping, despite the fact that I have worked it hard for two weeks. In the taxis, I find that I'm unruffled by traffic delays and angry drivers. And when a waitress gets my lunch order wrong between tight appointments, I wait patiently and engage in a pleasant conversation with the couple at the next table. By the end of each day, still buzzing with energy, I'm anxious to tell Chris about this new magical dimension. But he doesn't understand.

"Okay, so on a scale of one to ten, how does he rate?!" Trish asks in a phone call.

"Trish. Shhhhh." I glance at Chris, who is still sleeping beside me.

"Well?" she giggles.

"Okay. Four, maybe five tops," I whisper with regret. How unfortunate, considering that I feel more sensual than ever, having spent two weeks in the Outback.

"Oh, no! I hope you're still coming to my dinner party tomorrow." Trish's voice crackles with her usual passion.

"Yes, yes, we'll be there!"

We have a great time at Trish's party; however, when I catch her eye from across the room she slowly shakes her head—as in "No, he's not for you." She knew the moment we walked in the door. She is the perfect hostess—generous, charming, funny—and a wonderful cook. By the end of the evening, though, she is so supercharged by all the energy that she begins to feel euphoric and becomes manic, launching into a cryptic, breathless monologue like she did in the Outback. My heart floods with compassion, and I don't want to leave her. But Chris convinces me that her other friends will take care of her.

The meltdown comes in a house near Bondi Beach. Given the short time Chris and I have known each other, I'm rather surprised to find myself sitting in his parents' living room trying to make conversation, a frustrating task. Trish was right; Chris and I are not meant to be together. I've known it all along; I just couldn't admit it to myself, so desperately had I hoped we would be a match.

Though I am exhausted, I sleep fitfully that night—unlike Chris, who appears to be anesthetized. But predawn, I awaken.

I'm drenched with sweat. I begin to shiver. I feel weightless, then heavy, and weightless again. More hot flashes, then chills—the same sensations I had in the Outback. Only this time, they are more severe. Can I be ill? My ears are ringing, and my head is throbbing with scattered bursts of pain. It's as if the very circuits of my brain are being rewired. Images and sensations of the Outback flash through me: the vast starry skies, the early-morning screech of cockatoos, the crackle of dry bush grass, clouds of red dust, and the rush of spring water over my head. A piercing, bright light spreads through my mind, then my body; I'm ecstatic. Tears flow. My awareness, my heart, and my mind are blown wide open.

"Are you okay?" asks Chris.

"All this light and clarity." My words race, though I can barely speak above a whisper. "I must nurture it, share it, be responsible to it and with it."

"What?" He gazes at me with a puzzled, helpless look.

"My vision is clearer; my focus is sharper. It's as if the old me, or who I thought was me, no longer exists. Taking small steps for the past five years, but now . . . I've really opened a door. And the light is brighter than ever before." My heart is pounding.

"Uh huh. Maybe when I come to New York you'll tell me more about it, sweetheart." He kisses my forehead and falls promptly back to sleep.

New York? I realize the futility of trying to make him understand. I feel very lonely and want desperately to talk to Trish, who understands everything. Then it hits me. What if I have lapsed into some kind of a hyper-agitated state? I'm gripped with fear.

Wait. I take a few deep breaths and check in with myself again. I am firmly anchored here in this room, in this bed next to Chris.

My body feels very real. No, I have not lost control of myself. Trish showed me what it's like to inhabit the extremes of consciousness, to lose touch with this earthly plane in a way that can cause great pain to oneself and loved ones. Having suffered so intensely for her own gifts, she inadvertently showed me that the real challenge is being able to connect with Spirit while remaining grounded, here and now. This new dimension of being is all about balance and my staying centered within myself no matter what the circumstances. My powerful physical experience just now has reminded me that I'm blissfully, divinely embodied. I am both pure consciousness *and* the sensual being I experienced in the timeless Outback. I am both passion and stillness.

I smile at Chris sleeping peacefully. He is a mirror reflecting back to me the work I need to do, which is nothing less than marrying within myself all of life's dualities—male and female, spirit and matter, time and eternity, the sensual and the sacred— if I am to become a whole, fully integrated person. "Thank you, Chris," I whisper. "Thank you." The Aborigines have always known about and practiced this dance of integration.

The next morning, teary-eyed, I call Trish to say good-bye. She has been such an unexpected gift, showing me the great joys of a true soul friendship, perhaps the most exalted of human relationships. I leave Sydney knowing that we will remain friends for a very long time. On the plane home, I begin writing her a letter about my revelations, as much for myself as for her. Some lines from one of my favorite poems, T. S. Eliot's *Four Quartets*, come to mind: "At the still point of the turning world. Neither flesh nor fleshless; / Neither from nor towards; at the still point, there the dance is."

I gaze down at the Earth, its rocks and trees and bodies of water forming a series of interconnecting circles. I see now that we are all circles whose center is everywhere. What is happening "out there" is not separate from what is happening inside me. All is one with the infinite Divine. That is simply and most profoundly what Aboriginal wisdom has taught me. I want Trish to know that I have touched the still point of the circle, and I have been both shattered and awed by what I have found there.

Meditate on the Guide, the Giver of All, the Primordial Poet, smaller than an atom, unthinkable, brilliant as the sun. . . . I am the beginning and the end, origin and dissolution, refuge, home, true lover, womb and imperishable seed. I am the heat of the sun, I hold back the rain and release it; I am death and the deathless, and all that is or is not. . . . In this sad, vanishing world turn to me and find freedom.

—Bhagavad Gita

2

THE HEART
OF ANGKOR

Surrender

A fter four flights and more than twenty-four hours of continuous travel, I am weary and anxious as our jeep bumps along the primitive roads of northwestern Cambodia in the heart of Southeast Asia. The fiery sun beats relentlessly on my shoulder. The floodplains extending from Phnom Penh to the provincial town of Siem Reap unfurl in a patchwork of lush rice paddies and blackened, scorched earth punctuated here and there with scraggly, lone sugar palms. The contrast between the alternating fertile and lifeless landscape is both striking and unsettling. Bob, a tall, gracious British conservation architect working for a nonprofit international preservation group, is both my driver and my guide.

I have traveled to this far-flung outpost to write about conservation efforts at Angkor—the legendary ancient capital and spiritual center of the Khmer Empire from 802 to 1432 CE that sprawls deep within the tropical jungle near Siem Reap and the great Tonle Sap Lake. Given Cambodia's violent recent history, I naturally met with a deluge of puzzled expressions and warnings from friends and family before I left New York. Why, they wondered, would I want to subject myself to the triple threat of land mines, tropical disease, and the notorious Khmer Rouge—the homegrown Communist group responsible for one of the worst genocides of our time, whose last remaining holdouts continue to undermine the country's stability? Surely there are more agreeable places to travel. Whether I was foolishly naïve or overly enthusiastic, I saw things differently. This was the assignment of a lifetime, and nothing was going to stop me. After all, I reminded loved ones, I'm not a war correspondent. I write about culture. But I never suspected that my assignment would be a catalyst for a much grander adventure than I had imagined.

I listen attentively as Bob fills me in on Angkor's history. Angkor, the Khmer word for city, was erected at the same time as the cathedrals of Chartres and Canterbury in Europe and rivals the Egyptian pyramids in scale. It is one of the archaeological wonders of the world, comprising the ruins of more than a thousand temples and monuments that cover an area of 120 square miles. Built of huge blocks of sandstone without mortar by thousands of local craftsmen for a succession of extravagant Khmer kings, Angkor's mammoth structures are the repository of some of the world's greatest art and architecture, hailed by scholars as works of genius. They represent the cultural zenith of the Khmer Empire, which for more than five hundred years extended from Vietnam to Burma. The great age of Angkor ended when Thailand invaded in 1431, and the capital moved south to Phnom Penh. As the Khmer Empire declined, Angkor's temples were abandoned to the ever-encroaching jungle.

Cambodians have always cherished Angkor as a symbol of national pride. Yet, despite the accounts of early Chinese travelers and a few European missionaries and traders in the sixteenth century, it was little known in the West until the publication in 1863 of the illustrated travel diaries of the French naturalist and explorer Henri Mouhot. In the following decades, artists, writers, and intrepid travelers began visiting Cambodia in search of this mysterious lost city swallowed by the jungle. Beginning in the late 1960s, Angkor became inaccessible once again due to the turmoil of the Vietnam War and civil chaos culminating in the murderous reign of the Khmer Rouge (Red Cambodians), under whom more than one million people perished from 1975 to 1979 in Cambodia's infamous "killing fields." It wasn't until 1991 that United Nations peacekeeping forces reopened Angkor to tourists and allowed international preservation groups to continue their restoration work. At the time of my visit, Pol Pot, the brutal Khmer Rouge dictator, is still alive and hiding out near the Thai–Cambodian border, as are many of his henchmen and a corps of loyal soldiers. (Later, I would learn that Pol Pot died in his sleep, regrettably without being tried for war crimes.) There is also an active Khmer Rouge contingent based in the Kulen Hills not far from Siem Reap.

"Are there Khmer Rouge *in* Siem Reap?" I ask warily, a wave of fear coiling through me.

"Haven't heard of any," Bob says. "Let's not dwell on that. There are so many treasures awaiting you. But you've had a long trip. You need to rest first."

"I can't wait! What are we doing tomorrow?"

"Don't worry yet about tomorrow." His expression suddenly dims. "There has been a slight change in plans, however."

"I see," I hesitate. "Is everything all right?" The serious tone of his voice makes me uneasy.

"Yes, yes, everything's fine. But we won't be going to Banteay Srei, unfortunately."

"Banteay Srei," I repeat slowly.

"One of the temples. A jewel of Khmer art and architecture, known for its many beautiful sculptures of women."

"Why can't we see it?"

Bob considers his response. "Out of the way, won't have time."

The small town of Siem Reap is nestled among tall gum, fig, and kapok trees and an abundance of colorful tropical foliage—bougainvillea, banana plants, red-leafed flame trees, and fragrant frangipani. Crude, thatched-roof huts on stilts are scattered along the roadside and throughout the rice paddies that stretch like an emerald carpet to the horizon. Some peasants swing lazily on hammocks inside their open-air huts, which bear few furnishings or necessities, while others toil in the paddies, their conical straw hats shielding them from the sun. Extremely thin, scantily dressed children run and shout and beg on the dusty, unpaved streets, trafficked by old, worn bicycles; rickshaws pulled by motorcycles; and wooden carts hauling fruits and vegetables. Mothers swaddle babies in red-checkered scarves called *kramas*. Many others wear the kramas around their necks and heads or carry them as food sacks on their way home from the market.

We meet with generous smiles as we pass into town and then through patches of charred earth pockmarked with bombed-out concrete buildings recalling the massive destruction of the war years. It is as though whatever peace and harmony may now exist among Cambodians is overshadowed by a lingering sorrow, which has already penetrated my heart with a profound, unyielding heaviness. I know that Cambodia is one of the world's poorest countries, and it is painfully obvious that these people are barely surviving. Despite my fatigue, my senses are heightened; I have entered a hauntingly exotic land.

"The killing fields," Bob solemnly points out, as if reading my thoughts. "Don't forget, there are still a lot of land mines around Siem Reap and Angkor, leftover from the war. You have to be very careful."

"I know. I saw the film. It was horrifying." I stiffen. Even though I have prepared myself for an adventurous trip, Cambodia's dangers have suddenly become an unsettling reality.

"No telephones or hot water in Siem Reap," he adds. "And most people have no electricity. Which means no air conditioning. And you won't find any newspapers either. Takes some getting used to." Bob's dignified bearing and demeanor belie the fact that he has spent most of his life working on conservation projects in harsh third world conditions. Either despite or because of this experience, he has a relaxed, even-tempered nature that comforts me.

We pull up to a compound of modest teak bungalows on stilts. The Auberge D'Angkor, a French-owned guesthouse, occupies a secluded spot at the edge of the jungle. Shrouded by jackfruit and litchi trees, banana plants, and pink and purple bougainvillea, it does not appear to be within walking distance to anything. Bob explains that unfortunately there is no room for me at the conservation house where he and his wife, Norma, and other international conservators are staying. He helps me inside with my luggage, promising to pick me up the following morning to begin our tour of Angkor.

"How far away is your house, Bob?" I'm reluctant to say good-bye.

"Not far, about twenty minutes. Enjoy the evening, get some rest." He waves politely and drives off.

"Wait!" I call out, realizing that I don't have his address or telephone number. Then I remember that there are no phones here. No phones, no electricity, no hot water. This mantra of unpleasant inconveniences is just beginning to sink in. But given the hardships that Cambodians face daily, I remind myself that I should feel grateful for the opportunity to be here.

To my delight, the Cambodian proprietor, Madame Sokha, speaks French. This vestige of colonialism, however oppressive that history may be, is especially welcoming, since I learned the language while living in Paris. A slight, jovial woman eager to be of service, Madame Sokha shows me to my room, which seems more like a monastic cell with its tiny twin bed, single nightstand, makeshift muslin drapes, and crude toilet and shower stall. I unpack, shower, and climb into bed for a nap, but I can't fall asleep. So I wander back to the lobby veranda, which is decorated with beautiful ruby-red and indigo silk wall hangings and cushions in the woven tie-dyed-like ikat designs for which Cambodia is famous.

A breeze filters through the teak shutters, offering some relief from the oppressive heat. Despite the refreshing shower, my body is once again damp with sweat. Madame Sokha quickly arrives with a Cambodian version of planter's punch. I thank her and relax on the sofa sipping my drink, a ceiling fan whirring softly above my head. A footbridge leads from the lobby to the inn's thatched-roof restaurant, which is perched on a small island surrounded by a fish-filled pond. The lazy, tropical ambience is charming. Yet I feel tentative and disoriented, as though I am viewing everything through a dreamy haze. I want to blame it on jet lag because I am obviously exhausted, but there is something else going on. The auberge is oddly silent. I suppose that I must be one of few guests here, for I have not seen a single person other than Madame Sokha.

My mind drifts to the short, tense flight from Phnom Penh to Siem Reap on an old, crumbling Russian Aeroflot plane bereft of seat cushions and arm rests and with mysterious wires dangling from the cabin ceiling. An ominous entrée, perhaps? With that thought comes the alarming question: what on earth am I doing in Cambodia? I am here alone without any means of communication with the outside world! I can't believe Bob left me. I could use a tranquilizer, though I have never taken one. There is a bronze Buddha statue in an alcove. His serene smile momentarily calms me. Two men scurry through the lobby dressed in army fatigues. Upon noticing me, they stop to introduce themselves. Jean and Benoit are French doctors volunteering for Médecins Sans Frontières, or Doctors without Borders, the international relief organization that provides free medical care throughout the third world. I'm relieved to see other guests and happy for the unexpected company.

"Are you alone?" Jean inquires in English. He seems visibly surprised. He is tall and lanky with a close-trimmed beard.

"No, my colleague lives close by. I'm a journalist writing about Angkor." I realize that a young, single American woman must look out of place here. It is 1996 and sophisticated tourism has yet to infiltrate this corner of the world. Jean glances sternly at the ruggedly handsome Benoit, who is listening to an old shortwave radio perched on his shoulder.

"Don't venture too far outside Siem Reap," Benoit warns. "It is not safe." He offers a tentative smile.

"I'll keep that in mind," I reply with confidence. "I'm sure my friend will take good care of me." I don't want to be stereotyped as a damsel in distress by some macho French men, even though I'm certain that I have just turned whiter than a sheet.

"But didn't you hear?" Jean says with urgency.

"Hear what?"

"A British anti-mine personnel was kidnapped by the Khmer Rouge yesterday."

I'm stunned.

"At Banteay Srei," Benoit interjects.

"Oh, no!" I croak. So that's why Bob cancelled our visit. He didn't tell me, because he didn't want to scare me.

"And take care about the mosquitoes," says Jean in a fatherly tone. "Malaria and yellow fever are rampant."

"Thanks for all the good news, guys." I try to muster a smile as they start out for their jeep. "Leaving already?"

"Our last night here, on our way to Vietnam." Benoit shakes my hand good-bye.

"Good luck, then."

"Remember, *faites attention!*" they shout in unison, speeding off in a cloud of dust.

I return to my room, very much on edge, wishing the doctors were still here. Between the suffocating heat and looming threats it is nearly impossible to sleep.

Bob arrives early the following morning, as planned, and honks his horn. It is a relief to see him. I tell him about my visit with the French doctors, and he reassures me that I'm in good hands. As we head toward Angkor, my anxiety from the previous night soon fades into anxious anticipation. That is, until we are halted at a number of military checkpoints patrolled by tanks, army trucks, and stone-faced Cambodian soldiers bearing rifles. Bob produces documentation and a soldier waves us forward into the archaeological zone. My pulse quickens as I spy the dazzling stone spires of Angkor Wat piercing through the jungle's morning mist. I feel like a child discovering a magical fairyland.

"In the province bearing the name *Angkor*... there are ruins of such grandeur, remains of structures which must have been raised at such an immense cost of labor; that, at the first view, one is filled with profound admiration and cannot but ask what has become of this powerful race, so civilized, so enlightened, the authors of these gigantic works? One of these temples—a rival to that of Solomon, and erected by some ancient Michelangelo—might take an honorable place beside our most beautiful buildings. It is grander than anything left to us by Greece or Rome," the late nineteenth-century French explorer Henri Mouhot wrote in his diary.

We begin our visit at Angkor Wat (*wat* means "temple" in Khmer), the largest and best preserved of Angkor's temples, whose most salient feature is a crown of five towers shaped like lotus buds, surrounded by numerous courtyards and chambers. Walking toward the temple on the long causeway that spans what was once a vast moat, I'm conscious of leaving the familiar world for another space and time. Giant stone lions guard the steep stairways, and covered galleries of bas reliefs (carved wall sculptures) flank the ascending terraces. Several orange-robed Buddhist monks acknowledge us with generous smiles.

My heart sinks at the sight of children with missing arms and legs; they are begging around the temple. Victims of exploding land mines, many of them are orphans whose parents died in the killing fields. Their eyes are round and wide and hopeful, and they are obviously malnourished. The simultaneous presence of tranquil monks and suffering children, evoking the extreme conditions of war and peace, are graphic reminders of the often harsh dualities that define our earthly existence—a theme that will come to dominate my journey, as it did in a less threatening way in the Outback.

As we climb the terraces, Bob explains that Angkor Wat was built in the early twelfth century as a funerary temple for King Suryavarman II and dedicated to the Hindu god Vishnu. Khmer kings believed in the *devaraja*, or "god-king," legend—a religious belief introduced by Jayavarman II, the first ruler of the Angkor period—whereby they identified themselves with a particular deity whom they believed would protect them and with whose spirit they wanted to merge. These kings are believed to have been perceived as the earthly incarnations of Hindu gods such as Vishnu and Shiva, or the Buddha, endowed with divine power to protect their kingdom. In a refreshing example of religious tolerance, Hinduism and Buddhism coexisted peacefully at Angkor. Freestanding sculptures of their representative divinities, as well as idealized, deified portraits of the Khmer kings and their ancestors, once adorned Angkor's temples. I have long admired the ethereal grace and beauty of the Khmer sculpture on display at New York's Metropolitan Museum of Art and the National Museum of Asian Art Guimet in Paris.

Each ruler of Angkor consolidated his power by erecting a temple mountain in honor of his chosen god. A symbol rooted in Hindu and Buddhist myths, the temple mountain represents the cosmic Mount Meru—the center of the universe and the mythical dwelling of the gods. The outer enclosing wall symbolizes the mountains around the earth, and the surrounding moat is the cosmic ocean. Like other temple mountains at Angkor, Angkor Wat was inspired by Indian and Javanese prototypes. Its construction reflects a complex system of cosmological and religious beliefs, incorporating calculations based on the seasons and movements of the planets, all meant to ensure that the temples were in harmony with the cosmic order. In Hindu and

Buddhist mythology, spiritual beings inhabited different levels of the mountain. Devotees ascended the levels of the temple to gain spiritual enlightenment, but only the priests were allowed in the innermost sanctuaries. Like the pyramids of Egypt and those of the ancient Maya in Central America, whose builders were also master astronomers, Angkor's temples represent the interface between heaven and earth. To enter these structures is to move from an earthly to a spiritual realm.

For several hours, we navigate Angkor Wat's dusty corridors and deserted chambers, some of which bear crumbling statues of Vishnu and smooth, pillar-like lingams mounted on pedestals. (Lingams, or erect phalluses, are Hindu symbols of the creative life force.) Around them are scattered the remains of offerings—burnt incense sticks, fruits and flower petals left by worshippers. In the long covered galleries, elaborate bas reliefs narrate Hindu epics, such as the Ramayana and Mahabharata, and depict historical Khmer battles. Hindu deities, Buddhas, mythological beings, and ornate foliage and scroll motifs also animate the lintels, walls, pillars, and pediments of this majestic temple, revealing the sophisticated artistry and cosmology of the Khmer civilization. I rapidly take notes as Bob points out the details of Khmer sculpture, much of which was meant to depict the spiritual quality of the gods in anthropomorphic terms. Ranked by scholars as among the finest in the world, this sculpture has an otherworldly presence, yet also incorporates the naturalistic detail of the human form. I am entranced.

We pause in front of a massive bas relief depicting the churning of a milky ocean, which gave birth to the universe, according to Hindu mythology. Numerous gods pull at a long snake-like rope in what appears to be a tug of war. One team represents darkness and evil, the other goodness and light, and together they churn the elixir of immortality from the ocean. All around them float numerous Apsaras—sensual celestial dancers adorned with complex layered crowns, pleated skirts, and elaborate jewelry—who serve as mediators between heaven and earth. I study the scene closely, for it appears to hold an important message. For me, the message is that the dualities that define our earthly existence and cannot exist without each other must be continuously reconciled or integrated in order to transcend what the sacred Hindu Bhagavad Gita calls "this sad, vanishing world." The Bhagavad Gita, which means "Song of the Blessed One" in Sanskrit, is both a love song to God and a manual for how to live in a transient world of seemingly endless sorrows.

In the Gita, the young warrior Arjuna is stalled, refusing to enter a battle he is meant to fight, when his charioteer, the god Krishna, teaches him how to become a warrior of the soul, a truly enlightened being. Arjuna comes to realize that what is most important is to confront and win the battles within his own heart and mind, to connect with his essential Self, or *atman*. For therein lies the seat of his divinity. This is the ultimate quest, the true mission of our lives on Earth, which requires sustained awareness, discipline, and much hard work. Our belief that we are separate from the perfection of the Absolute, or Godhead, gives rise to our daily struggles and their attendant fears, guilt, and chaos.

Krishna advises Arjuna that the key to overcoming our greatest enemies—hatred, ignorance, and selfishness—lies in the simple yet profound spiritual practice of letting go of the desire for specific outcomes from our actions. We must, therefore, perform our daily tasks with a kind of detached attachment, which brings inner peace and freedom. "You have a right to your actions, but never to your action's fruits," the Gita says. "Act for the action's sake. And do not be attached to inaction. Self-possessed, resolute, act without any thought of results, open to success or failure. This equanimity is yoga."

It is difficult to reconcile the sublime wisdom of the Gita and the Hindu belief system, which so inspired the artists, architects, and inhabitants of Angkor, with the present-day horrors that have plagued their descendants, both as victims and as perpetrators of unspeakable violence. How could all of this misery have been avoided? Exactly how do we let go? How do we become the spiritually enlightened beings that the Gita exalts? Krishna, who represents God and thus our highest Self, tells Arjuna: "Abandoning all desires born of his own selfish will, a man should learn to restrain his unruly senses with his mind. Gradually, he becomes calm and controls his understanding; focusing on the Self, he should think of nothing at all. However often the restless mind may break loose and wander, he should rein it in and constantly bring it back to the Self. When his mind becomes clear and peaceful, he enters absolute joy; his passions are calmed forever; he is utterly absorbed in God. . . . For men whose minds are forever focused on me, whose love has grown deep through meditation, I am easy to reach, Arjuna."

Beyond meditation, the best practice is simply to "surrender," according to the Gita. The man [woman] Krishna loves best is "He [She] who has let go of hatred, who treats all beings with kindness and compassion, who is always serene, unmoved by pain or pleasure, . . . He who neither disturbs the world nor is disturbed by it, . . . The same to both friend and foe, the same in disgrace or honor, suffering or joy, untroubled, indifferent to praise and blame, quiet, filled with devotion, content with whatever happens, at home wherever he is."

We climb to one of the top-level terraces of Angkor Wat, where Bob allows me some time alone to enjoy the magnificent vista. I perch on the ledge of a stone window facing the sun, an orange fireball hovering like a ripe nectarine above the horizon. The ancient city below seems to extend infinitely in all directions and is veiled by a dusky, gauze-like haze. From this perch, Angkor appears like a fleeting figment of my imagination. The undercurrent of unease that has haunted me since my arrival evaporates into a comforting serenity; my everyday concerns seem insignificant, even nonexistent. This is a temporary relief from the restlessness and vague dissatisfaction that I have been feeling lately, the pervading sense that something is missing.

Some of my restlessness has had to do with the daily challenge of trying to survive as a freelance writer. I've had to work around the clock just to stay afloat, the pay is lacking, and I've been unable to sell a proposal for my first book. Everything feels so frustratingly tenuous, and I've been impatient to move forward. Perhaps Angkor holds some answers.

"This fleeting world is like a star at dawn, a bubble in a stream, a flash of lightning in a summer cloud, a flickering lamp, a phantom, and a dream," says the Diamond Sutra, a sacred Buddhist text.

Okay, I get it. As long as I'm in the dream, and the dream doesn't last, I might as well try to worry less and enjoy each moment more fully, not as a means to a desired outcome, but as an end in itself, wherever it may lead. Not so easily achieved. Fortunately, I recently attended a retreat center in New York, where I learned how to meditate in the Buddhist tradition of Vipassana, or insight meditation, which trains one "to see" using direct perception. This ancient meditation technique, supposedly developed by Siddhartha Gautama Buddha himself, cultivates self-transformation through both introspection and experiential observations about the self, mind, and matter. The particular form of Vipassana I learned emphasizes an awareness of breathing as a gateway to higher consciousness based on insight into the impermanent nature of reality. At the most basic level, it is supposed to help me tame my raging thoughts and remain more consistently calm and centered in the midst of perceived turmoil. Of course, this takes considerable time, practice, and patience.

As we drive back to town through the vast, empty, scorched fields, my heart grows heavy again. I think about T. S. Eliot's poem *The Wasteland*, whose haunting evocation of a disintegrating civilization mirrors the desolation that surrounds me. But even *The Wasteland*, where thunder eventually brings cleansing rains, ends with a Hindu prayer of peace: "Shantih, shantih, shantih" (the peace which passes understanding). I repeat those lines to myself like a magic spell, as though they have the power to protect me against the darkness that looms so heavily here.

"Over there," says Bob, pointing to a narrow dirt road leading into the jungle. "At the end of that road is a big pile of bones. Do you want to see it?"

"No!" I blurt. "I mean, I can't. I just can't go there."

"It's okay, I understand." Bob is possessed of a preternatural calm and composure that is starkly at odds with the alarming realities and the remnants of the killing fields surrounding us. It would be easy to misinterpret this poise as cool indifference, but I suspect that Bob has had to develop an emotional shield in order to carry out his important, compassionate work.

Much of my unease stems from guilt—as both an American citizen and a privileged tourist who cannot begin to imagine the deprivations to body and soul that scar life in a war-torn country.

The United States' covert bombing of Cambodia beginning in 1969 during the Vietnam War contributed greatly to destroying and destabilizing the country, helping to pave the way for the Khmer Rouge's genocide and then the subsequent occupation by Vietnam. Though I was a young girl at the time, I cannot help but feel an unnerving complicity. It is the same feeling I had years ago when I visited the beautiful Vietnam War Memorial in Washington, D.C. As I read the names of the fallen soldiers, I couldn't help but notice my reflection on the Memorial's smooth granite surface. It was like coming face to face with my shadow.

Because I think of myself as a good, well-meaning person, this realization of my lurking shadow is especially difficult to accept. But no one is an isolated entity exempt from participation in the greater whole with all its uncomfortable dualities. The American physicist J. Robert Oppenheimer, one of the creators of the atomic bomb, famously recognized the overwhelming power of his own shadow side. "I am become Death, shatterer of worlds, annihilating all things," he said, quoting the Bhagavad Gita upon witnessing the first atomic explosion in New Mexico in 1945. Granted this is an extreme example, but Oppenheimer must have believed that his intentions were noble when he invented the bomb.

The contemporary tragedy of Cambodia has fascinated me since I was a teenager, when it unfolded before my eyes on television. When Pol Pot and his Communist Khmer Rouge regime came to power in 1975, after a debilitating five-year civil war, they wanted to transform the country into an agrarian society of worker-peasants. But their "utopian" experiment soon became a horrific nightmare for the Cambodian people. During their four-year reign of terror, religion was abolished, schools were closed, and families were separated, according to reports in the *New York*

Times. Intellectuals, Buddhist monks, and minority groups were killed, and everyone was forced out of the cities to work in the countryside, mostly by hand in dreadful conditions from morning to night. Holidays and entertainment were banned. Children informed on their parents, and those who refused to comply were brutally murdered, sometimes buried alive or fed to crocodiles. Many thousands died of starvation, disease, or overwork. Others were tortured and executed.

The Documentation Center of the Cambodia Genocide Program, which is administered by Yale University, estimates that a quarter of the country's population in 1975—about 1.7 million people—perished from these atrocities. The bones and skulls of the dead lie in heaps on thousands of Pol Pot's killing fields around Cambodia. Many of those responsible for the genocide have yet to be brought to justice, and torturers still live among their victims, while political instability, corruption, and intermittent violence continue to plague the country.

Surrounded by the ghosts of this grisly past, I am overcome with anger. If a benevolent God truly does exist, then how could he have let this happen?! It is a question that many of us have asked at one time or another about all varieties of senseless suffering. And it is a main theme of Fyodor Dostoyevsky's *The Brothers Karamazov*, one of my favorite novels, in which Alyosha, a young seminarian seeks wisdom from his teacher Father Zossima, who says that evil exists to present opportunities for love and forgiveness: "If the evil doing of men moves you to indignation and overwhelming distress, even to a desire for vengeance on the evil-doers, shun above all things that feeling. . . . Remember particularly that you cannot be a judge of any one. For no one can judge a criminal, until he recognizes that he is just such a criminal as the man standing before him, and that he perhaps is more than all men to blame for that crime. . . . Though that sounds absurd, it is true. If you can take upon yourself the crime of the criminal your heart is judging, take it at once, suffer for him yourself, and let him go without reproach. . . . 'What is hell?' I maintain that it is the suffering of being unable to love."

When I first read these words, I thought Father Zossima was asking too much. But it makes more sense to me now that Cambodia is reflecting to me the frightful face of unimaginable evil. There is nothing left to do but to surrender to the darkness and be liberated by it. Not only does this apply to darkness on a grand scale but to all the instances in my life when I've felt mistreated by others who do not show me the kindness and consideration I would like. The Gita, too, offers consolation through Krishna, the living embodiment of the Absolute—an infinite wholeness that is neither benevolent nor malevolent but holds within itself both good and evil and the power to extinguish them altogether.

Over the next few days, Bob and I trek further into the jungle to explore more of Angkor's temples. The roots of towering fig and gum trees strangle fallen stones and collapsed porticoes like the tentacles of a massive octopus. Cryptic Sanskrit and Khmer inscriptions hint of untold mysteries. It is like a scene from an Indiana Jones film. As we investigate the temples' secret chambers, axial staircases, and soaring tower shrines, I walk only along marked pathways, carefully sidestepping the stray land mines that Bob warned me about. Swarms of mosquitoes are on the attack, and I constantly sip water to keep from dehydrating. Bob has given me a krama, which I use to dab my sweaty face and body. My eyes tear, as usual, at the sight of several maimed, barefoot children begging for food and money. I take some bills out of my pocket and fold them into a little girl's hand. She lowers her eyes, as if embarrassed, and smiles gratefully.

Local craftsmen haul, chisel, and replace stone fragments, directed by several international conservators, whom I interview for my story. They explain that the temples were surprisingly little affected by the upheavals of war, having succumbed over the years to more primary threats: damage caused by the suffocating jungle and monsoon rains; looters who sell artifacts on the international art market; and, only recently, more tourists. While these massive structures are clearly deteriorating, they nevertheless have remained largely invincible to the ravages of time.

At the breathtaking monastic complex of Preah Kahn, an enclosure wall bears numerous intricately carved sandstone Garudas—anthropomorphized birds that function as guardian protectors of the site. Its shrines, halls, and pavilions are decorated with sensual deities and the familiar Apsaras, the celestial female dancers that burst forth in graceful profusion on so many walls at Angkor. Another striking sculptural feature at Preah Kahn and other sites at Angkor is the Naga—a mythical serpent supported by rows of gods and demons flanking the long causeways leading to the monuments. The Naga is said to represent a rainbow uniting the worlds of man and god, much like the Aborigines' Rainbow Serpent. Walking among Angkor's ruins, I feel as though I have entered a privileged sanctuary that has been long protected by an otherworldly presence. As Bob explains the intricacies of conservation work, I momentarily forget about the land mines, the Khmer Rouge, the kidnapping, and the French doctors' warning.

"When I first arrived, the jungle had completely taken over," he says, guiding me through Preah Khan. "Huge gum trees were growing over and around the stones, and there was grass up to my head. The Cambodians were struggling to rebuild their country after years of destruction, and most of the educated population, including conservators, had died in the killing fields. I realized that we had to help these people." He speaks urgently and excitedly, waving his arms like a man possessed of a great mission. I admire his passion and dedication.

"Most importantly, we're training Cambodian craftsmen and architecture students who will be able to carry on conservation work at Angkor after our group pulls out," Bob adds, as I continue scrawling in my notebook. "Hopefully, these new jobs and skills will contribute to the future peace and economic stability of the country." He wipes his forehead with his handkerchief. Relaxing his professional tone, he turns to me. "You must be hungry by now. C'mon, let's get some lunch!"

Each day, Bob and I and the other conservators return to the conservation house in Siem Reap for lunch. We dine in a modest room at a long table on delicious grilled fish, rice, and vegetables with a subtle sweet and sour flavor, which the Cambodian cooks prepare in an adjacent open-air kitchen that also happens to accommodate three toilets! (I try not to think about this.) I enjoy conversing with Isabel, a French architect; Juan, a charismatic stone specialist from Guatemala; and Nala and Sophea, two bright young Cambodian architects. It feels good to be part of a community, after focusing so much on my work and being alone at the bungalow each night. Sometimes we eat dinner together, too, after which Bob and Norma, a generous, good-natured woman who looks after me with a quiet maternal charm, invite me to their apartment upstairs for a nightcap. We relax on the veranda with a few beers and talk and laugh about our travels. The nights are humid and extremely dark, infused with the sweet scent of jasmine and illumined only by the distant glimmer of starlight.

After lunch one afternoon, Nala, Sophea, and I take a walk along the dirt road near the conservation house. Recent graduates of Cambodia's School of Architecture, they are petite, attractive, and clever. Sophea is slightly taller and more reserved than Nala, who asks me many questions about life in America. Their English is excellent, and they have radiant smiles. Of course, I'm also eager to learn from them. Though they were just children during the Khmer Rouge's reign, they still remember the chaos and destruction. Sophea's father, a doctor, died in the genocide, as did many of their relatives.

"I worry so much," Nala says. "The situation here is still not stable. I'm afraid everything will be taken away from us again." Her face tightens with anxiety. Sophea nods in agreement, her eyes tearing.

"I'm sorry." I don't know what else to say, realizing that any attempt at consolation must seem empty and inadequate.

Sophea links her arm in mine. "Don't worry." She smiles lovingly.

"I wouldn't blame you for not liking us very much," I say, ashamed.

"Who, you mean the Americans?" Nala asks.

"Yes, all of us who contributed to what happened."

"Oh, no, we like the foreigners," Sophea says.

"Cambodians think they are good people," Nala chimes in, without the slightest trace of resentment.

I'm surprised by this unexpected show of compassion and forgiveness.

"C'mon," Nala grasps my other arm. "Let's go to the temple!" She points down the street to a whitewashed, bell-shaped structure crowned with a tapering spire.

"But what about the Khmer Rouge and Pol Pot?" I ask. "How can you forgive them?"

"What's done is done," says Sophea, waving her hand as if banishing forever all painful memories. She meets my eyes with a sparkling smile.

"Married?" Nala asks.

"No, not yet." I'm surprised yet tickled by her instant familiarity.

"Good. Neither are we," Sophea says.

"Men. Too much trouble!" Nala giggles.

"But you must have a boyfriend." I glance at each of them. "You're both beautiful."

"No boyfriends," Sophea states flatly.

"Not good to have a boyfriend unless you want to marry," Nala adds.

"I understand. So you are true feminists," I tease. Then I realize that this word likely does not exist in the Khmer language, so I explain it.

They nod in agreement, and we burst out laughing as we walk arm in arm to the stupa. Once inside, we light some incense sticks and place them before the Buddha statue, which is surrounded with additional offerings of colorful flowers and fruits.

"We came last week," Nala whispers, as she and Sophea bow their heads in prayer. "When our friend died."

"Hepatitis," Sophea adds solemnly. "We all passed around a candle and blew the flame toward her ashes in a jar."

"Why?" I ask.

"Because we are blowing in her spirit for her next life," Nala replies.

"We don't believe life ever ends," Sophea reflects. "Unless you become enlightened and don't have to reincarnate." In Cambodia, I have been continually reminded of the fine line between life and death. At times, the two have seemed almost indistinguishable.

The following morning, we all take an excursion to Rolous, one of the oldest temple sites at Angkor, dating to the ninth century. It is less intact than the others and farther afield. We are planning to spend the day there, and Norma has packed a picnic lunch. Though I'm excited about the adventure, I have never been so anxious about a casual drive through the countryside. For about an hour we bump along in the scorching heat in a big pick-up truck. The dirt roads are particularly rough as we head into what seems like an infinite no-man's-land of dry, lifeless fields. We pass several military checkpoints and bunkers with machine guns pointed toward the road. I shudder as a tank rolls past. Again, the reality of this lawless, war-scarred country weighs heavily. And again, I wonder what I am doing in such a strange, inhospitable place. I remain slightly on edge the rest of the day, as we wander about the ruins inspecting the preservation work.

That night I can't fall asleep. Images of tanks, machine guns, and the begging children at the temples besiege me as I toss and turn. It is hotter than usual, and I feel clammy and nauseated. I wish I weren't so alone. I have not noticed any additional guests since the French doctors left. Suddenly a loud boom breaks the silence, and then another. Could it be a land mine or machine gun fire? There's the revving of engines on the road and then some shouts and scuffling. I pull my sheet over my head and freeze. My heart races. The doctors were right. It is definitely not safe here. Soon, all is silent again. I peer out from beneath the sheet. A stray breeze rustles the muslin drapes, behind which palm fronds and banana plants billow and sway in shadowy silhouettes. Then I see what looks like a hand waving to someone along the veranda surrounding my bungalow on stilts. A crouching figure appears to creep forward in the shadows, followed by another. They halt, then move forward again. I can't make out the faces or figures. I want to scream, but I dare not. I am certain they are Khmer Rouge prowling for intruders on their turf. For an instant, I question my sanity. Perhaps the heat and stress have made me delusional. Then again, I remind myself, there was a kidnapping at Angkor just days ago.

To say that I'm terrified is a gross understatement. I tremble; my heart feels like it's pounding right out of my chest. I slip under the sheet again and hold my breath for as long as possible so that my bungalow will appear empty through the teak slatted windows and drapes. Growing more panicked by the minute, I reach for the phone, but there is no phone! And there is no other way to contact anyone in the hotel. At any moment these men (I assume they are men) may break into my room and haul me into the jungle, never to be seen again. I gasp, then hold my breath again. I cannot believe this is happening. Something is amiss here. At the age of thirty-five, when most women are worried about their biological clocks, I am in the jungles of Cambodia sick with fear, worried about being kidnapped by the Khmer Rouge! The crouching figures appear to have halted. Then a hand waves, and they begin inching forward.

You must collect yourself, I think in despair. Still trembling, I remember my Vipassana training and begin to meditate—eyes closed, I try to keep my attention focused on each extremely quiet breath. As I meditate, I repeat The Lord's Prayer: "Our Father Who art in heaven, hallowed be Thy name . . ." Although I was raised a Catholic and recited this prayer often as a child, I don't practice that religion anymore. Why did that come to me? Eventually I become exhausted from my relentless adrenaline rush. Though I no longer detect the crouching figures, I am still immobilized. I just can't take it anymore! As if possessed by a superhuman force, I leap out of bed, run to the door, and swing it open, prepared to confront my perceived enemies. Considering the extent of my fear, most people would classify this as madness.

I'm blinded by a beam of light through the early-morning darkness. "*Retournez dedans!*" a stern voice shouts. "*Tout est bien!*" As my eyes adjust, I notice a young man on the lawn below shining a flashlight. He is one of the staff, telling me to go back inside; everything is okay.

Okay?! Dazed, I turn to inspect the wrap-around veranda. There are no crouching figures. But that does not mean they were not slinking around earlier. Breathing a huge sigh of relief, I wave "thank you" to the young man. My entire body instantly relaxes as the blood flows back into my extremities. I scan the surrounding jungle flora, wondering whether the figures are hiding there. But, too tired to care, I crawl back into bed, hoping to salvage an hour or two of sleep.

Later that morning, as we head out on our final excursion, I recount the previous night's ordeal to Bob. I'm still haunted by the possibility that I could have been kidnapped.

"I'm sorry," Bob says. "That must have been terrifying. But you were probably not in danger. I have a feeling it was just the shadows from the plants."

"But . . ." I hesitate, deciding not to pursue the issue. His remark seems a bit flippant, considering what I've endured.

Even though I don't believe Bob, I know he means well. And I know I must try to forget that dreadful episode if I want to enjoy the rest of my trip. Then something occurs to me. If those shadows in the curtains weren't the Khmer Rouge, or even the plants, then what were they? Perhaps they were a reflection of the shadows inside me—my own buried anger and grief, grievances and anxieties, doubts and fears. Perhaps the shadows were a powerful message for me from Spirit. This thought makes me considerably uncomfortable, and I want to banish it. Yet as the Swiss psychologist C. G. Jung once said, "One does not become enlightened by imagining figures of light, but by making the darkness conscious." The great mystics have long taught that darkness is fear, and that enlightenment means to see in light. For the Hindus and Buddhists, in particular, enlightenment means being in a continuous meditative state, in constant contact with a higher intelligence, which produces an empty, peaceful mind free of distractions. They believe that the entire world itself is only a shadow, an illusion called *maya*. This illusion is the medium through which we undertake a journey to respiritualize ourselves, to reconnect with what the Hindus call the essential Self, our true, divine nature. I begin to wonder whether my instinctive impulse to meditate and pray at that time of extreme fear has not, in fact, saved my life. And, despite all appearances to the contrary, whether I may have experienced a brief moment of enlightenment.

We pass through the usual military checkpoints, an unpleasant ritual that continues to ruffle me, on our way to Bayon, a temple mountain within the ancient walled city of Angkor Thom.

"I guarantee you're going to love this one!" Bob says with enthusiasm, as we hike through tall grass and thick masses of kapok and fig trees. Like other sites at Angkor, gigantic creeping tree roots and vines strangle massive stones and majestic monuments. Bob walks briskly, in his usual purposeful gait, and I struggle to keep up. Not only is he made of heartier stock, he is obviously more acclimated to the energy-sapping heat and humidity than I am.

When Bayon first appears from behind the trees, I stop in my tracks. Looking back at me are more than two hundred serene, smiling, Buddha-like faces carved on fifty-four soaring towers. Bob explains that the faces are meant to represent Lokesvara, a god possessing the compassionate qualities of the Buddha. The faces also have been said to represent Jayavarman VII, the last great builder king of Angkor and a devout Buddhist, who continued construction in the twelfth and thirteenth centuries. The entire site is like an enormous sculpture. Bob appears equally awed, though he has seen it many times.

"Bodhisattva," he says with reverence.

"What do you mean?"

"A bodhisattva is a being who has attained enlightenment, or *bodhi*, and is on his way to becoming a Buddha himself." He pauses. "Or herself, of course. But he postpones his freedom from the cycle of rebirth to help others attain enlightenment. It is the ultimate act of compassion."

"What a great idea. I wish I had my own bodhisattva, like a personal trainer or shopper," I joke. "We need a lot of them in New York City, considering what we have to endure just to mail a package or cross the street!"

Bob lets out a deep belly laugh as he leads me to a magnificent sculpted wall. Like Angkor Wat, Bayon is noted for its stunning galleries of bas reliefs. But unlike the ancient myths and battles depicted in the sculpture at Angkor Wat, the Bayon reliefs illustrate refreshing scenes from everyday life among the Khmer who lived at Angkor, including activities such as festivals, cockfights, and even getting a haircut. These reliefs have obviously benefited from ongoing preservation efforts. After we inspect the sculpture, Bob agrees to let me explore on my own while he chats with the workers and conservators. But he asks me not to wander too far away.

I'm happy for some time alone among the smiling bodhisattvas. Searching for an ideal spot to meditate, I ascend a crumbling staircase leading to a small chamber strewn with incense sticks and flower petals—more offerings left by visiting pilgrims. The accumulated dust of centuries sends me into a coughing fit. Not a good place to meditate. It is too dark and suffocating.

So I continue to wander among the stone-faced towers, which appear to be surveying my every move. From a distance, the faces appeared serene and comforting, but close-up they are unnerving, haunting even, now that I'm alone with them. A slight shiver shoots down my neck and back. It is late afternoon and the sun has cast a golden glow upon the bodhisattvas, speckled here and there with gray- and green-toned mosses and lichen. I sit down at the base of one of them, close my eyes, and try to observe my breath while allowing my thoughts to slip away. A high-pitched howl startles me. I open my eyes to find two thin, long-tailed monkeys scampering among the ruins. Smiling, I close my eyes and again begin counting my breaths—one, two, one, two—noting the length of the interval between them. I succeed at focusing for several minutes, but again I lose my concentration.

One would think it would be easier to meditate here than in my room. I shudder, recalling the crouching figures at my window. Only now, in addition to fear, I'm aware of other emotions, equally intense. Anger bubbles up like a long dormant volcano, as it did during our drive through the killing fields. I'm still angry at the killers—the Khmer Rouge and all the suffering they've caused here; still angry at my country for allowing it; angry even at myself for taking for granted the many blessings of my own life. This anger is accompanied again by a deep sadness, as I think about the begging children at the temples, each individual face and deformed body. I feel like I have to vomit. I lean forward and open my mouth, but nothing comes out.

The Bayon is eerily empty. Bob and the workers are out of sight, and the monkeys have disappeared. Loneliness, helplessness, and despair consume me. I glance at all the smiling bodhisattvas; they offer no solace. How can they be smiling? "Who, if I cried out, would hear me among the angels' hierarchies?" the poet Rainer Maria Rilke wrote in *Duino Elegies*. It seems that no matter where I go or what I do here, I am continually forced to confront my own heart of darkness—which makes focusing on my writing assignment all the more challenging. I take a deep breath, close my eyes, and begin meditating again.

After some time, a question arises: Isn't my anger toward and disdain for the Khmer Rouge just another side of the same hatred that resulted in the deaths of more than a million people? Just as there is no greater or lesser magnitude of goodness, nor is there a greater or lesser evil, which is simply darkness made visible. Even something as simple as my frustration with the maid who forgot to clean my room the other day is a mild form of hatred, because any thought or feeling not rooted in love issues from its opposite, which is fear. And fear feeds separation, which, in turn, feeds hatred. Separation is the lack of insight arising from an erroneous perception that reduces everything into a "you versus me" or "us versus them" equation. The real enemy lies within, and the battlefield is my own heart. That is what the Gita says, what Father Zossima meant in *The Brothers Karamozov,* and what the Buddhist sages believe. Okay, I get it. It is as though a disembodied voice has spoken to me. I gaze up at the bodhisattva smiling down upon me; perhaps he delivered the message.

I feel unexpectedly inspired, thinking of the Cambodian people and all that they've endured and overcome. And my heart aches for them. The only way, then, to survive the inevitable brutalities of life, however they may affect us, is to let go and persevere, as the Gita keeps reminding me. In his own way, the poet Rainer Maria Rilke, to whom I have often turned in moments of despair, offers the same transcendent wisdom. "Be ahead of all parting, as though it already were behind you, like the winter that has just gone by. For among these winters, there is one so endlessly winter that only by wintering through it will your heart survive," he wrote in *The Sonnets to Orpheus.*

Having stood witness to centuries of destruction by both man and nature, the bodhisattvas, in all their stony impassivity, are a symbol of such strength and endurance. They seem to pull me deeper into meditation. Breathing slowly, while continuing to observe each inhalation and exhalation, I practice what the Buddhists call "mindfulness," envisioning my mind as a clear, still pond, undisturbed by roiling waves of emotions and attachments to desired outcomes and rewards. And gradually my heart expands.

I have often thought that a more accurate term for this process would be "mindless-ness," given meditation's emphasis on stopping the mind and detaching from thoughts, which, in turn, stir emotions. But I see now that the word *mindfulness* refers to a mind that is fully focused in the present moment, because there is nowhere else to go. And when practiced consistently, mindfulness allows me to be more attentive to whatever task I undertake in each moment, whether it's eating a meal, washing the dishes, or drinking a cup of tea. The architects of Angkor obviously knew something about mindfulness. An awesome edifice like Bayon is meant to take one on a sacred journey. Just walking through it and beholding all the bodhisattvas is an active meditation that cultivates both focused awareness and compassion.

"When your mind is liberated your heart floods with compassion," wrote Buddhist monk, poet, and Vietnamese peace activist Thich Nhat Hanh in his book *The Miracle of Mindfulness*. "Compassion for yourself for having undergone countless sufferings because you were not yet able to relieve yourself of false views, hatred, ignorance and anger; and compassion for others because they do not yet see and so are still imprisoned by false views, hatred, and ignorance and continue to create suffering for themselves and others."

Our liberation from suffering, according to Hanh, comes from reaching a level of wisdom in which we perceive reality in its ultimate perfection, free from all false views produced by the imagination, when "there is no longer any distinction made between subject and object." He claims that we can all attain at least a taste of this state if we persist in practicing meditation, particularly meditation on the concept of interdependence. "People normally cut reality into compartments, and so are unable to see the interdependence of all phenomena," he wrote. "To see all in one and one in all is to break through the great barrier which narrows one's perception of reality. . . . A person isn't some private entity traveling unaffected through time and space as if sealed off from the rest of the world by a thick shell. . . . We are life, and life is limitless. . . . The suffering of others is our own suffering, and the happiness of others is our own happiness."

I continue to meditate, adopting the serene smile of the bodhisattvas, while observing my breath and focusing on the concept of interdependence. I try to perceive that my existence is dependent upon the condition of everything else in the world at this moment as part of an intricate web of cause and effect. Meditating in this way, according to Buddhism, I will come to understand that because all phenomena are conditioned and in a constant state of flux, they are, therefore, impermanent and have no independent identity or self. As such, all phenomena are what the Buddhists call "empty." This understanding will allow me to see things as they really are and not as the ordinary mind perceives them. When I do so, I will be able to let go of desires (attachments) and fears (aversions), which cause suffering. The truth and experience of suffering, along with that of impermanence and of non-self (emptiness), are what the Buddha, upon awakening after much meditation, perceived as the three marks of physical existence. We can also meditate on each of these characteristics.

When I am able to stop suffering, then I will have attained wisdom and compassion, which will lead me to *nirvana*—the "other shore" beyond our transient, painful, day-to-day existence, or what the Buddhists call *samsara*. For only the blissful realm of nirvana can bring lasting peace and happiness. I open my eyes, uplifted by my meditation, which seems to have taken me deeper inside than my many previous attempts. I glance at my watch; I've lost track of time. I can't even remember when I sat down here. A familiar anxiety slowly creeps back as I jump to my feet and begin running toward the conservation site where I left Bob. But I'm not sure I'm heading the right way, and I become more anxious. What happened to that inner calm? I hear Bob's voice calling for me and follow the sound through the trees.

"I hope you enjoyed yourself," he says when I find him.

"Sorry I was gone so long." I'm relieved to see him. "I didn't realize . . ."

"Oh, you weren't gone more than twenty minutes. I was just about to show you something else. Your timing is impeccable."

I smile to myself, grateful for those few blissful moments in eternity.

Later that evening, Bob and Norma and I and some of the other conservators enjoy our last dinner at an outdoor restaurant in town, complete with card tables and plastic chairs, before winding up at the local disco. I am delighted to discover that even Siem Reap has stayed in step with the times (albeit a few decades behind). I dance joyfully alongside my new friends underneath a huge mirrored ball, feeling forever connected to the haunting landscape of Cambodia, the grand stones of Angkor, and all those I have encountered on this emotionally demanding yet exhilarating journey. As my body effortlessly moves to the pulsating music, my mind sinks into a soothing stillness. Having let go of all thoughts and expectations about the future, I feel serenely present and content. Nothing seems to be missing.

I am grateful for the many gifts of Angkor. This great monument to the spirit, as well as the Cambodians themselves, has led me into my own dark depths to confront my worst fears and misguided thoughts and perceptions. I have learned how to surrender more readily to an all-pervading Oneness, where I can always find inner peace, knowing that I exist as everything everywhere. As a result, my anger and grief over the needless destruction that has occurred here, while still acknowledged, has lost much of its initial charge. For Cambodia has expanded my heart, allowing me to make as much room for the darkness as for the light. Having passed through this harsh terrain, both outwardly and inwardly, even the challenges of my own day-to-day survival seem less overwhelming, my urgent need to publish my book less all consuming. As a result, I feel that I have developed an even greater compassion for myself and others.

Outside the disco, the most beautiful full moon I have ever seen glows with an unusual smoky orange color against the indigo sky. The faint, seam-like line snaking through its center from top to bottom transforms it for a moment into a celestial Yin-Yang symbol, whose twin wholeness reminds me of the inevitable transience of life and nearness of death, hovering thick and heavy like the heat.

I am she who separated the heaven from the Earth. I have instructed mankind in the mysteries. I have pointed out their paths to the stars. I have ordered the course of the Sun and the Moon. I am queen of the rivers and winds and sea. I have brought together men and women. I have caused truth to be considered beautiful. I am she who is called the goddess of women. I, Isis, am all that has been, that is or shall be; no mortal man hath ever me unveiled. The fruit which I have brought forth is the Sun.

—Inscription on the Temple of Isis at Sais

3

EGYPT TO ETERNITY

Remembering

A preternatural calm washes over me as I watch the sun rise over the Nile, fringed with graceful date palms and glistening brilliantly just beyond my hotel terrace in Luxor, a town at the center of a region known as ancient Thebes. In the distance, on the river's West Bank, tower the arid limestone cliffs of the Valley of the Kings, one of the world's most important archaeological sites, where many of Egypt's greatest pharaohs lie buried in massive subterranean tombs. Antiquated white-sailed feluccas ply the water, while peasant farmers work the cotton fields along the fertile riverbank as they have for millennia. An early-morning haze casts an unearthly aura upon the stunning scene, and, for several moments, time seems to stop, as though waiting for a long-submerged memory to resurface.

I feel such a surprising and overwhelming familiarity with my new surroundings that I barely hear the telephone ring. Nor do I feel moved to speak; I am so completely awed by this strange sensation that silence seems the only appropriate response. I hear a voice whispering, "Wherever you are, be the soul of that place."

These are the words of the thirteenth-century Sufi mystic and poet Jelaluddin Rumi. I'm suddenly tumbling backward to a time when the banks of the Nile were teeming with throngs of people celebrating the arrival of a large boat, its narrow prow bearing an effigy of the goddess Isis standing with outstretched arms, holding an Ankh sign (the Egyptian symbol of eternal life) and wearing a headdress comprising a solar disc between two cow horns. I have seen many such images of Isis—the universal mother goddess of creation, fertility, healing, and magic—in books and museums and have been long captivated by her compelling presence. The boat appears to be carrying someone or something significant after a long journey. I strain to capture the details of the occasion, but the phone will not stop ringing. I answer with frustration at having been interrupted from my dream-like state. It is the American archaeologist Kent Weeks.

"I'm afraid there has been no change," he reports. "The Antiquities Department refuses to make an exception. They will not allow anyone in the tomb at this time. I'm sorry."

I'm crestfallen. This is not what I expected to hear. I have traveled to Egypt on an assignment to write about Weeks's latest discovery—the largest and most unusual tomb in Egypt, KV-5 (designating tomb number five in the Valley of the Kings). Hailed as the biggest archaeological find in Egypt since Howard Carter discovered nearby King Tutankhamen's tomb and its priceless treasures in 1922, the 3,200-year-old KV-5 is thought to be a family mausoleum for up to fifty sons of Ramesses II, Egypt's greatest pharaoh, who ruled from 1279 to 1213 BCE.

Granted, I was informed just before I left New York that I would likely not get into KV-5, because, as a newly excavated site, it had been deemed unsafe by the Egyptian authorities. But I've invested so many months in trying to contact Weeks, secure the magazine assignment, and plan my trip. I cannot bear to forfeit what I have been anxiously anticipating as an incredible opportunity. Nor do I want to disappoint my editor. These factors, combined with my inability to take "no" for an answer, lead me, after several sleepless nights, to a simple conclusion: I will take the trip anyway, hoping that everything will work out as I have planned. I will clench my teeth and pray.

"But what about my story?" I plead nervously. "You said you thought my getting permission to enter the tomb wouldn't be difficult, Dr. Weeks."

"You knew you'd be taking this chance when you decided to come." His tone is polite and conciliatory.

"Yes, I know." I fall back onto the bed, staring helplessly at the Nile flowing serenely in its upward course toward the Mediterranean. It is one of the few rivers in the world that runs south to north in what seems like a defiant snub to geologic convention.

"I'll show you some of the other tombs," he tries to comfort me. "I'm sure you'll find something else to write about. You're in Egypt, after all!"

"Okay, sure . . . thanks." My words fall flat. I can't seem to muster any enthusiasm.

"Who knows," Weeks replies. "Maybe, by some stroke of luck, you *will* be able to see KV-5. This is a magical place, anything could happen." He stops, perhaps realizing that he has overstepped his authority. "But don't get your hopes up."

We agree to meet the following day in the Valley of the Kings. Despite the disappointing news, I'm grateful that Weeks is willing to make time for me. His discovery has catapulted him to celebrity status. He has been interviewed numerous times in the press and on television and doesn't really need more publicity. The image of Isis that I saw moments ago reappears before me. She seems to be beckoning me into an enticing mystery that has long remained hidden from me. Perhaps there will be more to this journey than my now precarious assignment. Perhaps the article was simply a vehicle to bring me here for a grander purpose. But what?

I rest in bed, drained by the long flight. Though my life in New York now seems like a desert mirage, recent events keep racing through my mind: the contract I have just signed for my first book, a long awaited fruition; more lucrative and fulfilling magazine assignments; and my re-ignited relationship with a man with whom I have a passionate connection on many levels. There appears to be much to celebrate, and yet I feel oddly vulnerable and discontented, as though everything could be snatched away from me in an instant. I make a mental note to check my telephone messages every few days.

Later, after a quick lunch at the hotel café, I meet my guide/ escort, Samy, who is waiting for me in the lobby. He greets me warmly with a wide smile, as though we are old friends or family. He appears to be about my age—late thirties—and is darkly handsome with kind, expressive eyes.

"Welcome to Egypt, Dana!" he says buoyantly, leading me outside. "Today, we see the great temples Karnak and Luxor and then . . . well, let's just take it one step at a time. No need to race ahead. Everything will unfold exactly the way it should. *Insha'Allah.*"

"Insha'Allah?"

"God willing." He helps me into the car. "You will hear that expression a lot here. Nothing happens without his help, you know."

"Yes, I like that idea." I'm struck by Samy's easygoing attitude. He exudes a peaceful, unselfconscious charm—a refreshing quality that I will come to experience in many Egyptians, who consistently greet me with grace and generosity.

Samy introduces me to our driver Mohammed, a wiry, older man who nods and smiles sweetly. I notice the military truck parked directly behind us. In it sit two burly soldiers with rifles.

"Who are they, Samy?" I ask anxiously.

"They're our chaperones."

"Chaperones?"

"You heard about the massacre a few weeks ago at Hatshepsut's Temple? Here in Luxor."

"Yes." I wish he had not reminded me. "It was all over the news before I left." Given my preoccupation with the present obstacles, I thankfully had not dwelt on this unnerving fact.

"Over forty tourists died. Terrorists shot them point–blank." He bows his head mournfully.

My heart pounds.

"Of course, we want to protect you," Samy continues. "Not many tourists here now. The soldiers will escort us wherever we go. And we will be safe." He pauses, scratching his head. "Insha'Allah."

"I appreciate that." I wave politely to the soldiers. They wave back, expressionless. Great. "All I need is something else to worry about," I mumble as we drive into the blinding sunlight.

My trepidation soon fades, however, as Luxor comes alive with vivid bursts of color and the bustle of commerce. In the open-air markets, vendors hawk gold jewelry, fake antiquities, and other souvenirs along with spices, nuts, dried fruits, pastries, and an array of fresh fish, meats, and produce. Some men are squatting and sorting beets and radishes. Human- and horse-drawn carts piled high with olives, dates, eggplants, and okra zigzag through the congested, narrow streets, populated by wandering goats. Mud-brick tenements stand side by side with posh tourist hotels. Veiled women stroll arm in arm, while men in white turbans and long blue robes called *galabiyya* sit smoking long, snake-like water pipes, or *shisha*, in cramped coffee shops. The mosques, with their ornate minarets, preside like stern sentinels over this sensual feast, as if reminding us mortals how easy it is to be led astray by coarser appetites. I begin to loosen under the spell of Luxor. And, like my first impression of the Nile, this exotic, time-capsule town seems oddly familiar. I feel at home here.

For centuries, luminaries ranging from the ancient Greek historian Herodotus to the French writer Gustave Flaubert have been captivated by Egypt's timeless charms. "So here we are in Egypt, land of the Pharaohs, land of the Ptolemies, land of Cleopatra," Flaubert wrote in a letter to a friend in 1850. "Here we are and here we are living, our heads more hairless than our knees, smoking long pipes and drinking coffee on divans. What can I say about it all? . . . As yet I am scarcely over the initial bedazzlement. It is like being hurled while still asleep into the midst of a Beethoven symphony, . . . each detail reaches out to grip you; it pinches you; and the more you concentrate on it the less you grasp the whole. But the first days, by God, it is such a bewildering chaos of colours that your poor imagination is dazzled as though by continuous fireworks."

My heart races as the massive sandstone walls of the sprawling Karnak Temple complex and its processional avenue of ram-headed sphinxes greet me with the mystical grandeur that has characterized Egypt's awe-inspiring monuments for more than five thousand years. At least that is the historical timeline assigned by conventional archaeology. Some iconoclastic Egyptologists date Egyptian civilization to thirty-four thousand years or older. The striking contrast between the immortality of ancient Egypt and the frenzied daily life becomes blatantly apparent as we explore the numerous pylons and temples, vast pillared halls and courtyards, and inner chambers, chapels, and sanctuaries that comprise what was once the most important temple complex in Egypt. This dramatic interplay between the eternal and the ephemeral gives me a heady sensation.

Built, restored, and decorated by a succession of pharaohs over two thousand years, beginning in the Middle Kingdom period (c. 2055–1650 BCE) and continuing through the New Kingdom (c. 1550–1069 BCE), when Thebes rose to new heights of power and prosperity, Karnak was the main place of worship of the Theban gods Amun, Mut, and Khons. As such, it is also called the Great Temple of Amun. The creator god Amun was the ruling god of Thebes. In the relief carvings and paintings adorning the temples, he is typically displayed wearing a crown with two tall plumes and holding a crook and flail, symbols of kingship. Associated with the sun god Re, he is also known as Amun-Re, King of the Gods and symbolic father of the pharaoh. Amun's wife, the war goddess Mut, who wears a vulture-shaped headdress, was Thebes's principal goddess and mother of the pharaoh. Their son, the moon god Khons, is often portrayed as a hawk-headed man wearing a crown topped with a crescent moon supporting a full moon.

Statues of this sacred triad journeyed down the Nile on a large boat from Karnak to Luxor Temple during the Opet Festival, an annual celebration marking the flood season and ensuing crop cycle. In another popular yearly celebration, a boat traveled from Dendara carrying a statue of Hathor, goddess of love and joy (who, bearing a crown of cow's horns enclosing a solar disc, was a manifestation of Isis) to Edfu, where she joined with her husband, Horus. God of light and the sky, Horus was depicted as a falcon or falcon-headed human with a solar disc on his head. As the son of Isis and her brother/husband Osiris, god of the underworld, fertility, and grain, he was also regarded as the divine manifestation of the pharaoh.

The numerous gods worshipped by the ancient Egyptians each had their own particular role to play in preserving the cosmic order. Often depicted as human-animal hybrids, they could assume many forms, be both beneficent and destructive, and adopt each other's characteristics, reflecting the multiplicity, dualities, and contradictions of life itself. Some gods, like the Theban triad, were local to various regions, while others, such as Isis, Osiris, and Horus, held universal significance. In order to ensure a harmonious relationship between the earthly and heavenly realms, the gods continually had to be appeased with offerings and rituals, overseen by the pharaoh, who himself was regarded as a god.

As with other ancient religions, creation stories were a central component of the Egyptian worldview. Thebes was one of the four great initiatory spiritual centers of ancient Egypt, along with Heliopolis, Memphis, and Hermopolis, each of which developed its own cosmogonies. But they all shared the belief that a creator god (Amun, in the case of Thebes) arose from the chaos of a great primordial ocean called the Nun, the infinite source of the universe, to create the world of men and gods. In addition to establishing moral order and investing the pharaoh with divine power, the creator god initiated the cosmic cycle of creation, becoming, and return, which all beings experience as an incarnation from Spirit into matter and then an eventual return to Spirit.

"The great mystery is the passage from invisible into visible, to be realized by the Power, which from the incomprehensible One will call forth the Many," wrote Lucie Lamy in *Egyptian Mysteries: New Light on Ancient Knowledge*. "When the One wished to know himself, he first of all created himself through the projection of his heart. Then came the first breath, inspiration then expiration, dilation then contraction. He conceived the world in his spirit (akh), then caused his ba [soul] to intervene to play the role of specification, determination and animation. Thus, little by little all the forms came into existence on earth, each according to its species. . . . The result is the Becoming, expressed hieroglyphically by the scarab Khepri: this insect passes through three essential phases, egg, larvae and nymph, before realizing its final winged form." The winged scarab god symbolized the rising sun and, therefore, resurrection. The Egyptians believed, then, that through metamorphosis and transformation the human soul could transcend the dualities that define its earthly existence—light and darkness, order and chaos, life and death—and eventually, if properly purified and prepared, achieve immortality.

Standing among Karnak's colossal statues of Amun, Mut, Ramesses II, Tuthmosis III, and other gods and kings; the soaring columns and obelisks; and the hieroglyphics, paintings, and carved reliefs depicting both religious rituals and the pharaohs' military conquests, I admire the artistic genius of their creators. The massive hypostyle hall, comprising a seemingly infinite forest of towering carved and painted stone columns with papyrus-shaped capitals, is most impressive. Halls such as these were supposed to represent the primordial marsh of creation from which all life arose. The ceiling is decorated with stars, the walls and columns with scenes from daily life. Wandering through here, I begin to feel dizzy and lean back onto one of the columns to steady myself.

"Everything okay?" Samy asks, concerned.

"Fine thanks. Still tired from the trip, I guess." I offer a tentative smile, sensing that it's not just the desert heat that has affected me. An ancient energy is pulsing through me, as I struggle to remember something. Something so familiar yet so distant. But I can't seem to focus. As we proceed farther into the complex, I notice that the rooms become smaller and darker. Samy tells me that all religious temples were built this way to convey a sense of mystery as one entered the innermost chambers and sanctuaries, the domain of the gods, where only the pharaoh and high priests were permitted to give offerings and conduct rituals. The sanctuaries once held statues of the gods, which were placed in tabernacles in small gold or gilt wood ceremonial barques, or barges. These long-prow barques were placed on the ships that traveled down the Nile in religious processions and festivals. Like other ancient peoples, including the Maya and the Inca, the Egyptians believed that the earth mirrored the sky. For them, the Milky Way was a great cosmic river upon which their gods sailed, and the Nile was its earthly reflection.

I feel dizzy again and slightly nauseated. It is as if the veils of time have momentarily parted and the distant past has seeped into my blood, affecting me on a cellular level. I have been here before! I have a vision of myself sitting in a candle-lit chamber in a temple, perhaps this one, writing down unfamiliar symbols on a papyrus scroll, a cloud of incense encircling me. I appear to be intensely engaged in my task, as if it is urgent and important. I strain to see more, but the vision quickly fades. Then a tingling sensation spreads through my body. Did I just glimpse eternity?

Our final stop at Karnak is a large stone statue of a scarab near the sacred lake, where the priests purified themselves before their rituals.

"Go ahead, walk around it for good luck," Samy urges. "Three times if you want to get married." He raises an inquisitive eyebrow. "Are you married?"

"No, not yet."

"Women here marry young. A lot of men do, too. Devout Muslims aren't supposed to sleep together before marrying." There is a mischievous twinkle in his eye. "Not so easy."

Though Samy has so far proven to be a gentleman, treating me with a brotherly, protective quality, I feel compelled to change the subject. "You know, I'm thinking of getting some souvenirs," I say, making one pass around the scarab.

Just then, a young man approaches me seemingly from out of nowhere. He is selling necklaces with oblong silver cartouches that can be engraved with your name in hieroglyphs. (Cartouches, which often appear in tomb and temple paintings and inscriptions, encase the hieroglyphs of divine and royal names.) I'm surprised by this timely response to my request, as I did not notice any vendors nearby. I order some cartouches for my three nieces and one for myself, which will be delivered to my hotel. After a visit to Luxor Temple, on the bank of the Nile, another astonishing edifice that bears the architectural imprint of a number of pharaohs (in addition to Alexander the Great and the Romans), I ask Samy to take me to the nearest post office. I want to check my telephone messages, secretly hoping for word from my boyfriend. There are a few work-related calls, but nothing from him. That sinking feeling returns. I wonder if he has left me again. He could have at least checked in with a simple "I miss you." No, even better, "I can't wait for you to come back!" Something does not feel right. Then I stop myself, realizing that I have become obsessed. Wait a minute. I'm in Egypt! Who cares about him anyway?

Later, Samy and I have dinner at a cozy restaurant overlooking the Nile, where I enjoy delicious grilled squid and musaga, a baked, spiced tomato and eggplant dish. We exchange pleasant conversation about work and family and, of course, our wildly divergent cultures.

"What is the most sacred place in Egypt?" I ask. "A temple, a tomb, the Great Pyramid?"

"Everything is sacred," he replies with authority. "Everything! Even death."

"Well, I'm not exactly looking forward to that!" I gaze at the river, reflecting the golden-pink light of dusk. A flock of herons descends upon the far bank, while two feluccas sail by lazily.

"Truth be told, there is really no such thing as death . . . the way we think of it." Samy sips his coffee slowly, as though savoring each nuance of taste. "Ahhhhh." He pauses. "We live forever."

"Perhaps . . . but we don't know for sure, do we? There is no real proof." I'm aware that the methodical, fact-crunching journalist in me is talking now—flaunting the day's glimmerings about eternity. I've read about past lives, and for the first time I've been given the opportunity to experience what has formerly seemed only like a distant, murky possibility. So why am I resisting it?

"The proof is in your own heart," Samy says knowingly. "You'll see. Insha'Allah."

I wonder whether my fear of losing my boyfriend is really just my fear of death playing out on a more mundane level. Death misperceived as the ultimate descent into loneliness. Then my anxiety about KV-5 resurfaces, along with thoughts of the recent terrorist attack.

"Any more news about the terrorists?" I scan the restaurant with suspicion. "I mean, this place could easily be blown up in a second! Where are our chaperones?!"

"Dear Dana." Samy reaches for my hand. "Stop worrying so much. When you allow yourself to surrender to the flow of life, everything will seem effortless. You don't have as much control as you think."

"Easier said than done," I quip, knowing that Samy is right. I take a deep breath. The fragrant scent of oil, garlic, and mint infuses the dry evening air. I'm suddenly startled by the plangent sound of the muezzin at the nearby mosque calling faithful Muslims to prayer, as he does five times each day.

Samy bows his head and murmurs a few words. "Better to be at the mosque," he says afterward with a trace of guilt.

It is a beautiful ritual, repeatedly having to drop whatever you're doing and take time to connect with God. I'm beginning to understand what Samy meant about everything being sacred. How could one not believe this to be so, especially here, if only because of this single constant reminder? I reflect sadly on the visible lack of public rituals reaffirming the constant presence of the sacred where it is perhaps needed most, in the Sodom and Gomorrah of all cities, my home, New York.

The following morning, Samy and Mohammed, accompanied, of course, by our ever-present military chaperones, take me to the secluded Valley of the Kings on the Nile's West Bank. In this barren, forbidding canyon, fringed with craggy cliffs and a pyramidal mountain peak, lie more than sixty excavated tombs, many of them the final resting place of the New Kingdom pharaohs. The western location of the necropolis is significant, because the setting sun symbolized death. In keeping with the pervasive Egyptian belief in the immortality of the soul, the pharaoh was thought to be reborn each day with the rising sun in the east. The New Kingdom pharaohs, who devoted much of their great wealth and resources to the quest for eternal life, built their elaborate tombs underground in an attempt to stave off the grave robbing that had desecrated the monumental pyramid tombs erected by earlier pharaohs. That effort, however, met with little success, as these later tombs also suffered a similar fate over the millennia. Pharaohs were buried with myriad treasures, ranging from magnificent jewelry, furniture, and statues of deities to clothing, food and drink offerings, and huge boats on which they "traveled" through the underworld—everything they would need to survive in the afterlife. Among the most prevalent of these treasures were *ushabtis*, small statues of servants who carried out manual labor for the pharaoh in the afterlife.

At the modest, rock-hewn entrance to the celebrated KV-5, a tall, suntanned Kent Weeks is directing a group of Egyptian workers who are hauling sand and rubble out of the tomb in large leather satchels and plastic buckets. Nearby, a tent-like structure shades a dusty, old trailer and picnic bench. The sun is blazing with its usual intensity. I stand at a distance observing the scene, not wanting to interrupt. Upon noticing me, Weeks rushes to my side.

"You must be Dana. So pleased to meet you, finally!" His smile is full of childlike enthusiasm, the perfect complement to his blond, boyish good looks. Not at all the crusty, dry academic type I expected from our phone call.

"Thank you for taking the time to see me, Dr. Weeks." I shake his hand, secretly hoping for a miraculous shift in fortune regarding KV-5.

"Kent, please. Sorry, I don't have any good news for you." He answers my thoughts. "But, don't worry. We'll spend your time wisely, starting with King Tut!"

Visibly pleased that I'm in good hands, Samy waves good-bye, as Weeks leads me down a path to the entrance of the fabled tomb of the child pharaoh Tutankhamun, who reigned from 1336 to 1327 BCE.

"Tombs were built to mirror the underworld," Weeks says. "The Egyptians believed that the deceased had to travel through the underworld before he could be reborn in spirit."

We enter the truncated doorway, which is essentially a hole cut into the cliff, and descend into the tomb via a dark, narrow corridor, which ends in a cramped space comprising several small chambers that once housed King Tut's dazzling treasures. The elaborate furniture, musical instruments, inlaid jewelry, and weapons, along with his renowned gold mummy case and gold and lapis lazuli funerary mask—all of which came to public attention in 1922, when English Egyptologist Howard Carter discovered the tomb—are now on display at the Egyptian Museum in Cairo.

The tomb is very plain, much smaller and less imposing than I had imagined. The air is stale and musty. In the burial chamber, Weeks shines his flashlight on a beautiful mural painted in white, red, and black of the mummified Osiris, god of the underworld, who is shown wearing his tall white crown and embracing Tutankhamun. The figures stand in the iconic Egyptian pose— three-quarter view, the head in profile.

Another scene shows the mummified young king taking part in a funerary ritual called the "opening of the mouth," in which a priest touched his body with special instruments designed to restore his voice and senses, as he would need these to survive in the afterlife. In this way, his body would become a vessel for his *ka*, or the part of his soul that functioned as a double for him in life and ultimately survived death. When the ka united with the *ba*, the part of the soul that animated his body during his existence, they became *akh*, or "spirit," through which the deceased achieved eternal life with the gods. I take notes as Weeks explains these mysterious funerary beliefs.

Part of the overall process known as the "judgment of the dead," the "opening of the mouth" allowed the deceased to speak and, therefore, to defend himself to a tribunal of fierce gods against any wrongdoings he may have committed in his life. The opening of the mouth was followed by a "negative confession," in which the deceased declared that he had committed no sins. Then came the famous "weighing of the heart" ceremony, presided over by Anubis, god of embalming, depicted as a man with a black jackal head in funerary texts collectively called *The Egyptian Book of the Dead*. Anubis weighed the deceased's heart—considered the center of the intellect and emotions—on a pair of scales against the feather of Maat, goddess of truth, justice, and order, who is depicted either as a woman with an ostrich feather on her head or as the feather itself. If the deceased's heart weighed heavy from sin, he was devoured by the crocodile-headed monster, Ammut. If his heart did not outweigh the feather, then the deceased was led by Thoth, the ibis-headed god of wisdom and writing who records the judgment, to meet Osiris, with whom the deceased becomes identified, so he can complete his dangerous journey through the underworld. This journey requires that he utter specific magic spells that will safely lead him to life everlasting with Osiris in the Happy Fields, a paradise version of the Nile Valley, scenes from which are often depicted in tomb paintings.

Imagining the ceremony, I place my hand on my heart. How light is it, I wonder? Would I be allowed to pass through? I am a good, well-meaning person. Then again, I'm not free of the worries, doubts, and fears that plague all of us now and then and make our hearts heavy. I will try to remember to weigh them against Maat's feather whenever they threaten my peace of mind. I like that image. Someone once said that the greatest things are accomplished with a light heart.

"Do you know the story of Osiris?" Weeks points to a relief of Isis as protector endowed with long outspread wings, as divine beings were often depicted.

"Vaguely, but I could use a refresher."

He proceeds to recount the legend as transmitted by the Greek historian Plutarch. Osiris, son of Nut, the sky, and Geb, the earth, ruled peacefully over Egypt together with his wife and sister, Isis, civilizing the land and teaching Egyptians how to grow crops, obey the law, and worship the gods. But his evil brother, Seth, god of chaos and discord, and Seth's accomplices ambushed him at a banquet, sealed him alive in a coffin, and threw it into the Nile. The coffin washed up in Byblos (now Lebanon), where Isis found it and returned it to Egypt. During that journey, she perched upon Osiris's body in the form of a kite and miraculously conceived their child, Horus, who eventually grew up to avenge his father by defeating Seth. Though Isis had hidden her husband's coffin, Seth discovered it, hacked Osiris's body into fourteen pieces, and scattered them throughout the country. Isis and her sister, Nephthys, who also happened to be Seth's wife, discovered all these pieces and resurrected Osiris as lord of the underworld. It is not surprising that the Egyptians equated themselves with Osiris upon their death, for his death and resurrection was a powerful metaphor for their own belief in life after death.

"Wow, posthumous conception!" I joke, when Weeks finishes the story. "There was no end to their imagination." He laughs in agreement.

"In there, King Tut's mummy." Weeks shines his flashlight on the large granite sarcophagus at the center of the burial chamber. "Egyptians preserved the body through mummification, so the soul could recognize it in the afterlife. Did you know it takes about seventy days to mummify someone?"

"No, I did not." This is not a fact I ever thought I would need.

"Well, first, the vital organs were removed, and then the body was dehydrated and preserved using the natural salt natron. The heart was left inside the body, because the deceased needed it in the afterlife."

My stomach churns as he explains more grisly details. The other organs were stored in canopic jars whose lids were sculpted to resemble each organ's protector god. These jars were also buried in the tomb. Afterwards, the corpse was packed with linen, resins, spices, and sawdust, anointed with fragrant oils, and coated with resin. It was then bandaged with swathes of linen and decorated with amulets that would protect the deceased on his or her journey to the afterlife. Mummification is perhaps the most extreme expression of the Egyptians' belief in eternal life and thus their ultimate oneness with the gods. Unlike people in our modern culture, they were supremely aware of their own divinity and dedicated much of their lives to expressing it through funerary and temple rituals.

I'm claustrophobic. My palms are sweating. The hot, dust-choked darkness fills me with an eerie foreboding. I long to run straight back out of this underground prison as fast as I can. Weeks instinctively places his hand on my shoulder, as if to comfort me. A shiver runs down the back of my neck. The nearness of death is suffocating.

"Can we go now?" I ask anxiously.

Weeks hesitates, lost in thought. "Yes, yes, of course."

We scurry up the corridor and out into the brilliant sunlight. I shield my eyes until they readjust, gratefully inhaling the fresh air. It is a relief to see the beautiful turquoise sky and to feel the scorching heat on my skin, reminding me that I am, indeed, alive. Down the road, Weeks's crew is still excavating debris from KV-5, an arduous task. Again, I'm seized with anxiety about my presently nonexistent assignment. I take a few deep breaths and try to calm down.

"Wait until you see the next one!" Weeks says, hastening his pace. "Then I have to get back to work, unfortunately. But you can come back tomorrow." His passion is contagious.

Despite my trepidation about entering the other tombs, I am beginning to feel like a treasure hunter myself. A tourist stops to ask Weeks for his autograph and he kindly obliges. At the tomb of Ramesses VI, the walls of the corridors, vestibule, and pillared burial chamber are beautifully carved and painted with hieroglyphics and images of gods and the pharaoh. It is so exquisite that I am determined not to get claustrophobic again. New Kingdom tombs are noted for their elaborate decoration. Highly skilled artisans carved reliefs either directly onto the limestone walls or onto applied plaster. The scenes in this tomb are from various funerary texts, including the Egyptian Book of the Dead and the Amduat.

The Egyptian Book of the Dead, also known as the Book of Coming Forth by Day, contains numerous magic spells and formulae, prayers, hymns, and incantations that were supposed to aid the deceased's safe passage through the perilous underworld to resurrection in the afterlife. The Amduat, also known as the Book of What Is in the Duat (*duat* being the Egyptian word for "underworld"), was the main text for those who worshipped the sun god Re. A guidebook to the afterlife, primarily for pharaohs, it describes the sun's twelve-hour nocturnal journey from dusk to dawn, death to resurrection. On this dangerous journey, Re and the deceased pharaoh travel on a solar barque through the underworld, which is teeming with terrifying demons and other enemies that they had to vanquish, with the help of numerous gods, before they could be reborn. The journey ends at sunrise with the pharaoh's resurrection as Re.

In addition to adorning the interiors of pyramids (in the case of the Old Kingdom pharaohs) and the tombs of later pharaohs and nobles, Egyptian funerary texts were often painted on a roll of papyrus and buried with the dead—kings and commoners alike. These texts, however, were not solely reserved for the benefit of those who died. They were also "used as guides in the context of sacred mysteries and spiritual practice, and very likely describe the experiences of the initiates and practitioners," Stanislav Grof wrote in *Books of the Dead: Manuals for Living and Dying*. "It has become clear that these texts are actually maps of the inner territories of the psyche encountered in profound non-ordinary states of consciousness. . . . The sacred temple mysteries of Isis and Osiris gave neophytes the opportunity to confront death long before old age or diseases made it mandatory, and to conquer it and discover their own immortality. In initiatory procedures of this kind, neophytes not only lost the fear of death, but also profoundly changed their way of being in the world." This experiential practice of "dying before dying" was a key component not only of Egyptian mysticism but also of other mystery school traditions throughout the ancient world.

By the time I finish my first tour with Weeks, my mind is crammed with so much new knowledge that I can barely sleep. My dreams are now dominated by images of Isis and Osiris swirling around me in a glimmering vortex of colors.

Weeks and I spend another day together in the Valley of the Kings and the adjacent Valley of the Queens, traipsing from tomb to tomb. Walking the narrow roads and suspended metal bridges of these dry, forbidding cliffs, I notice that my hands have become sunburned from taking so many notes, despite the fact that I still don't have a clue as to what kind of story I will be writing. However fascinating my visit has been, everything I have learned so far is old news—very, very old news—and this frustrates me considerably. And each drop of sweat reminds me how much the heat is draining my energy. I wonder how Weeks can spend so much time frying in this death trap.

I leave the necropolis feeling incredibly enchanted and stimulated, but at the same time acutely disappointed, for I still have not been allowed access to KV-5. Nevertheless, I express my sincere gratitude to Weeks, whom I truly admire and who sees me off with an apologetic hug. Damn!!

Over the next several days, Samy escorts me to more magnificent sites around Luxor, sometimes in the expert company of local Egyptologists. Time continues to expand and contract—it's instantaneous and eternal all at once—as I become more attuned to this mysterious civilization. Rarely do I allow myself to sink deeply into the moment and enjoy its many gifts when I'm rushing around New York City. Indeed, I am enjoying myself more and more here. To my surprise, I begin to worry less about KV-5. Although I still secretly hope for a miraculous turn of events, I even stop mentioning KV-5 to Samy. What a relief.

The Mortuary Temple of Queen Hatshepsut, where so many tourists were recently murdered, is eerily silent and empty of visitors. Between the murders, tombs, and mummies, I am acutely aware of the constant hover of death, threatening at any moment to shatter my dream vision of the world. Needless to say, I feel extremely anxious as we explore the huge colonnaded terraces, courtyards, chapels, and long corridors of Hatshepsut's temple, a majestic architectural gem enveloped by the limestone cliffs of the Nile's West Bank. When she assumed the throne in 1473 BCE following the death of her father Tuthmosis I, the formidable, forward-thinking Hatshepsut declared herself pharaoh, becoming the first woman ever to reign as king. Depicted in reliefs dressed like a man and wearing the traditional pharaoh's beard, she ruled peacefully for fifteen years. I have always admired powerful, self-possessed women.

One afternoon, we stop at a mud-brick village near the tombs of the nobles, where we drink *karkaday*, a refreshing red drink made with hibiscus flowers, and have a great time smoking shisha with a few of Samy's friends. The water pipe is essentially a long, flexible tube connecting a water-filled glass vase and a small clay bowl containing burning charcoal and sweet tobacco. I smile at the thought of myself smoking this odd contraption in the middle of the desert with three Egyptian men, which is not exactly respectable behavior for local women. Yet I feel quite comfortable here. My first encounter with the pipe, however, is a bit clumsy, and I soon find myself gagging on the smoke. Samy rushes over to comfort me while his friends watch, concerned. I recover with a giggle, then we all burst out laughing. Samy kindly translates the conversation: most of his friends' questions are about me and life in the United States—all very respectful and punctuated now and then by the obligatory "Insha'Allah." The enchanting combination of piousness and worldliness in the Egyptians I've met, who appear to shift between these extremes with graceful ease, reminds me of a character in the novel *Palace Walk* by Egyptian writer and Nobel Laureate Naguib Mahfouz.

"His conduct issued directly from his special nature," Mahfouz wrote, describing a Cairo shop owner who is challenged by a zealous shaykh (holy man) for his love of women and wine. "His breast was not shaken by storms of doubt, and he passed his nights peacefully. His faith was deep. . . . Using it, he set about performing all his duties to God, like prayer, fasting, or almsgiving, with love, ease, and happiness; not to mention a clear conscience, a heart abounding in love for people . . . . With the same ardent overflowing vitality, he opened himself to the joys and pleasures of life. He delighted in fancy food. He was enchanted by vintage wine. He was crazy about a pretty face. He pursued each of these pleasures with gaiety, joy, and passion. His conscience was not weighed down by guilty feelings or anxious scruples. . . . The integration of all these within him was secure and carefree. His soul was not disturbed by any need to reconcile them."

For me, the shop owner is an admirable character, a refreshing reminder that the sacred and the sensual are not mutually exclusive, as my earlier journey to the Australian Outback had dramatically shown me. In the same way, my experience of the Egyptians is reaffirming that life is not about *either* this *or* that, it's about this *and* that. It's about integrating, allowing, accepting, and holding the space for paradox within oneself and others.

At sunset, Samy treats me to a magical felucca cruise on the Nile. I lie back upon a jewel-toned carpet and gaze dreamily at the shadowy date palms and lotuses along the riverbank, as a soft wind rustles my hair and the bright white sails. Samy smiles his brilliant smile, and the skipper makes me a cup of strong Egyptian tea. I think how I could lie here forever, drifting lazily on these serene ancient waters, tenderly attended to by two handsome young men. Unfortunately, my reverie is interrupted by thoughts of my phone messages, which I have not checked for days. I wonder whether I have been offered any new assignments or, more importantly, if my boyfriend has been trying to reach me. After the cruise, I stop by the post office to call New York again.

No assignments—not what I expected, given my recent productive streak. So, naturally, I begin to worry about my finances. Even worse, there is no word from *him*. My disappointment quickly turns to irritation and then distrust. I can't believe he doesn't miss me! He certainly has taken me for granted and is probably seeing someone else by now. I should never have given him another chance! Oh, no. Here I go again with these ridiculous obsessions. Where is my worry-free tranquility and present-moment mindfulness? Remembering Maat's feather, I ask myself, "How light is your heart now?" If only my mind could be as still as the Nile at sunset. I browse the tourist shops in Luxor, determined to distract myself from myself.

In one of the jewelry shops, the skinny, gregarious proprietor takes an interest in me, shows me around, and strikes up a personal conversation. I'm mildly flattered until I realize that this likely has nothing to do with any unique charms and talents he may have ascribed to me. After all, how many women walk the streets alone here? And, considering that I am now the only person in his shop, he is naturally trying to make a sale. In a dimly lit rear room, beside a glass case filled with lapis lazuli jewelry and faience ushabtis, he suddenly grasps my hands and gazes intently into my eyes, as though he is about to deliver an urgent message like, say, a terrorist alert.

"You give too much away to others and don't keep enough for yourself." He smiles knowingly. "You need love and nourishment, because people take it from you."

I am too surprised by this personal pronouncement to respond, though I will admit he's onto something. Instinctively, I pull my hands away. "Well, who doesn't need love?"

"You must balance your heart and your head."

"How do you know that?"

"I read palms." He winks. "Why don't you come back tomorrow night, and I'll give you a reading." Before I know it, he has trapped me in a desperate, disarming hug.

Nervously yet politely I push him away. "Sorry, I have to go now. Thanks." My pulse races as I head for the door.

I stay clear of the shop during the rest of my stay in Luxor, only to learn later from Samy that this man had been caught robbing people and was wanted by the tourist police. I feel that something or someone had been protecting me that night; perhaps it was Isis.

Early the next morning in my hotel room, I'm awakened by the telephone. It is Kent Weeks.

"I know you're heading to Cairo today, but I have some good news."

I hold my breath.

"Ask Samy to bring you to the Valley right away. It looks like I can get you into KV-5!"

For a moment, I'm speechless. "Are you serious?! How did that happen?" My entire body is buzzing.

"Don't worry about the details," he laughs. "Now, you have something to write about, after all."

I thank him profusely, quickly dress, and then gulp down a fruit salad in the hotel café before I meet Samy in the lobby.

"Wait, where's your luggage?" He looks puzzled.

"You won't believe it, Samy. Dr. Weeks called this morning. We have to go back to the Valley of the Kings!"

"Excellent!" He smiles with self satisfaction. "I said that if you just tried to let things take their own natural course and not worry so much, then it would all fall into place."

It is another sweltering spring day, when we arrive at the necropolis. Outfitted in a hard hat and khakis, Weeks greets me with his customary warmth and enthusiasm.

"Here, better put this on," he says, handing me my own hard hat. "Still dangerous in there, so we have to make it quick. I, personally, and the authorities want you to be safe. Always the threat of a collapsing ceiling, small avalanche, whatever, God forbid."

Am I crazy? I take one last breath of fresh air and follow Weeks into the dark hole in the sun-scorched cliff. Slowly and carefully we make our way through a vast labyrinth of narrow dusty corridors, half-buried doorways and staircases, and numerous chambers packed with centuries-old layers of silt, rock, and rubble washed in by flash floods. The cracked, caving-in ceilings are supported by timbers and steel beams. It's hot, and the air is thick and suffocating. There is an odor as mysterious as the passage of time; it's the smell of history decayed. The only illumination comes from the dim yellow glow of a few light bulbs. Weeks points out hieroglyphics on the limestone walls that spell the names and titles of four of the sons of Ramesses II, the most prodigious and industrious builder to occupy Egypt's throne. Ramesses II not only created monuments to himself throughout the Nile Valley; he also sired more than one hundred children (to eight principal wives) to further ensure his immortality. Weeks says that when he found a one-hundred-foot long, T-shape corridor here filled with debris and flanked by dozens of additional chambers, he knew he was onto something extraordinary.

"It was unlike anything I had ever seen," he says, as we stoop to enter a small, formerly buried doorway at the end of a huge hall supported by stone pillars. "We were crawling with flashlights over rubble on our stomachs. It was claustrophobic and unnerving to see nothing but the ceiling. I was astonished by the tomb's enormous size and unusual layout. It was more intricate than I initially thought. We've found 108 rooms and expect to unearth as many as 150! I believe it's a family mausoleum for up to fifty of Ramesses's sons. The only known tomb of its kind!" He grins widely, his eyes sparkling with excitement.

I suddenly crave a rock-carved window revealing a patch of blue sky to alleviate my claustrophobia. I struggle to take notes in the dim light, as Weeks explains that these rooms probably functioned as offering chapels and storage chambers for the worldly goods of the deceased princes. Like those of other tombs in the necropolis, most of KV-5's treasures were plundered by ancient grave robbers. Yet Weeks's excavation has turned up many valuable artifacts, including alabaster and faience ushabtis, pieces of canopic jars, and pottery shards bearing inscriptions signifying that choice wines, beers, and oils were among the buried foodstuffs.

As we creep farther into the tomb, Weeks shines his flashlight on a rare life-size statue of Ramesses II portrayed as Osiris. The living pharaoh was a manifestation of Osiris's son, Horus, who had the power to subdue chaos and maintain the cosmic order; at death he became Osiris himself.

"Over there," Weeks says, peering through the dust of three millennia. "Those beautiful reliefs depict Ramesses presenting his sons to various gods in the afterlife."

My claustrophobia turns to nausea, which I try to conceal from Weeks, who abruptly walks into another chamber to direct his workmen.

I stare into a long, dark corridor, wondering where it leads. The idea of venturing farther into KV-5 fills me with anxiety. My palms are sweating, and I begin to tremble. It is the same sensation I had in King Tut's tomb. Only this time I feel worse, completely trapped. I don't want to make a scene, but I'm struggling to breathe. Weeks has gone to so much trouble to get me in here. I sit down on the rubble and close my eyes. My body feels lighter, almost weightless, as though it is dissolving and I am losing track of myself. In the adjacent chamber, Weeks's voice trails off into what sounds like radio static. I can't seem to speak or even move. All is silent. I am terrified. Then, slowly, I begin to let go and feel myself floating in a warm cloud of light. It is surprisingly peaceful. I feel as though I now exist as everything everywhere and have no need of a body. There is nothing to fear. How wonderfully liberating. The experience feels strangely familiar.

"Okay, ready?" calls Weeks.

I open my eyes to see him walking towards me as if through a thick haze. I look down at my body, which seems to have miraculously rematerialized, and touch my arms and legs. Everything appears to be in order. Then a huge surge of energy pulses through me like an electrical current. I jump to my feet, glancing at my watch. Barely five minutes have passed.

Weeks leads me back out of the tomb. I brush a thick layer of dust off my clothes as I emerge from the darkness, grateful again for the warm caress of sunlight on my skin. This time, though, I'm aware that something has shifted inside me, like I have remembered something significant and essential to my very being. It is a memory of existing in an eternal, all-pervading oneness, being in sacred union with all that is. I had to experience a little death of my own to realize that there is no beginning or end to my soul. I, too, am immortal, just as the Egyptians believed.

"This mystery *must be* unveiled some day," wrote H. P. Blavatsky in *Isis Unveiled*. "The answers are there. They may be found on the time-worn granite pages of cave-temples, on sphinxes, propylons, and obelisks. . . . The key was in the keeping of those who knew how to commune with the invisible Presence, and who had received, from the lips of mother Nature herself, her grand truths. And so stand these monuments like mute forgotten sentinels on the threshold of that *unseen* world."

I am filled with emotion as I hug Weeks good-bye, promising him a great article. And, of course, I'm saddened to be parting ways with Samy, who is certain that he knew me in another lifetime in ancient Egypt and that we are destined to meet again. He has no idea how much I have learned from him in his own unassuming, wise, and magnanimous way.

I spend the next few days in Cairo, immersed in an exhilarating, chaotic swirl of life that leaves me feeling at moments incredibly grounded in my body, with all my senses fully activated and heightened, and at other times like I am floating blissfully above my earth-bound experiences. I'm walking with more grace and confidence, feeling with greater depth and appreciation. It is truly as if one of Isis's veils has been lifted, as if I have transcended my former self and any illusions I may have had about my limitations.

I think of the word *transcend*: trance-end; end the trance. It makes perfect sense.

I remember the Sufi concept of *fana*—the continual, simultaneous dissolution and expansion of the self, like a raindrop, which does not disappear when it falls into an ocean but rather absorbs the entire ocean into itself. Like that raindrop, I am not only flowing through Egypt; it is flowing through me. And one emotion, which is really more a state of being, connects everything—*joy*. So many times I feel like laughing, even shouting to whoever is listening, "*Thank you. Thank you!*"

"There is a community of the spirit," the poet Rumi wrote. "Join it, and feel the delight of walking in the noisy street, and *being* the noise. . . . Be empty of worrying. . . . Why do you stay in prison when the door is so wide open? Move outside the tangle of fear-thinking. Live in silence. Flow down and down in always widening rings of being."

While visiting the Egyptian Museum, I finally see King Tut's stunning lapis and gold death mask, along with—among other glittering ancient treasures—numerous imposing limestone and granite sculptures of Egyptian gods and royalty. Spontaneously, I decide to pay a visit to the Antiquities Department. By some grand stroke of luck, the director happens to be available for a quick interview! This is not something I had arranged in advance or even expected, given the difficulties I encountered when seeking permission to visit KV-5. I had essentially written off these officials as potential sources for my story. I'm tickled by the incident, for fate does seem to be conspiring on my behalf. Is it because I'm finally in "the flow"? With each passing day, more synchronistic events seem to confirm that I am.

Another afternoon, I am suffering from a bothersome cold as I navigate the congested Cairo streets, teeming with exhaust-spewing traffic, donkey carts, dark-suited businessmen, white-turbaned street vendors, mud-brick tenements and modern office buildings, mosques and madrassas, and the occasional wandering goat. I can't seem to stop sniffling and realize, with some dismay, that I have no tissues. Just as I begin to wonder where I could possibly find something as insignificant as a tissue amid this overwhelming frenzy, someone taps me on the shoulder. To my astonishment, it is a young woman carrying a large basket of Kleenex packets! This can't be happening, I think, as I gratefully pay her for a few packets. I have never experienced such an instantaneous manifestation of a thought. I feel as though I have been invested with a magical, new power. Now, if I can only sustain it.

Later, I embark on a special mission at the Khan al-Khalili, Cairo's famous outdoor bazaar—a sprawling warren of local artisans and shops and stalls selling everything from silver and gold jewelry and Bedouin handicrafts to alabaster bowls, mother-of-pearl inlaid boxes, papyrus paintings, and faience ushabtis and scarabs. My editor asked me to buy her an Alexandrite ring at a jewelry shop called Nasser Brothers. Alexandrite is a beautiful lavender-colored stone that turns blue and green in the light. She had seen these rings on a trip to Cairo. So my lovely young guide, Leyla, and I wander the narrow labyrinthine streets of the market in search of this particular shop, stopping to buy souvenirs along the way.

Leyla's English is impeccable, and she has assured me that we will find the shop. But we pass several hours with no luck. I'm tired and disheartened. I don't want to disappoint my editor, though I know she would understand. Despite the fact that I don't easily give up, I stop abruptly and reluctantly tell Leyla that it's time to call off the search. Just then, I look up at the sign on the shop in front of us. It's Nasser Brothers! I cannot believe my luck. Just like the tissue incident earlier, I would never have thought this possible. I am so stunned that I'm momentarily immobilized. Leyla, too, is transfixed. We glance at each other, then howl with laughter. I rush into the store and happily purchase an Alexandrite ring for my editor, along with a beautiful Bedouin silver bracelet for myself. Once again, the power of my thoughts alone has led me to my object of desire. Someone or something beyond space and time seems to be making its presence known.

Feeling as though I have been transformed and reborn into a higher awareness by my experiences in Egypt, I notice that the synchronicities occur when my mind is serenely focused, not running rampant with scattered thoughts. I see that I literally must "stop" my mind in order to access and surrender to the universal flow. One side benefit of this new state of being is that for several days now I have felt no compulsion to check my phone messages. Nor does it matter that I have not spoken to my boyfriend. My fear of abandonment seems to have abated. I don't even care if he has lost interest. If so, I'll find someone better suited to me. And I'm not overly concerned for my safety. What a relief not to be on constant alert for a potential terrorist attack! How empowering to have stopped worrying so much! All I have to do is trust, trust, trust that all will be well, and so it is.

On my last day in Egypt, I am snaking through traffic in a taxicab on my way to the Great Pyramid of Giza, enjoying a pleasant conversation with my driver. Before I leave the cab, he asks me to sign his guest book. A taxi driver with a guest book? This takes Egyptian hospitality to a new level! I gladly pen my name, whereupon he gives me a small, worn faience scarab as a token of thanks.

"For good luck, Insha'Allah!" he says warmly. I smile, recalling the scarab Khepri, the Egyptian god of transformation and resurrection.

The Great Pyramid, which served as a tomb for the Old Kingdom pharaoh Khufu, is even more awesome than I had imagined. Built more than 4,500 years ago with 2.3 million limestone blocks by tens of thousands of skilled workers, it covers fourteen acres and stands nearly forty stories tall, reigning over the Sahara with a sublime presence that has defied time. Pyramids functioned not only as royal tombs but also as initiatory centers of esoteric knowledge, where the great mysteries of the universe were revealed to those deemed ready and worthy. Legend has it that spiritual adepts such as Pythagoras, Plato, and even Jesus were among those initiated here. Constructed in a triangular shape symbolizing the sun's rays, and with entrance passageways facing directly north towards the Pole Star, the Great Pyramid has several air shafts that were meant to allow the departed pharaoh's soul to ascend to his eternal home in the stars with the sun god Re. In this sense, pyramids were literally stairways to heaven.

The ancients also viewed pyramids as transmitters of cosmic energy, integrating heaven and earth, and spirit and matter. I think about this as I walk ever so slowly and carefully up the long, steep plank stairway to the burial chamber. The climb is challenging, and my steps unsteady. I grasp the flimsy wire railing with all my might to keep from slipping. Thankfully, there is no one behind me, though a few tourists are climbing back down alongside me. We exchange beleaguered smiles. Finally, I reach the small King's Chamber, at the center of which stands an empty red granite sarcophagus. I sit down on the hot stone floor, close my eyes, and try to absorb the ancient energy of the pyramid in the all-encompassing silence. Again, I feel the elasticity of time, which expands to encompass the present and the future as well as the past. The veils between dimensions seem to be continually thinning. I fidget and run my hand along the granite wall to ascertain that I'm still here, in physical form.

As my eyes open, they settle on the empty sarcophagus, and a thought occurs to me: Why is it empty? "Because there is no death," I hear a voice whisper, as if from a great distance. "There is no death . . . You live forever." For the first time, deep inside, I feel this to be true. And I imagine my own soul taking flight like the pharaoh's through the airshaft. Then an image of Isis, goddess of magic, rises up in my thoughts. She appears so real that I can almost touch her—her graceful, slender form, long gleaming black hair, and golden solar disc crown. She offers me a lotus, symbol of the awakening spirit and purification. I interpret this as a gift acknowledging that I have begun to reclaim, integrate, and literally re-member the disparate parts of myself—body and mind, heart and soul, male and female, the sacred and sensual—as one divine essence, the whole, true me. "Remember who you are," her voice echoes with urgency. "Remember who you are."

All existing things are transient. . . . All existing things are involved in suffering. . . . All existing things are unreal. He who knows and perceives this is no longer the thrall of grief.

—Buddha, quoted in the Dhammapada

4

TEN DAYS IN TIBET

Faith

I t is tempting to seek refuge in the Buddha's metaphysics. But the ragged children begging for food on my journey across Tibet won't let me. They are real, knocking on our van windows, pulling at our jackets. Our guide collects what is left in our lunch boxes, specially prepared by the tourist hotels, and tosses it to the children and their families, nomads, and villagers who seem to appear out of nowhere each time we stop to eat. A little boy catches a roll and stuffs it into his shirt, grasping it tightly. Some of those gathered around us smile appreciatively; others just stare.

It is not the first time that I have witnessed the crippling poverty of a third-world country. This is the travel addict's curse. In my perpetual quest for the next new frontier and the adrenaline fix provided by unfamiliar sights and sensations and a sense of connection with diverse peoples, cultures, and wisdom traditions, I am made painfully aware of the daily realities that build walls of separation.

There is an expected harshness to life in Tibet, a barren, windswept country surrounded by forbidding mountains, including the world's highest—the Himalayas—to the south. One of the few signs of life on this cold, largely treeless plateau, whose heights of more than fifteen thousand feet have christened it the Roof of the World, are free-roaming sheep and yak—long-haired oxen that have provided Tibetans with much of their food and wool for centuries. But the Tibetans are not merely victims of their geographical isolation, inhospitable landscape, and an ancient, agrarian-based feudal system that has long kept them out of step with modern times.

There is a peculiar heaviness to mountain air so thin that breathing becomes an effort without pills to prevent altitude sickness. There is an empty stillness in the majestic monasteries— the historic repositories of Tibetan religion, culture, and scholarship—even as life in Tibet ostensibly marches onward. There is a vacancy in the eyes of many Tibetans, even as they smile, as if the animating force of this country, its very spirit, is itself struggling to breathe. (Curiously, the word *spirit* comes from the Latin *spiritus*, meaning "wind" or "breath.") It is in this sense that the Buddha's words from the Dhammapada are tragically astute. If one looks closely enough, very little *is* as it appears today in Tibet. The cosmic irony is hard to digest—that a peace-loving country of Buddhists who value the ideal of universal compassion above all else should have, for the past fifty years, suffered the horrors of a tyrannical Communist regime that has perpetrated one of the worst genocides in recent history.

Since 1950, when the Chinese People's Liberation Army invaded and annexed Tibet as part of the newly established People's Republic of China, more than 1.2 million Tibetans (20 percent of the population) have died either by execution, torture, starvation, or suicide, in prison and labor camps, or in battle as a result of the Chinese occupation. Tens of thousands have been driven from their homeland, including the fourteenth Dalai Lama, Tibet's spiritual and political leader, who has established a government-in-exile in Dharamsala in northeast India, where many Tibetan refugees have settled.

In his book, *Seven Years in Tibet*, the Austrian explorer Heinrich Harrer recalls the twenty-five-year-old Dalai Lama's dramatic escape from the Potala in 1959, during a fateful uprising in Lhasa. "Should the Dalai Lama stay or flee? The Tibetan Government could not make such an important decision; the gods must have the last word. The State Oracle said 'flee.' The Dalai Lama's flight was kept strictly secret. For the last time high officials drank butter tea in the Potala, and then their cups were refilled and left standing as a charm to bring about a speedy return. . . . Sixteen days after leaving Lhasa the caravan halted in the Chumbi Valley on the borders of India. I stayed with his Holiness in the Chumbi Valley for three more months, still believing that we might be able to return, but I soon realized that was the end of the old Tibet."

Like other Western pilgrims, I have traveled to Tibet in search of Shangri-La, a mythical place of peace and enlightenment, an exotic land of snow-capped mountains, monks, and meditations. It has been a long-held dream. And having just turned forty, I like the idea of literally being on top of the world. I also urgently need an exhilarating distraction from my work, whose increasing pressures have left me exhausted. I had read early explorers' accounts of Lhasa—the Forbidden City, "ground of the gods" (in Tibetan), and "the furthest goal of all travel," according to the pioneering Tibetologist Csoma de Koros, who never got there. My pulse quickened as I imagined the mystical delights that awaited me. What I see now instead is a surreal, Disney version of this fabled land, most glaringly apparent in Lhasa, which has become a capital of Chinese kitsch and commerce, masking the true plight of the Tibetan people, who walk about like actors in a staged event, visitors in their own home.

Where once stood Tibetan villages of whitewashed farmhouses with colorful, rooftop prayer flags, there are dreary, homogeneous concrete buildings; broad, symmetrical streets; and Chinese-run factories, hotels, shops, restaurants, cinemas, casinos, and discos blaring heavy metal music—frequented mostly by Chinese. I am reminded of Chengdu, the city in western China, where we boarded a plane to Lhasa along with hundreds of Chinese tourists on holiday.

Modernization has certainly come to Tibet, but at what price? Over the years, the continuous influx of Chinese immigrants has flooded the job market, leaving most Tibetans out of work or underpaid in menial jobs. Many have become street hawkers and beggars, living in slums often deprived of electricity and running water (which are available in Chinese communities) and unable to afford the most basic amenities. Apartheid is indeed alive and well in Tibet under a policy the Chinese call "segregation and assimilation." "In reality, Tibetans are, at best, second-class citizens in their own country," the Dalai Lama has said.

For the past fifty years, Tibetans have also been denied freedom of speech and demonstration. Expressions of discontent and demands for independence are capital offenses, punishable by imprisonment, torture, and execution. Movement within and outside the country is severely restricted for Tibetans. Chinese soldiers patrol numerous roadside checkpoints, where tourist vehicles are also obliged to stop for clearance.

As I walk the streets of Lhasa within the confines of my tour group, I feel trapped, as if I have become an unwilling participant in a charade devised to conceal the truth of the Tibetans' daily existence. I have never been tolerant of untruths. As I sink down through my antipathy for the layers of obvious deceit, I am overcome with rage—a rage that, simmering without release, transmutes into nausea. I am fairly certain that it's not the kind of nausea triggered by high altitudes, because I'm taking Diamox and the tingling in my fingers and toes confirms its effectiveness. It's a visceral nausea. My own personal concerns—whether the stressful demands of my work and its accompanying financial uncertainty or my tiresome, ongoing search for a so-called soul mate—seem so inconsequential here, compared to what the Tibetans endure on a daily basis.

I am wary of sharing my innermost thoughts and feelings with my travel companions, who have been mostly silent about all matters political. We are strangers, after all, and we will be spending nearly every waking hour of ten days together. It is in everyone's best interest to be as agreeable and accommodating as possible. And we have been forewarned by the tour operator to keep our political opinions to ourselves, particularly when we are within earshot of Chinese officials. It's just a trip, I tell myself. I'm not here to take action. Or am I?

So I simmer in silence. But then something shifts inside me. I become increasingly aware that I may not be as different from the oppressors as I might have believed. I see in them a side of myself, dark and buried, that is uncomfortable to acknowledge. I sometimes express it in conscious and unconscious judgments and stereotyping, which fuels perceptions of separation. At the extreme, this state of mind can validate mistreatment of others, as it has in the case of the Chinese's treatment of Tibetans. One of the essential teachings of Tibetan Buddhism is that we are all linked in a continuous chain of cause-and effect-energies. Interconnection is inescapable. I realize that while I don't have to condone the incomprehensible sufferings of the Tibetans, neither should I allow my rage to perpetrate further illusions of separation as well as blanket assumptions about the Chinese.

As stated in the book *The Meaning of Life from a Buddhist Perspective*, a collection of lectures given by the Dalai Lama, anger and aggression are not permitted on the Buddhist spiritual path. Though under certain circumstances it may be necessary to take counteraction to stop a wrongdoing, the Dalai Lama believes that such measures can be enacted without anger. This "is much more effective than when your main mind is governed by a strong afflictive emotion, because under such influence you may not take the appropriate action," he says. "Anger destroys one of the best qualities of the human brain—judgment, the capacity to think, 'This is wrong,' and to investigate what the temporary and long-term consequences of an action will be." He counsels that a daily meditation practice in which one continually focuses on the benefits of love, compassion, and kindness and the disadvantages of anger "has the effect of creating dislike for hatred and respect for love," so that "even when you get angry, its expression changes in aspect and diminishes in force."

Given that the problems in our world, whether global or personal, are the result of what Buddhists call afflictive emotions, such as anger, hatred, jealousy, pride, desire, doubt, etc., the main focus of Buddhist practices is to still one's mind through meditation, which is supposed to breed nonviolence and compassion. "Since the root of suffering is ignorance, suffering stems from an untamed mind," says the Dalai Lama. "Correspondingly, since relief from suffering stems from purifying and destroying the ignorance that is in the mind, it stems from taming the mind. The taming of the mind is to be done mentally by training. . . . As practitioners our real target or battle should be within ourselves."

Afflictive emotions from the Buddhist perspective result from the ignorance that conceives objects/phenomena as inherently existing in and of themselves, independent of other causes and conditions. Because all objects/phenomena are, in fact, dependent on infinite causes and conditions, a concept the Buddhists call "dependent-arising," they are devoid of "being under their own power," according to the Dalai Lama. "Also, because in this context of dependence, help and harm arise and exist, objects do *not* not exist—their performance of functions is feasible, as is the I that is the basis of them. When one understands this, one is released from the extreme of non-existence, nihilism." The same conceptual framework, of course, applies to interpersonal relationships.

"When we reflect on our own desire and hatred, we see that they are generated within a conception of oneself as very solid, due to which there comes to be a strong distinction between oneself and others, and consequently attachment for one's own side and hatred for others," the Dalai Lama says. Contemporary quantum physics has validated the Buddhist concept of "dependent-arising" by proving that something exists only because it has been perceived by the consciousness of an observer, effectively obliterating the distinction between subject and object. This, of course, has extraordinary spiritual implications, reconfirming what the mystics throughout the ages have always known: All human beings are one and the same; therefore whom we perceive to be "others" are deserving of the same compassion we would want for ourselves. It is the same moral code upon which all spiritual traditions are founded and was perhaps delivered most simply and eloquently by Jesus, who said, "Love one another as I have loved you."

I see the last vestiges of old Tibet at the Barkor—the pilgrimage route surrounding the Jokhang, the country's holiest temple, which Tibetans continually circumambulate in a clockwise direction. Fanning out from the Barkor are narrow, cobblestone streets and winding alleyways lined with some of the last remaining Tibetan townhouses. Here, merchants sell large slabs of yak butter, vegetables, household items, and other goods from their humble stalls. There are small tearooms, machine shops, and even a "dental office" displaying tooth specimens and cryptic dental treatment descriptions. Goats, sheep, dogs, bicycles, and tourist rickshaws ply through this ancient market maze, once crowded with traders and pilgrims from all over Asia.

Around the Barkor and the adjacent, modern plaza, punctuated with gaudy street lamps, are hundreds of stalls. Many are manned by Chinese vendors skilled in the art of bargaining, fueling the tourist trade with Tibetan souvenirs. Here are the ubiquitous, sacred prayer wheels that are endlessly twirled by devout Tibetan Buddhists; turquoise jewelry; carved yak-bone bowls; and dorjes (ritualistic Buddhist implements shaped like thunderbolts and symbolizing the creative male energies of the universe). There are also wood-block-printed prayer books; decorative thankas (intricate religious paintings of Buddhist deities, lamas, and Buddhas that serve as aids to meditation); Tibetan wool hats and boots; and cheap trinkets made in China. Plain-clothes Chinese operatives with video cameras patrol the area for Tibetans fraternizing with foreigners.

I inspect one of the prayer books and ask its price. Deciding that it is too high, I try to bargain with the anxious vendor. We do not arrive at an agreement, and she is visibly annoyed as I return the prayer book to her table. She shouts some harsh words at me, which, of course, I do not understand. Stung by this outburst, I am tempted to shout back. But I can almost hear the Buddha, the Awakened One, whispering, "All that we are is the result of what we have thought; it is founded on our thoughts, it is made up of our thoughts. If a man speaks or acts with a pure thought, happiness follows him, like a shadow that never leaves him." I smile and walk away.

Many of the Tibetan women at the Barkor are outfitted in colorfully embroidered black boots, black woolen tunics, and turquoise jewelry. They offer a warm "*tashi deleg*" ("hello" in Tibetan) as children, wearing dusty old sweaters and pants with slits at their behinds to facilitate mother nature's call, gather around me chirping, "Hello, money," like parrots. I want to give them some of the felt-tip pens I have brought along as gifts. "Don't indulge them," advises Kumar, our jovial Nepalese group leader. "It only encourages aggressive begging that hassles tourists." I reluctantly put the pens away. On the streets of Lhasa, men huddle around public pool tables. I pause at the irony. Although many Tibetans do not have electricity or enough food to eat, their oppressors have allowed an outlet for recreation.

I am saddened to find that Lhasa's major landmarks—the Jokhang Temple; Potala Palace, sacred home of the Dalai Lamas since the mid-seventeenth century; and the great Drepung, Sera, and Ganden monasteries—are little more than vacant museums, supplying a significant flow of tourist dollars to the Chinese economy and thereby validating their continued existence. There are so many Chinese tourists on the rooftop of the Potala the day we visit that it is nearly impossible to frame a photograph.

From any vantage point, the Potala stirs emotion. A white and red, four-story complex of more than one thousand rooms, it sits majestically atop a rocky outcrop overlooking all of Lhasa. Its austere architecture and massive proportions endow it with an earthly solidity that evokes a sense of order amidst chaos. Yet at the same time, as if containing within its walls all the otherworldly yearnings of generations of Tibetans, it appears to be surging upward toward the heavens. Inside the seventeenth-century palace, a solemn grandeur permeates its labyrinthine chambers, chapels, and corridors; its grand audience halls and shrines; the towering, bejeweled burial chortens of past Dalai Lamas; and the ornate quarters of the thirteenth and fourteenth Dalai Lamas.

Although Tibet has been open to foreign tourists since the early 1980s, in recent years it has been possible to travel only as part of an official tour group. Most groups stay at the Chinese-owned Lhasa Hotel, the best in the city, complete with its very own "Hard Yak Café" and a large gift shop selling thankas, Tibetan carpets and jewelry, and other souvenirs. The hotel is comfortable enough, but far from luxurious. Its rooms are spacious and equipped with oxygen tanks, which I fortunately do not require. Nor do I feel the need to sample a yak burger, despite occasional protein cravings and prodding from my companions. My diet on this journey is strictly vegetarian—varied combinations of rice and cabbage, spinach, bok choy, carrots or broccoli when available, hard-boiled eggs, and peanuts. We eat buffet-style. As time wears on, I tire of this culinary asceticism. Julia, a spunky younger woman in our group, and I playfully taunt each other with our cravings, calling out delicacies like banana cream pie, chocolate chip ice cream, and pinot noir when we need an imaginary indulgence.

On our last night in Lhasa we find ourselves in a cramped, smoky disco not far from the hotel. The crowd is young and energized, the music ear-splitting and distinctly familiar. As we sit talking and imbibing the local beer, a young Tibetan man approaches our table and whispers something to Kumar.

"He's asked for your hand in a dance," Kumar laughs heartily. "I said okay."

"Why not?" I say, with some trepidation.

Before I know it, my partner and I are soon dancing and sweating and smiling at each other like old friends. After a few numbers, he nods politely and leads me back to our table. "Don't worry," says Kumar, who is clearly enjoying his new role as my surrogate father. "He won't agree to marriage, not even for five yaks!"

I would like to feel as though I am dancing across Tibet, not bodily of course, but rather in mind and spirit. I find, however, that the spontaneous openness with which I greeted my dance partner that evening can be stingy in its expression. The following day, as we stand in one of the secluded, ornately decorated chapels at Sera Monastery listening to our excellent Tibetan guide, Denzin, who, in his late twenties, conducts himself with a maturity far beyond his age, a German woman breaks away from her tour group and joins ours. She soon begins asking questions that monopolize Denzin, which annoys me.

"Why couldn't she have stayed with her own group?" I whisper to Julia.

"We *are* learning something from the woman's questions," she replies politely. "Maybe you should be more tolerant."

I am initially offended by her blunt honesty, but I soon realize she's right. We are, after all, in Tibet, and a good Tibetan Buddhist would not seek to exclude but willingly accept diversity. In perceiving the German woman as an intruder on my territory, am I not, in microcosm, adopting the same misanthropic view as that of the oppressors who have made life miserable for the Tibetans? I am humbled. I obviously need to work on that pesky virtue, patience—one of the "six perfections" that the Buddhists believe we need to master on the road to enlightenment. The other five in fixed order are charity (liberality), ethics and manners, effort (strenuousness), meditative concentration, and wisdom (discriminating awareness), each one proceeding from the mastery of the former, with patience following ethics.

According to *The Jewel Ornament of Liberation* by sGam. po.pa, the great eleventh–twelfth-century Tibetan Buddhist monk, philosopher, and teacher: liberality abolishes poverty; ethics leads to coolness; patience endures harshness; strenuousness applies itself to what is most sublime; meditative concentration holds mind in its own inner sphere; and discriminating awareness allows the ultimately real to be known. "Fixed order means the succession in which the perfections arise in our life," sGam. po.pa wrote. "By liberality, not counting how much enjoyment we give, we bow to ethics and manners. Following these rules we grow patient and so become strenuous. This in turn develops the power of meditative concentration. When we enter the latter state we acquire discriminating awareness born from wisdom and see things as they really are."

So I will try to use patience and effort to quiet my ego and dwell more deeply in that still place within myself that remains unperturbed by external events. Upon leaving the chapel, I pass a monk sitting crosslegged and chanting mantras over a prayer book. He does not seem to mind our intrusion in his sanctuary, with all the low-pitched bantering and shuffling about. He has centered himself in a single-focused awareness.

Having encountered few monks in Tibet, I consider myself fortunate to witness a large group of them vehemently debating Buddhist philosophy among the willow trees in an outdoor courtyard at Sera Monastery, each one clapping loudly as he makes his point. Some occasionally even push one another away, which does not coincide with my image of the gentle, taciturn monk. This rare showing, however, barely conceals the truth. The Sera, Drepung, and Ganden monasteries (all within about twenty-five miles of Lhasa) have each once housed thousands of monks, whose numbers have diminished to the low hundreds since the Chinese invasion. Like the Potala, Tibet's religious structures are mostly absent of monks. Except for a few wandering caretakers, their cavernous, pillared assembly halls are dark and silent. Red monks' robes lie in heaps on the cushioned benches, surrounded by colorful embroidered hangings resembling elongated lampshades that are meant to transform and spiritualize the space. Instead of the deep, droning chants uttered for the spiritual benefit of mankind, there are the hushed voices of tour guides.

Branded as "counterrevolutionaries" and "enemies of the people" for practicing their Buddhist faith, an entire generation of monks, inheritors of centuries of scholarship, perished due to extended imprisonment, torture, execution, suicide, and bloody massacres that marked Mao Tse Tung's Cultural Revolution from 1966 to 1976, when many of Tibet's monasteries were deliberately destroyed. Another wave of slaughter swept Tibet during the late 1980s, when the Chinese military suppressed demonstrations for Tibetan independence. Monks and nuns, who are the majority of political prisoners, continue to be arrested, tortured, and subjected to political re-education for speaking out against their oppressors and refusing to renounce the Dalai Lama, public enemy number one. The education campaign against the Dalai Lama has been so strong in recent years that many of the remaining monks have fled Tibet, according to the Tibet Information Network, which is based in London and Jackson, Wyoming.

"Caught in a fresh tidal wave of repression, the country seems to be battling now for its very existence," wrote Mary Craig in her 1999 book *Tears of Blood: A Cry for Tibet.* "But what the foreign governments perhaps do not realize (or do not care to think too closely about) is that a Tibetan caught singing or playing a cassette of national songs, reading a book about or by the Dalai Lama, putting up his picture, or writing a leaflet in praise of freedom, whether civil or political, is 'endangering national security.' A tortured monk or nun enduring long solitary confinement in prison shouts an independence slogan and has his or her sentence prolonged by a number of years for 'attempting to overthrow the state.'"

In order to ensure the extinction of religion in Tibet, the Chinese government has also resorted to the nonviolent tactic of imposing strict quotas on the number of monks permitted to enter each monastery. As we proceed through the dim, empty corridors and elaborate chapels of Drepung Monastery—inhabited by massive gilt, jewel-encrusted Buddhas and lamas, serenely impervious to the sufferings of their people—my heart weighs heavy. Tears fill my eyes, as they have so many times these past days, for my initial rage at the cruel injustices perpetrated against this great culture has frozen into a deep sorrow. The rancid smell of yak butter—an offering poured by pilgrims from small chalices into the candle-lit cauldrons—interlaced with the burnt, sweet scent of juniper incense, nauseates me. One kindly monk presiding over the kitchen offers me some steaming yak-butter tea. I politely decline.

I am keenly aware of the surveillance cameras and Chinese guards hovering like watchdogs here, lest a Tibetan tour guide or a pilgrim circumambulating the holy shrines fall prey to a politically incorrect encounter with a foreign tourist. We were warned before leaving for Tibet not to display or distribute photographs or information about the Dalai Lama or even to utter his name, which could result in detainment or deportation and seriously endanger the Tibetans in our midst. Tibetan tour guides are particularly suspect and frequently interrogated.

Flashlight in hand, I inspect Drepung's intricate frescoes and thankas, marveling at their complex Buddhist iconography. No surface, whether a ceiling beam, cornice, or lintel, is left uncolored. I recall the *horror vacui* (Latin for "fear of empty space") attributed to medieval artists who would not risk leaving any unpainted space on their canvases, for to do so was to admit, perhaps, a gap in faith. There is no room for such gaps in Tibet. Faith is perhaps the one thing that the Chinese cannot take away from the Dalai Lama and his people, the faith that they will prevail in their struggle for freedom, despite seemingly insurmountable obstacles. I am momentarily distracted by a monk who is trimming the wicks and stirring the yellow wax of one of the many enormous bronze, candle-lit cauldrons that illuminate the monastery's dark recesses. It is his job to ensure a constant flame. This simple ritual, reenacted daily, is itself a powerful reminder of the steady attention that faith requires.

I have always believed in the presence of a divine healing force in the universe, which guides us to the proper people and experiences necessary for our own individual and collective spiritual evolution. Yet I also sometimes doubt that the universe will provide; it's as if I fear the very ground I'm treading will give way beneath me. Similarly, I can suddenly glimpse eternity in meditation, and when my ego momentarily dissolves in union with the cosmos, I'll experience a frightening, shaky sense of no-self. The Tibetan Buddhists might say that in such moments I am having a bardo experience. *Bardo,* as explained in *The Tibetan Book of the Dead,* literally means "gap," an interval of suspension that occurs in both death and life. My fluctuating feelings of doubt and uncertainty are the psychological fallout from the birth and death transitions that I am continually undergoing in my everyday life. These recurrent deaths and rebirths are necessary for our spiritual development. We are having bardo experiences all the time.

The bardo we enter after physical death and before our next rebirth initially makes itself known through a bewildering and terrifying panorama of colors, lights, and sounds, all of which are projections of our own mind, as is this earthly plane of suffering. The key to enduring what seems like a bad "acid trip" is recognizing that we have, indeed, created it, while releasing thoughts of fear and keeping the mind focused in a meditative state, according to *The Tibetan Book of the Dead*, whose wisdom applies equally to the living.

I realize that my wakeful bardo experiences are often intensified by a clouded view of reality—as a continual conflict between, rather than an integration of, opposites such as life and death, good and evil, pleasure and pain, and so on. This theme continues to revisit me throughout my travels, in an effort, I suspect, to lodge itself permanently in my consciousness. For wisdom typically is not gained in one dramatic moment but through a series of ongoing lessons, many of them repetitive yet delivered in an infinite variety of circumstances so that we don't get bored, I suppose. One of the keys to an enlightened consciousness, Tibetan Buddhists believe, is to experience the dualistic world from a clear, nondualistic view of all-encompassing oneness. Such dualities exist, then, not as conflicts but as complementary aspects of a larger whole. In this state, the confusion that causes uncertainty and dissatisfaction disappears.

I see this belief expressed, metaphorically, in the many thankas that enliven the walls of Drepung Monastery. In these cloth scroll paintings, which have been used for centuries by Tibetan Buddhists as aids to meditation, both peaceful and wrathful deities burst forth in a profusion of color. In some thankas, male and female deities are depicted in sexual union. Referred to as a yab-yum (father-mother) pair, the male symbolizes compassion, while the female symbolizes wisdom. Their union signifies enlightenment. They challenge us to integrate the male and female energies within ourselves.

Most Tibetan art, including thankas, murals, and the ornate sculptures of Buddhas and lamas that adorn Tibet's monasteries and temples, has a religious function. Thankas, in particular, serve as sources of spiritual energy that represent the mystical visions of monks. Few original artworks housed in Tibet's religious structures remain, however; most of these centuries-old treasures were carted off to China as spoils of the Cultural Revolution. By the early 1980s, Tibet's monasteries and temples were being rebuilt by Tibetan monks, and the looted art was gradually replaced with replicas.

It is one thing, of course, to read reports about the tragedy of Tibet and quite another to witness it. The cultural destruction wrought by the Chinese is particularly noticeable at Ganden Monastery, where, with the exception of a few partially rebuilt structures, a barren cliff side impressed with the faint outlines of former dwellings is the only evidence of the hundreds of buildings that once stood here. Again, I'm overcome with emotion. According to the Tibet Information Network, of the more than six thousand monasteries that existed in Tibet before the Chinese occupation only six remain.

We embark on a ninety-minute pilgrimage walk around the bombed-out remains of Ganden. The trail is narrow and rocky with steep precipices. At one point, I slip, and my water bottle tumbles out of my backpack over the cliff. My heart races. Another false step and it could be me. I think of all the freedom-fighting Tibetans who are in constant danger of being killed. Yaks graze the mountainside studded with ashen heaps of burning juniper and small, stone stupa-chortens that look like miniature Buddhist temples and represent enlightenment. There is also a fair share of human debris—torn cardboard, paper wrappers, and colored plastic bags—that has increasingly littered the Tibetan countryside. Obviously, no effort is being made to clean up after the eagerly sought tourists.

The only stirrings on the mountain, aside from the yak and our small group, are two Tibetan boys from a nearby village who have joined our trek and a tattered, cross-legged holy man chanting and reading scriptures in a cloud of incense under a rocky overhang. Each bend in the trail brings a new vista of dusty, wind-swept plains and snow-capped peaks. Multicolored prayer flags flutter around us, inscribed with sacred mantras that are symbolically scattered by the wind throughout the world. It is yet another irony. Even as they themselves suffer, the Tibetans pray for all living beings.

Denzin points out a sky burial site in the distance. Tibetans usually dispose of their dead on a mountaintop, leaving cut-up remains to nourish birds of prey as an act of generosity. Since Tibetan Buddhists believe that all beings are continually reborn for the sake of their own spiritual progress, they view death as a transforming experience that is not to be feared. The ultimate goal, however, is to transcend *samsara*, the ceaseless round of reincarnations on this plane of suffering, and attain nirvana, the state of complete enlightenment and spiritual liberation from rebirth. The sky burial site is a powerful reminder, like my misstep moments earlier, of the fragility of life and the impermanence of all things—my awareness of which is often obscured by the habitual drone of daily activities. Impermanence is an important concept underlying the Buddhist dharma (the teachings of the Buddhist tradition in its entirety), which holds that conventional reality as we know it is an illusion. That does not mean, however, that Tibetan Buddhists have renounced their involvement in the world and its sufferings. Their reverence for life is so intense, in fact, that they will not even kill insects.

The type of Buddhism practiced by Tibetans, known as Mahayana, stresses the interconnection of all life and the imperative to discover the meaning of one's own participation in it, the Buddhist scholar Stephen Batchelor explains in *The Tibet Guide*. Compassion and love, versus renunciation, detachment, and the self-centered desire to achieve only one's own spiritual enlightenment, are central to Tibetan Buddhism and embodied in the bodhisattva—a person who aspires to realize enlightenment for the benefit of others.

It is this very idea of contemplation in action, engaged awareness, which the Dalai Lama has embodied in his nonviolent struggle to save Tibet. At the heart of his message, and of Tibetan Buddhism itself, is the belief that enlightenment, and hence peace, comes with the integration of wisdom and compassion—the wisdom that we are not isolated, separate selves, and the compassion that motivates action for the benefit of others. But even as millions in the West flock to his sold-out lectures and appearances, that message has fallen largely on deaf ears; Tibet is still an occupied country whose two-thousand-year-old civilization is on the brink of extinction.

Throughout my journey, I witness many acts of compassion, however small, that leave me with a renewed faith in their combined power to bring about positive change in Tibet. There is the primal compassion of Tibetan mothers begging for food for their children, even as they themselves go hungry. There is the tender compassion of our Tibetan guide, Denzin, who is so concerned when my camera malfunctions that he offers to give (not loan) me his extra camera. There is the noble compassion of the American couple who have sent a $5,000 check to Kumar to present to the head nun of Ani Sangkhung Nunnery, the only active nunnery in Lhasa, which we visit after touring the monasteries. The money is to be used for the care of a sick, elderly colleague who needs medical treatment and a wheelchair. The nun smiles ebulliently, poses for a photograph with the check, and then drapes each of us with a white kata (the traditional greeting scarf) as a blessing.

At the nunnery, painted a cheerful yellow and bedecked with potted flowers, we visit a workshop where several young, hair-shorn nuns sit all day performing assembly-line tasks. On this particular occasion they are printing prayers onto tiny rolls of paper. These scrolls are placed inside hand-held prayer wheels and the large, bronze cylindrical wheels adjacent to religious structures. The spinning of the prayers inside the wheels brings additional merit to the devotee. The nuns smile cheerfully, and some converse with us in English, to my surprise. I'm struck by their warmth and openness even in the midst of their duties.

"Americans are too isolated from each other," Denzin observes, curiously tapping into my thoughts. He told me earlier that he had visited both New York and Los Angeles. "They're afraid to interact and connect." He looks to me for affirmation.

"More isolated than we need to be, especially in the cities," I say, saddened by his perception, limited as it is.

I vow to open my heart more fully to each moment, to take the time to make connections, beyond friends and family, as I go about my daily life. I remember missed opportunities—an interaction with the cashier at my neighborhood grocery store or the waitress who serves me Sunday breakfast. I will try to release all judgmental, critical thoughts as barriers to a clear mind open to the positive potential in each person and situation. Denzin tells me that many of the nuns here have demonstrated against the occupation and have been imprisoned. Upon hearing this, one of the young nuns catches my eye. My heart aches as she says softly, "We Tibetans may be smiling on the outside, but we're crying on the inside."

Despite the traumas of the occupation, the single most enduring image of Tibet is the spiritual fervor of its people. Their Buddhist faith permeates every aspect of their lives, which manifests in everything from the ceaseless whirling of prayer wheels and murmuring of mantras to prostrating pilgrims and the ubiquitous prayer flags waving at mountain passes and on the roofs of Tibetan houses. Throughout the Tibetan countryside, incense fires burn and colorful Buddha images enliven rock faces. The omnipresent Tibetan words *Om Mani Padme Hum* (Hail to the Jewel in the Lotus), a mantra recited by devotees, is carved and painted on mani stones scattered around monasteries, roadsides, and mountain passes, and spelled out with small white stones on hillsides.

This mantra, which holds within it many layers of esoteric meaning, can also be translated as "within your heart there is a lotus, and within this lotus there is a diamond." The diamond (*mani*) represents the void, or source of creation, which is associated with the male principle of the cosmos, while the lotus (*padme*) is associated with the enfolding form, or female principle, through which the void is made manifest. And because all phenomena are interrelated, there can only be one lotus. *Om* means the infinite totality of existence, while *Hum*—as the expression of the infinite in the finite, spirit in matter—represents our potential for enlightenment. These simple words thus contain within them the wisdom of the universe.

From morning till night, devout Tibetans circle temples, monasteries, and the numerous chapels within them, making offerings of yak butter, incense, flowers, and katas to the Buddhist deities enshrined on their altars. And they walk the Lingkor, the old holy route around Lhasa (much of which has disappeared with modernization), chanting "Om Mani Padme Hum" as if such devoted acts of faith alone will deliver them from their plight. These popular public displays of faith began to resurge in the early 1980s, when the Chinese government relaxed restrictions imposed during the Cultural Revolution, and are viewed by authorities as folkloric practices.

As I watch the Tibetans endlessly circumambulating the Jokhang Temple, they inspire me to fortify my own faith—faith in Spirit, myself, and others; faith that all the events and experiences of my life, no matter how painful, are happening for my highest good and that of others. I recall the Four Noble Truths at the center of Buddhist teaching: All life is suffering. Suffering is caused by cravings (or desires and attachments). We can end suffering by ceasing to crave. The way to do this is to follow the Buddha's Eight-Fold Path—practicing right views (understanding), right thought (motive), right speech, right action, right livelihood, right effort, right mindfulness (full awareness of all thoughts, words and deeds), and right concentration (meditation). If properly understood and consistently practiced, the Eight-Fold Path can lead us out of ignorance and the relentless demands of our egos to a state of deep inner peace and tranquility.

Perhaps it is their acceptance of such truths that enables the Tibetans to endure the difficult circumstances of their existence. I believe I, too, can benefit from this philosophy and practice as I negotiate my own daily struggles and challenges. As the Buddha said in the Dhammapada, a collection of verses also known as The Path of Truth: "From craving comes grief, from craving comes fear; he who is free from craving neither sorrows nor fears. Good people walk on, whatever befall; the good do not prattle, longing for pleasure; whether touched by happiness or sorrow, wise people never appear elated or depressed."

One bright afternoon in Lhasa, in a small temple courtyard behind the Barkor, hundreds of elderly Tibetans who have traveled here on a forty-nine-day pilgrimage sit huddled together in clusters, reciting mantras and spinning all varieties of wood and embossed metal prayer wheels in a trance-like state. Some Tibetans smile warmly, others look away as I snap a few photographs, feeling like a voyeur. I am eager to record their noble faces, deeply creased with the wisdom of age and experience. Although photos are permitted here, I hastily put my camera away; it is an intrusion on this holy occasion. Entranced, I return the following day to the temple courtyard, crowded once again with pilgrims. Whatever the depth of the common people's spiritual understanding, Tibet is surely one of the few places on Earth where life and spirit are so manifestly one. I have had my glimpse of nirvana, however fleeting. The Chinese may crush the hearts and minds of the Tibetans but not their souls.

Our minibus route, southwest through the Tibetan countryside—along winding, unpaved roads ringed by snowy mountain peaks and past barley and buckwheat fields, grazing sheep, nomads pushing ornately decorated yak-plows, and a sparkling turquoise lake—leads us first to Gyantse, historically Tibet's third largest city after Lhasa and Shigatse. Gyantse has suffered a fate typical of other old Tibetan towns around which a Chinese "new town" has been established. Gyantse old town is a scenic relic of the past, a cluster of muddy streets, wandering goats, donkeys and chickens, and whitewashed, earthen dwellings in various states of disrepair, whose squared rooftops are piled high with clumps of yak dung used for fuel. An old man in rags pulls a wooden cart, while a few Tibetan women stare from their darkened doorways and windows. The Chinese quarter of town does not show such signs of deprivation and neglect. Its inhabitants appear to be better clothed and fed. Its newly built shops and restaurants benefit from the tourist trade.

Gyantse's crowning glory is the Pelkor Chöde Monastery and the Kumbum, one of Tibet's most famous temples, a spiraling, vividly painted, dome-shaped chorten whose gilded crown glitters in the bright afternoon sunlight. Painted high up on the Kumbum is a large pair of eyes, gazing upon the city below with enigmatic indifference. Although the fifteenth-century Kumbum and adjacent Pelkor Chöde Monastery (both of which contain many of their original paintings and statues, though some were defaced) were miraculously spared the destruction wrought by the Cultural Revolution, most of the monastic buildings that once comprised this walled complex no longer exist.

Outside the monastery, a Tibetan man carving a mani stone with the mantra "Om Mani Padme Hum" has misspelled one of the syllables. Kumar notices the mistake and shows him the proper pronunciation. The man graciously acquiesces. The destruction of Tibet's monasteries, which housed extensive libraries and functioned as the traditional education system, has also led to the erosion of the Tibetan language. Most of Tibet's greatest teachers and scholars were monks, and Tibetan families usually sent at least one son to a monastery for schooling. Today, few young Tibetans are able to read or write in their native language. And all the shop signs in Tibet carry Chinese names. Their former Tibetan names are either barely visible under layers of whitewash or appear in small script above the much larger Chinese characters.

Many times during my journey across Tibet, I recall the sand mandala that I had watched Buddhist monks patiently construct for a Tibetan art exhibition in New York City years ago. For hours, they tapped grains of colored sand from small rods onto a circular board stenciled with geometric designs of squares, circles, and Buddhist deities symbolizing the dwelling of an enlightened being to be visualized during meditation. Once the ceremony was over, the monks destroyed the mandala. It was a symbolic act affirming the transitory nature of existence. The continual cycle of creation and destruction finds a perverse mirror in present-day Tibet. Like the mandala, Tibet is being obliterated, not as an example of cosmic law but of earthly brutality.

The golden-roofed Tashilhunpo Monastery in the modern town of Shigatse, about 247 miles west of Lhasa via Gyantse, is another of the few Tibetan monasteries that survived the Cultural Revolution relatively unscathed and is therefore an obligatory stop on most travelers' itineraries. Its centerpiece is an enormous, gilded and bejeweled figure of Maitreya, Buddha of the future.

Leaving Shigatse, we rumble westward through the vast, craggy landscape laced with glaciers and break for lunch near a mountain stream. As usual, some Tibetan villagers have spotted us and gather around to beg for food. And, as usual, we collect what we haven't finished and watch helplessly as Kumar distributes yak butter and cheese sandwiches, apples, cakes, and hard-boiled eggs. My friend Julia and I exchange beleaguered glances. Headed for the small, remote town of Shekar, a launching point for expeditions to nearby Mount Everest, we cross one of the highest mountain passes in the world—the Gyatso-la at 17,200 feet—and stop to take photographs of each other surrounded by poles of fluttering prayer flags. Upon our descent, we stop again, this time for our first thrilling view of Everest (its Tibetan name is *Chomolungma*, "Goddess Mother of the World") in the far distance. This massive white fang puncturing the heavens is every bit as ominous as I had imagined. There is nothing whatsoever maternal about it.

"Why would anyone want to risk his or her life scaling Everest?" I wonder out loud. The mountain is, of course, littered with hundreds of corpses. I would rather meet my match with Yeti, the furry mountain-stalking beast of legend.

"You'll never understand," teases one of my fellow travelers, a skilled climber. The conversation turns to the deadly 1996 climbing expedition documented in Jon Krakauer's *Into Thin Air*. As if the Buddhist theme of impermanence had not yet sufficiently impressed itself upon me, I later learn that a sherpa, who had accompanied that fateful expedition and held the record for the fastest Everest ascent, recently slipped into a crevasse on that very mountain and perished.

In Shekar, I have my first close contact with the Tibetan people, impoverished farmers living just beyond our deteriorating hotel, a modest concrete-block structure which seems more like a prison camp with its lack of heat and hot water and intermittent electricity. Our accommodations have progressively deteriorated as we've ventured farther into the heart of Tibet, and the food has become, at least to my taste, considerably less appetizing.

"Pinot noir," Julia says longingly at dinner one night.

"Banana cream pie," I sigh.

I am now surviving on rice and cooked cabbage and the last of the energy bars and dried fruit rolls that I packed. My vitamin C tablets have run out. I am still drinking one to two quarts of water each day, a necessity at high altitudes. I've developed a lingering chill from days of biting cold, despite my winterized layered clothing. I detect an oncoming sinus infection and barely sleep in the frigid hotels. In short, I feel miserable. And then there is that one annoying traveling companion continuously monopolizing conversations and spouting arcane facts.

It is time to still my thoughts. I commit to morning meditations with increasing discipline, recalling the Buddha's words: "It is good to tame the mind, which is difficult to hold in and flighty, rushing wherever it listeth; a tamed mind brings happiness." Gradually, my sundry annoyances loosen their grip, and my mood lifts. I stop clinging to what has been and how I think things should be. I am embarrassed to have been derailed by such minor discomforts, especially here, in Tibet. I am, however, pleased to find myself at one point hugging that formerly bothersome bloke.

Cutting across the fields to explore Shekar, we happen upon a group of young boys playing soccer. Several disengage to follow us. Like all boys, they are rambunctious and playful. I strike up a rapport with one, who tightly grasps my hand and walks beside me, smiling proudly. We buoyantly exchange our names and continually repeat them to each other in a mantra of comradeship and intuitive understanding. He points toward his home in the distance, speaking rapidly and waving his hands. From his gestures, I decipher that his mother is sick. He wants to take me home. But then his father calls, and off he dashes. I continue walking, feeling his absence. Minutes later, to my delight, he sneaks up behind me and clasps my hand again.

I am saddened to have to say good-bye to my new friend at the wired entrance gate separating the hotel from the village. From the hotel steps I can see him still silently clutching the gate, his forlorn, weathered face now permanently emblazoned in my memory.

Our perilous descent along rocky, hairpin roads from Shekar to Zhangmu, a commercial, unattractive Chinese border town perched on a cliff, takes us through the breathtaking Himalayas toward Nepal. The landscape changes dramatically from the barren Tibetan plateau to lush foothills carved by waterfalls, gorges, and the Tibetan River, surging with melt-water from the mountain peaks. Suddenly, after days of near freezing weather, we are warmed by the moist air. After a night in Zhangmu and one last encounter with PLA soldiers who inspect our passports, we descend farther along a spiraling muddy road and the small Friendship Bridge, crossing the "forbidden border" into Nepal.

The forbidden border is so named because Tibet, in an effort to counter the threat of colonization, had long closed itself to the West. Before the British invasion of 1904, led by Colonel Francis Younghusband, only a few Western missionaries and explorers had penetrated the Land of Snows. At that time, the British, along with the Russians and the Chinese, were vying for control over a geographically strategic Tibet in what became known as the Great Game to dominate Central Asia.

I glance back at the mountains. The Roof of the World, defined by its sublime, harsh beauty and contemporary tragedy, has disappeared in the mist. I have come in search of Shangri-La only to find that it doesn't exist in what the Buddhists would call the illusion of this impermanent, tormented Earth. I feel cheated. So I will try to look beyond the illusion to a place of endless wisdom and compassion, which the Tibetan people, with their uncompromising faith, fierce resilience, and expansive spirit, and the Dalai Lama in his passionate struggle for their freedom, consistently embody.

I am both pained and exhilarated by what I have witnessed and learned here. And my own worries and concerns have altogether evaporated. I wonder what to do next—not simply in the next hours or days but in the limited time horizon that remains for me now. What is important? How can I live peacefully with full, focused awareness and faith in the beneficent force of the universe, free of ego-centered doubts and desires while staying compassionately engaged in the world? "Be a lamp into yourself," I can hear the Buddha saying. "Work at your liberation with diligence. Speak the truth; do not yield to anger; give (of thy little) if thou art asked for little; by these three steps thou wilt attain the world of the gods."

By sacrifice alone, by genius alone they were made, they were modeled by the Maker, Modeler, Bearer, Begetter, Sovereign Plumed Serpent. And when they came to fruition, they came out human:... Perfectly they saw, perfectly they knew everything under the sky, whenever they looked. . . . The moment they . . . looked around in the sky, on the earth, everything was seen without any obstruction.... As they looked, their knowledge became intense.... They understood everything perfectly . . . they'll become as great as gods.

—Popol Vuh, the Mayan book of creation

5

MESSAGES FROM
THE MAYA

Initiation

I t is dark and cool inside the sacred Homun *cenote*, the Mayan word for "sinkhole," in an underground cave on the Yucatan peninsula of Mexico, not far from the ancient Mayan city and ceremonial site Chichen Itza. Water drips from stalactites in a measured rhythm as small bats screech overhead, piercing the otherwise all-encompassing silence. I stand at the edge of the turquoise pond, surrounded by twenty fellow travelers, a young Mayan woman, and our guide, the Mayan elder Hunbatz Men. We are dressed in white for the purification ceremony, a baptism of sorts into the sacred Mayan knowledge and rituals that will occupy the ensuing week. The women hold white carnations; the men hold candles. The haunting ambience of this unfamiliar subterranean world puts me slightly on edge, though I am also pulsing with anticipation and the sense that something magical awaits me.

This area of the Yucatan, where an abundance of colorful bougainvillea, palms, and acacia trees reflect a lush tropical beauty, is surrounded by many cenotes and is, therefore, associated with life-giving water. The ancient Maya believed that the rain god Chaac lived in the cenotes, and they often placated him with ceremonial offerings of gold, silver, jade, pottery, fruit, and seeds to ensure plentiful crops. Hunbatz Men, a charismatic, sprite-like man with sun-weathered skin and silvery hair, explains that we are all part of the cosmic family that includes Father Sun, Mother Earth, and Sister Moon. The Maya think of the pond—indeed, of any body of water—as Earth's sweat. So our ceremony here will also honor Mother Earth. Each of us women approaches Hunbatz Men, who helps us dip our carnations in the pond. We then traverse the cenote and anoint each other, tapping each face three times with the moistened flowers. I am struck by the simple beauty of this ritual, aware that we have already begun to unite our hearts and minds in a common purpose, to what end I am not yet sure.

There's a strange pressure on top of my head that seems to increase in intensity the closer I walk to the water. A few others experience similar sensations, and we share this in whispers. Someone says that our crown chakras are being activated and opened to receive more light. Hunbatz Men calls upon Hunab K'u, the Mayan creator god, to guide and protect us. In the Mayan language, *Hunab K'u* means the "One Giver of Movement and Measure," or "Absolute Being." He is the architect of the universe, symbolizing both form and energy, soul and spirit, according to Hunbatz Men. The Maya believed that the soul has material form, whereas they perceived spirit, or *k'inan*, as solar energy. *K'in* is the word for "sun," without whom no life would be possible. For the Maya, human existence was "a living reflection of cosmic consciousness, wherein energy—the spirit—conveys to all beings life, material existence," Hunbatz Men wrote in *Secrets of Mayan Science/Religion*. "This conviction came from the simple observation of our surroundings, the great environment wherein vibrates the essence of the Absolute Being, Hunab K'u." We remain silent as the young Mayan woman chants beautifully in her native language in an effort to connect with the ancient Mayan codes of wisdom. As she begins to cry, we all are overcome with emotion; my yearning transcends words.

After the ceremony, we solemnly climb the crude stone steps leading out of the cenote into the blinding rays of Father Sun. I am disoriented, and the metaphor is obvious: emerging from this deep, dark place into the light of day is like being reborn from the womb of Mother Earth. Something inside me has shifted; I'm vulnerable and exposed, as though any false conceptions I've had about myself—whether I am truly worthy to receive Earth's bounty, for example—have been stripped away, at least for now. Also gone are the phantom guilt and ego doubts that so often sabotage my—and everyone's—rightful claim to abundance of all kinds. I am grateful simply to be present and excited to begin my initiation in the Cosmic Mayan Healing For Humankind, as Hunbatz Men has christened the spring equinox journey we are about to undertake.

This trip has come at a time when I am feeling particularly drained. I have just published a book after an arduous course of research, writing, and editing within a very short time period— less than a year to be exact—meeting a deadline that initially had seemed impossible. But I pushed myself, working around the clock. I felt frustrated and enslaved by the project, and I desperately need to reconnect with my soul. I need joy!

As we head back to the bus, warmed by the morning sunlight, I recall some lines from Pablo Neruda's poem "If Each Day Falls" in *The Sea and the Bells*: "We need to sit on the rim / Of the well of darkness / And fish for fallen light / With patience." The symbolic life-and-death process we have just experienced at the "rim of the well," another meaning for *cenote*, reminds me of such dualities—light and darkness, male and female, spirit and matter, order and chaos—and their accompanying demand for balance and integration. This is a key component of the Mayan worldview, as it is with many other wisdom traditions I have encountered. Endeavoring to resolve our ingrained Western mode of dualistic thinking is not an easy task, but one that requires patience and discipline and perseverance—qualities required of every initiate on a spiritual path.

The ancient Maya, like other indigenous peoples, were acutely aware of their connection to nature, cycles of time, the cosmos, and the underlying unity and divinity of all creation. Throughout our journey, which alternates between classroom study at the hotel and visits to the sacred Mayan sites Uxmal, Chichen Itza, and Oxk'intok, Hunbatz Men constantly reminds us of our obligation to reclaim this connection to our innate wholeness and divinity: "Everyone, do your work! Do your work!" he exhorts us.

Since well before my book project, work—the everyday bread-and-butter type—has been all consuming. Though I have deeply enjoyed my career as a freelance journalist, at this point in midlife I feel an urgency to pursue my *real* work—the difficult, demanding, frustrating, exhilarating work of self-knowledge. Socrates's imperative to "know thyself" has become more than an antiquated platitude. It is a promise that I have made to myself, one that appears to be increasingly and effortlessly supported by a higher power or intelligence. Perhaps as a result of my growing commitment to my spiritual path, my initiation into Mayan wisdom (and, by extension, into some of the universal secrets of existence long taught by the ancient mystery schools) began before I even set foot in the Yucatan.

For years, during each visit to my favorite, now-defunct Manhattan spa, Carapan (a Native American word meaning "place of healing"), I found myself reading *The Mayan Oracle: Return Path to the Stars* by Ariel Spilsbury and Michael Bryner, one of many inspirational books lining the bookshelves of the cozy waiting area. As its name implies, *The Mayan Oracle* is a divination tool that offers inspirational answers to pressing questions, from the cosmic viewpoint of the Maya, of course. The more I read the *Oracle*, the more I felt a need to visit the Mayan homeland. But I did not want a typical tourist trip. I wanted something deeper, out of the ordinary. For weeks, I researched my options, without success. Feeling frustrated, I finally gave up, and a week or so later, I was stunned to receive a brochure about Hunbatz Men and his spiritual pilgrimages. I had never before heard of him, and this was exactly the kind of adventure I had envisioned.

Mayan prophecies predicted that the ancient Maya, who developed one of the most scientifically and spiritually advanced civilizations on Earth, would one day return to their homeland to help usher in a new era of elevated consciousness for humanity. Whether groups like ours are among these reincarnated souls, as Hunbatz Men believes, cannot be proven, of course. Yet, from the moment I step off the plane in Merida, the charming colonial gateway city to the Yucatan that serves as our base, I sense that I will be reuniting here with members of a long-lost family. Indeed, I came hoping to find a "light circle," described by *The Mayan Oracle* as "a gathering of beings with a shared spiritual purpose . . . a common spiritual lineage, often called a soul group."

Though my chosen home, New York City, is overflowing with many diverse spiritual teachers, lectures, workshops, and retreats, after more than a dozen years I am still searching for a community of like-minded, spiritually inclined individuals. My brother recently adopted two beautiful Mayan children, who undoubtedly have helped to ignite stirrings of remembrance that seem to be propelling me on this journey.

Jimmy, a handsome middle-aged man from Oklahoma with intense blue eyes, was the first person from this light circle to greet me. When I arrived, he was standing at the airport baggage-claim area, as if he were waiting for me. Oddly, as soon as our eyes met, I knew he would be one of my fellow travelers. We exchanged introductions and shared a taxi to the hotel in Merida, chatting with warm familiarity like old friends. I sensed instantly that Jimmy was not your average, everyday man. Everything about him, from his impressive knowledge of metaphysical matters to his extensive life experience and the many risks he has taken, was imbued with an otherworldly wisdom that I have rarely encountered. When you add to these qualities his openness and sensitive, heart-centered nature, Jimmy seemed to be the ever-elusive ideal man. "What a miracle!" I thought, as our taxi sped through the sunny Mexican countryside. "I have been searching for the man of my dreams my entire life and I had to leave the country to find him. I can't believe my luck!" Then, remembering how easily my enthusiasm is aroused, I tried to tame it.

Even so, I was surprised to develop such a strong connection with Jimmy so quickly and now—just a few days into the trip—I can't help but wonder how it will unfold. I am not thrilled at finding myself without a significant other in my early forties. In fact, along with my commitment to self-knowledge, my quest to find a lifetime partner has taken on an increasing urgency over the past year. Though I came to Mayaland for the first quest, the possibility of romance intrigues and excites me.

It is during our bus ride back to the hotel from Homun cenote that I learn Jimmy's marital status: unattached, having been married twice and recently divorced. He falls silent upon revealing this to me.

"I'm sorry," I say, not knowing how to respond.

"Don't be," he answers with an expression that hints of sadness. "It's my fault. I gave it all up, my business, everything, to pursue a life dedicated to Spirit. Neither wife could handle it. Thought I was 'too out there.' So they divorced me. Guess I don't really blame them." He stares sullenly out the window.

My heart fills with compassion for Jimmy, as I suspect that he must feel very lonely. Of course, I don't know him well enough to make conjectures, but I can't help thinking about the proverbial isolated genius—how some people can be labeled outcasts simply because of their unusually refined consciousness; and how these individuals are often unfairly misperceived by the masses as eccentrics, fringe dwellers, and, worse, delusional. I wonder if Jimmy sees himself in this way. Whatever he thinks, I believe that I have just met someone extraordinary.

The following morning, we gather in a conference room at the hotel for Hunbatz Men's teaching. The women outnumber the men. Otherwise we represent a diverse mix of ages, backgrounds, and geographical regions. Hunbatz Men is both a Mayan elder and a Day Keeper, an authority on the history, rituals, ancient healing techniques, art, and calendar systems of Mayan civilization. In the Mayan tradition, the Day Keeper is the carrier of an oral tradition of knowledge that has been passed down through a family over centuries.

Much of what we know about the Maya comes from four codices, or painted manuscripts, that survived destruction by the Spanish conquistadors. Though the Mayan civilization spans more than 2,500 years, its great cities—extending from Copan in Honduras and Tikal in Guatemala to Palenque in western Mexico and Uxmal and Chichen Itza on the Yucatan Peninsula—flourished in the tropical jungle from about 200 to 1200 CE. Each of the city-states had a ceremonial center dominated by temples, many of them pyramids that served as burial sites for their royal patrons. Mayan temples were also places of worship dedicated to various gods, who had to be placated continuously with offerings and sometimes sacrifices, including human blood. The Mayan cities began to decline in the early tenth century and were eventually abandoned completely. Scholars have attributed their mysterious demise to a combination of famine, overpopulation, epidemics, civil war, and excessive building and deforestation.

The ancient Maya had a holistic view of life. For them, science, religion, and art were intimately related. They excelled as astronomers and mathematicians and developed an advanced hieroglyphic language. They discovered the use of zero long before other cultures and invented a highly complex calendar based on precise observations of equinoxes, solstices, and the courses of the sun, moon, and planets that could project dates millions of years into the past and future. The Maya also used sophisticated urban planning and built massive limestone monuments without the use of the wheel or domestic animals. Constantly aware of their connection to the cosmos, they planned their lives around the movement of the planets, which were associated with various gods.

Mayan architecture was constructed to harmonize with cyclical time, the observable universe, and the four directions, with their attendant gods. Pyramids, temples, sprawling palaces, and vast ball courts were embellished with elaborate, brightly painted limestone and stucco relief carvings, mosaics, and gaping masks of gods that expressed the interrelationship between the human and the Divine. The concepts of harmony and balance permeated all aspects of Mayan art and life, which was informed and spiritualized by the simple yet profound metaphysical teaching "as above, so below." The realization that Earth and all its inhabitants, both animate and inanimate, are holographic reflections of the Absolute, or divine consciousness, and are therefore one with it, can be traced as far back as ancient Egypt, when the great sage Hermes Trismegistus inscribed this teaching on the Emerald Tablet. (The profound spiritual wisdom encoded in this green crystal tablet, which reputedly still lies buried in Egypt, is believed to have served as a foundation for alchemy and many other mystical traditions.)

"As a reflection of the Absolute, solar energy was particularly important to the Maya," Hunbatz Men says. "They harnessed it as medicine for healing. We can still use this medicine in modern times to heal ourselves and others." He then explains a Mayan healing technique that involves lifting one's chest upward as the sun rises, breathing in the wind, upon which the sun's energy travels, and then sending this energy to the heart, from which it enters the blood. This practice can be used to reenergize and is especially effective in reducing emotional stress and anxiety. We can help ourselves and others dispel heavy, or unwanted, energy, according to Hunbatz Men, by placing our fingers on the throat and chanting *k'in* (the word for "sun") seven times. This mantra also allows energy to flow freely throughout our bodies. Hunbatz Men says that all illness is simply the result of a loss of energy in a particular area of the body. He explains further that we can control the way we receive energy from others, which enters through the navel, our power center. If we want to prevent heavy energy from entering the body, we can either simply turn away from the energy source or cover our abdomen with our hand.

The Maya placed a lot of emphasis on sacred numbers, which, as components of sacred geometry, form the blueprint of the cosmos. Seven is one of these numbers. For the Maya, seven not only represented the seven stars of the Pleiades constellation, which they believed generated life-giving energy, but also the power or energy centers in the human body. These seven energetic centers are more commonly known in the yogic tradition as chakras, all of which must be consistently activated in order to achieve enlightenment. Familiar with this concept from my practice of kundalini yoga, I am intrigued by the unexpected connections between the ancient Indian and Mayan cultures.

Then there are the four seven-day cycles of the female menstrual period, corresponding to the cycles of the moon, to which the Maya were particularly attuned. In a simple yet brilliant application of cosmic knowledge, Mayan women practiced birth control according to the moon cycles. Considering the potentially harmful effects of the Pill, I wonder how we became so disconnected from this Earth-based wisdom. Because the moon represents both nighttime and feminine energy, and the sun represents both daytime and masculine energy, the spring and fall equinoxes (which typically fall on March 21 and September 21) were especially important to the Maya. These particular days, which are distinguished by equal periods of light and darkness, represent times when the masculine and feminine energies are balanced, indicating a concordance with the greater harmony of the universe. As such, the equinoxes were and still are considered to be especially propitious for marriages. I can't help but glance at Jimmy as Hunbatz Men delivers this teaching, playfully referring to the ancient Mayan art of tandla (similar to the Eastern concept of tantra), which involves balancing and mastering sexual energies. Fortunately, Jimmy does not notice!

Though I am thoroughly inspired by the new knowledge we are receiving from Hunbatz Men in our ersatz classroom, my brain has reached its limit. I am anxious to begin practicing the healing techniques and exploring the sacred sites. I rise early the following morning to try the sun/wind healing, which leaves me feeling simultaneously charged and peaceful as we head to Uxmal, one of the great historic Mayan city states and the site of a majestic temple complex. Hunbatz Men, dressed in his usual white slacks and shirt with a colorful woven banner around his head, leads us through a stone gate into the massive Nunnery Quadrangle, so named because its four sides form a cloister-like square.

According to anthropologists and other mainstream scholars, this group of interlocking buildings, with its many rooms and doorways, is believed to have housed Mayan sovereigns, priests, and high-ranking dignitaries. Its architecture is distinguished by complex geometric and anthropomorphic relief sculpture and intricate limestone latticework and mosaics on friezes adorning the upper walls. Like other Mayan palaces, the Nunnery Quadrangle was built on a horizontal axis, which contrasts with the verticality of the pyramids. The palaces were meant to house mere mortals— even though these inhabitants formed a small elite, while the populace lived in traditional huts—whereas pyramids, with their long stairways stretching toward the heavens, were the abode of the gods. Hunbatz Men, who possesses the oral knowledge of his ancestors and whose views, therefore, differ from those of the academics, says Uxmal functioned as a cosmic university for young girls and boys, with a special emphasis on sexual education. "Performing rituals in a sacred place activates the energy of that place," he adds. "This quadrangle is a repository of female energy. Here, the Mayan priestess Nak'in de K'inich Ahau will guide us to heal our own human experience and give birth to the life of the spirit." The sun is out in full force as our group gathers in a circle in the courtyard.

A beautiful Mayan priestess and a man whom we are told is her husband seem to appear from nowhere. She has long, silky black hair and wears a flowing white skirt and crystal necklaces. Her husband is also dressed in white. They place several vessels of burning copal, a type of incense that smells vaguely like camphor, at the center of the circle. Hunbatz Men blows through a conch shell to announce our presence and to call upon the assistance of Spirit. Then the priestess and her husband begin chanting prayers and blowing incense to the six directions (including up and down for heaven and earth). Afterward, they speak about the interconnection of all life and the necessity of treating each other and Mother Earth with consistent love and respect, which will advance the evolution of human consciousness that the ancient Maya prophesied for our time. We meditate silently upon this precept and the power of the receptive feminine principle of the universe.

I am transported by the mystical ambience, yet somehow I had hoped for more. We are being asked to acknowledge what seems to me a simple, natural inclination—love and respect. And though I barely know my fellow travelers, I assume that most people who embark on such a journey likely embody these qualities. Noticing this impatient judgment, I lower my expectations. I have come with such high hopes of receiving extraordinary wisdom that I have already set myself up for a perceived disappointment. How often, through my judgments, analyses, and projections, do I stand in my own way of receiving whatever I may need in the moment?

After our meditation, to prepare us to wander the quadrangle ruins on our own, Hunbatz Men delivers a few lessons about Mayan art and architecture. He explains that the many triangular doors here symbolize the position of hands held in prayer. "To enter a Mayan temple is to enter the sacred knowledge of Hunab K'u," he says. "The stucco cross symbols near the doors represent the sky and signify that you are crossing a threshold. When you come back through the door, you are bringing sacred knowledge out with you." Indeed, most of the detailed sculpture, or bas reliefs, adorning the monuments at Uxmal and other Mayan ruins have spiritual significance. According to Hunbatz Men, all Mayan art forms—ranging from codices and mural paintings to ceramics, textiles, sculpture, and architecture—emanate cosmic knowledge and energy. "Mayan artists also worked with space, dimensions, light, and shadow very precisely to ensure balance within their creations, which mirrored the balance of the universe," Hunbatz Men adds. "And each work was imbued with the artist's own spiritual vibration." I smile at the connection with the Aboriginal art I saw in the Outback.

The anthropomorphic relief sculpture at the ancient Mayan sites depicts sovereigns, priests, warriors, and deities in an intricate abstracted, naturalistic style. Portraits of Mayan royalty typically display elaborate headdresses and jewelry. Among the most prevalent deities is the rain god Chaac (sometimes conflated with the mountain god Witz), with its protruding eyes and long, trunk-shaped nose, who is often portrayed in obsessively repeating patterns. The letters G, T, and O are among the most important sacred symbols found in Mayan art. They appear in various stylized versions on the facades here at Uxmal. "The *G* is symbolic of the beginning, the germination, the Egg-Creator, the essence, the seed from which all life—human or otherwise—springs. . . . God; that which is sacred," Hunbatz Men wrote in *Secrets of Mayan Science/ Religion*. Notably, in Mayan mathematics, the zero is called *ge* and symbolized by the egg, the beginning of the universe. Ge, or the letter *G*, also symbolizes the Milky Way, which the Maya recognized as the generator of life. The *G* is depicted in both spiral and egg-shaped forms in Mayan art to represent both the Milky Way and the zero. In this way, Mayan art, religion, and science become one. Significantly, because the Maya connected the egg with the Milky Way, they viewed sex as a cosmic act that produced children of light. All human beings are, therefore, individual vibrations of the Milky Way—another reflection of "as above, so below."

The letter *T* is the symbol for *te*, the Mayan word for "tree," or "Sacred Tree," which originated from the Mayan words *teol* and *teotl*, the names of God the Creator. The tree, often symbolized by a cross, is a sacred symbol for many cultures throughout the world, from Asia to the Middle East and Africa. For the Maya, *T* also represents the air, the wind, and the divine breath of God, according to Hunbatz Men. "The human being, according to ancient Mayan philosophy, is a tuber of the cosmic root, of teol, the cosmic consciousness, the intelligent energy, God," he wrote.

The letter *O* and the circle represent the Mayan word *ol*, which means "consciousness," specifically "conscious recall or awareness of consciousness." "Only through consciousness can we attain the sacred state of sensing within ourselves the divine laws of Hunab K'u," Hunbatz Men wrote. This symbolism also extends to the sun, from which comes the essence of our consciousness, or spirit. Encoded with such sacred symbols, Mayan architecture was meant to activate and elevate the consciousness of those who came into contact with it. I wonder how much more evolved humanity might be now if modern architects had designed their buildings as transmitters of cosmic knowledge, if all our architecture and art were conceived of as sacred.

As we walk to the nearby Temple of the Sun (also known as the Palace of the Governors), Jimmy and I chat about the beautiful day and our mutual interest in meditation. Then I introduce myself to an eighty-seven-year-old woman named Geraldine, who is confined to a wheelchair. Her friend, Charlie, steers her from place to place.

"I admire your adventurous spirit," I say.

"Oh, this doesn't get in my way," she answers with an appreciative smile. "I've traveled all over the world, and I intend to keep on going!" Her patience stands in stark contrast to my impatience just moments ago.

The Temple of the Sun looks more like a Greek palace, perched on a platform high above a steep, stone stairway. We climb the steps to absorb the energy of the site on our own before Hunbatz Men calls us to begin another ritual. Jennie, a joyful middle-aged woman from New Hampshire, pauses to connect with an iguana, who appears stunned by the unexpected activity in his otherwise silent domain. She kneels down and says, "I love you," then kisses it—a gesture that both surprises and tickles me. I don't think I would ever feel compelled to react that way to a lizard. I admire her childlike wonder.

"Everyone, come close together, now!" Hunbatz Men shouts. "This temple symbolizes male energy. In Mayan religion, science, art, and architecture, everywhere in the Mayan world, there is a balance of the male and female principles. As we each integrate these within ourselves, we can transcend duality and become cosmic humans, at one with Spirit. In order to do this, humanity must continue the work of solar initiation."

By now it is midday, and the sun is blinding. I love the profusion of light and don't mind the heat, even though my clothes are damp with sweat. I feel cleansed by both. We raise our hands toward Father Sun, as Hunbatz Men leads us in chanting *k'in* fourteen times, seven each for the Earth and the cosmos. Then, sitting in a circle, we practice a meditation to balance the male and female energies within us. This involves simultaneously breathing in a golden light (representing Father Sun), from the heavens down through the top of our heads, and a silver light (representing Mother Earth), up from the earth, connecting both lights at the solar plexus, the spiritual/energetic center of our personal power. Entranced by the sunlight and the scent of burning copal, I feel energy buzzing through me as I do the meditation.

Hunbatz Men explains that the meditations we are performing will help us to create our light bodies. I am familiar with the light body from *The Mayan Oracle*, which defines it as "the 'body' that is crafted from the ignition and expansion of interstellar light within the chakra system and the cells of the physical body. This body exists both in and out of time and space and is able to travel freely between dimensions because of its demonstrated remembrance of its divine source." The concept had seemed so abstract, but now that I have been given practical instruction, it makes more sense.

What would my friends and family members think of my current explorations? Should I give them a detailed account? Of course, I never will, fearing that I will be judged as a hopeless eccentric at best.

After the meditation, I approach Jimmy, perhaps seeking affirmation that I am, of course, eminently sane. "Did you tell anyone you were coming on this trip?" I ask.

"Oh, whenever I do these things, I usually just tell people I'm going to a science conference." He smiles. "Which is not untrue, when you consider that what we are learning here is sacred science. Some people may be ready to hear about it, others may not be. How much I reveal depends on the person."

"Funny. I told my family the same thing."

"Dana." Jimmy sidles closer to me, as if to share a secret. "Don't ever let anyone inhibit your soul's expansion or define for you what is worth knowing, feeling, and becoming."

"Thanks. I won't." I appreciate his wisdom, which seems so natural and instinctive.

Jimmy is becoming more attractive to me with each minute. I recount the attributes I desire in a soul mate; it is likely an Everywoman's list: Wise. Sensitive. Kind. Generous. Sensual. Handsome. Physically Fit. Imaginative. Adventurous. Confident. So far, Jimmy seems to embody all of these qualities. Is this guy for real? I can't believe two wives left him. And I can't help but fantasize about more intimacy. *Oh, stop it*, I think, feeling slightly guilty that my hormones are running wild in a sacred place.

"People!" announces Hunbatz Men, interrupting my reverie. "We will now perform one last sacred ceremony before heading back to the hotel!" He instructs us once again to form a standing circle and asks Jennie to turn to her neighbor—a big bear-like man named Bill—look him in the eyes, and say, "*In Lak'ech*." This Mayan saying means "I am another yourself," or more simply, "I am you," which is, of course, the basis of the principle of universal love and compassion. Upon hearing Jennie's words, Bill responds,

"*A Lak'en*," meaning "you are me." Hunbatz Men explains that these words can also be interpreted as "I hurt you/I hurt me." We continue around the circle, each of us greeting our neighbor to either side in this way. I tremble slightly as I wait my turn, as though my body senses instinctively the power of these profound words. I think about how infrequently I look complete strangers in the eye, particularly on the streets of Manhattan—a reality that has often saddened me—let alone acknowledge our basic human interconnection.

My heart races and my eyes tear when I receive these words from Jimmy and then turn to the Mayan priestess. I begin to weep as the ritual continues around the circle. By the end, everyone is overwhelmed. We're all weeping as we embrace. I had not expected to be so deeply moved so soon. What the Mayan priestess said earlier about love does not seem like such a platitude now. I *feel* her words in the core of my being, as though my heart has instantly expanded. This ritual of love and compassion has bonded us as one family, one light circle. How tenderly the men and women are relating to each other. How polarized the sexes have become in our contemporary drama. How insidious are our incessant judgments and fears of each other. How separate we usually feel because of our distorted perceptions and behaviors.

Before we leave Uxmal, Hunbatz Men faces the sun and, with hands outstretched, recites one final prayer: "Oh, Father Sun, may man and woman bear children of the golden light. May we once again be in tune with you, so we may find peace and harmony on Earth."

That evening, Jimmy and I have dinner at a taqueria in one of Merida's charming Spanish-colonial plazas. We take a table outside on the patio. It's a beautiful, balmy evening, and the sky is filled with stars. Mariachi bands roam the streets, and the locals dance spontaneously. Merida seems constantly to be brimming with joy and celebration, such a marked difference from the hard-driving, work-oriented ambience of New York City. I'm uplifted and refreshed as we chat about the day's events. There is an ease of communication, as if we have always known each other. Jimmy is both gentle and intense, with a shy streak that makes him all the more appealing. His sparkling blue eyes have a curious hold over me.

"You were saying," he calls me back to attention. I am embarrassed by my obvious attraction to him.

"Right. I was just thinking about how today reminded me of some passages from *A Course in Miracles*, a spiritual text that I've been studying."

"Yes, the *Course*," he says knowingly. "Very powerful."

"It says, 'Love is the absence of fear,' 'Love holds no grievances,' and 'Anger is never justified.' Sounds simple in theory, but . . ."

He pauses to reflect for a moment. "I couldn't agree more," he says, easing into a wide smile. "What date is your birthday?"

I write it down on a napkin and slide it toward him. He does some quick calculations. "I'm not surprised. Your universal number is nine, which means that your lesson in this lifetime—if you believe in reincarnation—is unconditional love. I'm a nine, too."

"Interesting, considering our experience at Uxmal. You're a numerologist?" I'm enchanted, wondering what other talents he has yet to reveal.

"Dabble in it," he says modestly, holding up his beer bottle. "Another?" I nod, and he orders two more Carta Blancas.

Jimmy smiles as he pens another set of numbers on the napkin. "How about that! We also have the same self-expression numbers—one. That means we have both struggled in various ways to carve out our individuality."

"I can identify with that." I lean across the table and look him squarely in the eye, conscious that I am now flirting. "So what else do you have up your sleeve, Mr. Magician?" I am thinking now of my other romantic checklist—the more poetic, metaphorical one—which reads: warrior, meditator, dancer, and magician. Based on our conversations so far, it appears that Jimmy has nailed three of them. I can't wait to see if he can dance.

"Your soul number is eleven. It's a spiritual number meaning that you believe everyone should be enlightened." His eyes meet mine tenderly, and we both fall silent.

"Well," I clear my throat. "I'm not there yet, but I'll take it. Just imagine if everyone really *were* enlightened."

"Yeah, most of us have a way to go," he laughs.

Long into the night, we talk, and I feel that we are developing a special friendship. To his credit, Jimmy does not ask to see me to my room. In a way, though, I wish he had. My hormones are working overtime, and I realize that it will take considerable self-restraint not to give in to them. Of course, nothing is preventing me from seducing him. But I know intuitively that if I act too soon, I will become easily distracted from the Mayan teachings. After all, the journey has just begun.

The following morning, we meet again in the hotel conference room for another teaching from Hunbatz Men—this time on the astro-science behind the design and construction of the Mayan pyramids—in preparation for our upcoming outing to Chichen Itza, the Yucatan's most famous Mayan ceremonial center. This elegant complex includes an astronomical observatory, various temples, and a vast ball court, upon which the Maya played a cosmic ballgame that represented the dance of the planets and helped them to connect with their own divinity, according to Hunbatz Men.

The focal point of Chichen Itza, however, is the Pyramid of Kukulcan, a magnificent calendar in stone constructed to align with the position of the sun at the equinoxes and solstices, periods associated with powerful solar energy. This pyramid also measures cycles of Earth time, as mapped by the secular Mayan haab and sacred Mayan tzolkin calendars. Its four sides represent the four directions and seasons of the year. Ninety-one stairs on each side, plus the platform at the top, mark 365 days of the secular haab calendar, while the nine levels visible on each face of the pyramid represent the nine hell cycles (or periods of low consciousness) from which Earth is emerging. At the top of the pyramid are twenty G symbols, representing the number of days in each of the thirteen months of the sacred tzolkin calendar, which spans 260 days, or nine months in our present system—the cycle of human gestation. Thus a metaphor for birth, or rebirth, is encoded in the pyramid.

Tens of thousands of pilgrims from around the world flock to the pyramid each year during the spring and fall equinoxes to witness the legendary plumed serpent god Kukulcan slithering down the staircase as seven distinctive triangles of light, offset by seven triangles of shadow. According to Mayan cosmology, this event invites us to awaken our consciousness and, therefore, become Kukulcan himself, as Mayan initiates did long ago. Kukulcan, called Quetzalcoatl by the Aztecs, is associated with the planet Venus and the ritual of death and resurrection. Images of this half-bird, half-serpent deity adorn lintels, pillars, stairways, and applied stucco decoration throughout the ancient Mayan ceremonial centers.

Kukulcan has long been misunderstood by Western culture, according to Hunbatz Men. Beyond the many mythological and historical interpretations of Kukulcan as a supposed god-like ruler who brought wisdom to the indigenous people lies his true meaning as an esoteric symbol of the enlightened beings that we can all become. In order to do so, we must learn how to recognize and use the seven energies in our bodies (which correspond to the yogic chakras), as given to us by Hunab K'u, with the power of our minds. Mayan initiates tried to achieve this through their own brand of yoga, a form of controlled breathing.

The seven energies are symbolized by the serpent-like seven triangles of light that appear on the Pyramid of Kukulcan during the spring and fall equinoxes. Imbuing us with cosmic energy, they allow us to "feel the vibration of Hunab K'u as the only giver of life," Hunbatz Men wrote in *Secrets of Mayan Science/ Religion*. "When we fully comprehend the meaning of this seven in the geometric pyramid, we will enter the mouth of the serpent as Mayan initiates," wrote Hunbatz Men. "In doing so, we will fulfill the prophecies of the Itzaes [those Mayans who lived at Chichen Itza] when they return as luk'umen tun ben can, or 'those absorbed by the serpent of the sacred knowledge.' At that moment we will become buddhas, or as is said in Mayan, butz hah, 'those filled with the truth of the essence,' the ones who manage the seven powers." Throughout Mayan art and architecture, men and women are depicted emerging from the mouth of a serpent representing Kukulcan, essentially being reborn into a higher consciousness.

As Hunbatz Men explains in his book, the esoteric meaning of Kukulcan is encoded within the word itself. For example, the Mayan word *ku* means "God," "sacred," and "pyramid." *Kul* refers both to the vibration of God and to the coccyx, "the sacred place where solar energy is deposited at the base of the spine," the first, or root, chakra in yogic teachings. *Can* is the word for "serpent," "knowledge," and "wisdom." It also symbolizes the four manifestations of wave energy and how energy travels—in undulating waves, just as the snake moves. Thus, according to Hunbatz Men, *Kukulcan* can be interpreted as meaning, "God is the intelligent energy of vibration in its four manifestations and the serpent is the form in which that energy travels." Kukulcan is closely related to the Mayan word *k'ulthanlilni*, which means "coccyx of vibration" and knowing "how to breathe properly to generate movement of those faculties of Hunab K'u residing in the coccyx." This is the path to becoming Kukulcan or Quetzalcoatl, a true reflection of Hunab K'u. Not surprisingly, this word is similar to the Sanskrit word *kundalini*—the energy coiled at the base of the spine that travels up to the crown chakra at the top of the head when activated through yoga, meditation, and other spiritual practices, leading to enlightenment.

The serpent, called *naga* in Sanskrit, also represents the creative energy or knowledge stored inside pyramids. "During the day, pyramids absorb the energy of the sun; at night, they send it back out again," Hunbatz Men says. "As processors and transformers of energy, they serve as a connection between the earth and the cosmos, matter and spirit, the human and the Divine. Human beings also need to learn how to absorb and release energy. The best way to do this is to sit in a cross-legged lotus position, the typical yoga posture. In this way your body takes on the sacred geometry of the pyramid, and is able to absorb energy through the crown of the head more easily." Hunbatz Men describes various ancient sculptures that have been discovered portraying Mayan figures seated in this position while meditating to connect with the sacred power of Hunab K'u. Even the Sanskrit word *yoga* is similar in sound and meaning to the Mayan word *yok'hah*, which means "on top of truth."

Since the beginning of civilization, pyramids were places of initiation—which means going inside deep knowledge. Performing sacred ceremonies in or near pyramids not only can help us to raise our own energy to higher levels of consciousness and, therefore, connect with our divinity, but also can enable us to assist each other collectively in this mission. Much of what the Maya knew was taught in ancient mystery schools around the world. Some ancient philosophers have suggested that many thousands of years ago the Maya traveled to Egypt, India, Tibet, and Peru to share their wisdom, just as ancient peoples traveled to the sacred centers of Mesoamerica to learn from its indigenous culture, which accounts for the many parallels between spiritual traditions.

As Hunbatz Men keeps reminding us, the path to self-realization requires much conscious work, which can involve a certain amount of suffering. Okay, I accept the challenge. Years ago, I arrived at a crossroads—the place where one must either commit to awakening, no matter how difficult the obstacles and setbacks, or continue along the path of least resistance in perceived safety, security, and comfort. I chose the former, what the contemporary philosopher Alan Watts so refreshingly dubbed "the wisdom of insecurity." In his eponymous book, *The Wisdom of Insecurity*, he contends that because impermanence is inseparable from life, the only way to feel secure is paradoxically to embrace uncertainty, to ride the waves of the eternal present from one shifting moment to the next.

I have become accustomed to uncertainty, fueled by constant and extremely stressful financial insecurity, as I try to create each day from scratch in my small home office, conceiving and selling articles, never knowing when my next paycheck will arrive. This is what I have always wanted to do, and I've been determined to succeed. For the most part, I have walked my path alone, without the emotional support of a life partner, husband, or family in a city that, despite its many opportunities, can be downright harsh. Of course, I have often become weary walking the edge of my self-styled cliff, and I've wondered whether I was on the right track. I could have taken a "real job"—a steady, high paying, corporate position—gotten married, and had kids, as my mother has often reminded me. Though such choices invariably bring their own challenges, according to her view, my life would thereby have been more "normal."

When I read *The Wisdom of Insecurity* many years ago, it was as if Watts shined a light in the darkness. "The further the power of consciousness ventures out into experience, the more is the price it must pay for its knowledge," he wrote. "It is understandable that we should sometimes ask whether life has not gone too far in this direction, whether 'the game is worth the candle.' . . . If, then, we are to be fully human and fully alive and aware, it seems that we must be willing to suffer for our pleasures. Without such willingness there can be no growth in the intensity of consciousness. . . . Because consciousness *must* involve both pleasure and pain, to strive for pleasure at the exclusion of pain is, in effect, to strive for the loss of consciousness." It seems that Kukulcan has now come to encourage me to continue moving forward on the wild rapids of "insecurity," venturing beyond turbulent memories of the past and expectations of the future, so that I can move even deeper into the stillness of my true essence. And I am grateful for his blessing.

I am buoyant and buzzing with anticipation on the spring equinox, as we walk along the *Sac Be*, the sacred white road leading to the entrance of Chichen Itza.

"At the pyramid, we will perform a meditation to transform negative planetary energy so that we can help to heal humanity," Hunbatz Men proclaims. Other initiates, including a contingent of local Maya, several Mayan priests wearing bands of feathers around their heads, and the Mayan priestess we met at Uxmal, accompany us on this ritualistic walk. Attendants carry vessels of burning copal, while Hunbatz Men blows the conch shell to call upon the gods and guardians of Chichen Itza. "The Maya believed that men and women need the gods and the gods need us," says Hunbatz Men, his voice rising with the smoke curls of the incense. "We cannot exist without each other!"

It is a gorgeous, sunny day, as usual. By two o'clock, we are part of a huge sea of people, spilling out in all directions on the massive field surrounding the pyramid. Several salsa bands are performing. I am extremely agitated. Though I know we are taking part in a major celebration, I did not expect the site to be so noisy and chaotic. The commotion has undercut the sacred atmosphere. There is barely room to move, let alone find a reasonably good spot from which to view the solar light show on the pyramid.

"How disappointing," I say to Mira, a quiet, mystical Hispanic woman who has become a kind of mother figure to our group.

"Oh, don't let all this get to you," she smiles. "Just stay centered in your heart and mind, and you'll be fine."

"Does anything ever bother you, Mira?" I ask jokingly but with respect. She is the most peaceful person I have ever met.

"If my kids were here, they'd tell you," she quips.

"Oh, no!" I gasp, noticing that my expensive Indian silk shawl is missing. It is something that I always carry with me to avoid being chilled in the classroom and on our air-conditioned bus. At home, I wear it frequently.

"Don't worry," Mira comforts. "You'll find it. Try not to think about it."

Given the huge crowd, I suspect that the shawl is lost forever.

I roam around for about an hour, still overwhelmed by the crowd and annoyed about my shawl. Everyone in the group is careful to keep each other in sight. Hunbatz Men told us that the serpent of light would begin to appear on the north face of the pyramid at about three o'clock. I notice a young couple and their daughter, whom I had seen at the airport when I arrived, and wave hello. They smile and wave back. Later, I chat with two friendly Australian men, one of whom is an expert on pyramids. I am with Mira and Ginger, a free-spirited businesswoman from Manhattan, when I glance at my watch. It is just about time.

Hunbatz Men gathers us together again. "This pyramid represents the body of the Creator, Hunab K'u," he says. We chant *k'in* seven times as Hunbatz Men begins praying: "O, Master Hunab K'u! Let us remember why we came here. We are your children, pieces of the sun. Let us remember the wisdom of the universe." I gaze at the pyramid with expectation. But nothing happens. We all wait patiently. Twenty minutes pass, and still nothing. I become more anxious, wondering whether we have been duped. The crowd becomes restless.

"Look!" Hunbatz Men suddenly announces, pointing to the pyramid. "Here it comes!"

Everyone falls silent as triangles of light and shadow appear, one by one, along the side of the grand staircase, cascading down to the sculpted serpent head at the base. Hunbatz Men leads us in a meditation in which we ask Hunab K'u to allow the sacred energy of the seven triangles of light to help humankind.

I had not expected such a breathtaking spectacle. It is as though a door has opened to eternity, generously allowing me to experience, however briefly, infinite grace and beauty. I feel deeply connected to the Maya and their ancient wisdom, as if I have traveled beyond the confines of my body and our own space-time dimension. Even the madding crowd that so agitated me earlier now seems like a shadow. It is a fleeting but transforming sensation that I will never forget.

After the equinox celebration, Hunbatz Men guides us to a nearby field, where we gather in a circle to perform another meditation led by the Mayan priestess. It is similar to the one we experienced at Uxmal, during which we balanced our male and female energies, but longer, interwoven with the priestess's chanting in Mayan. The heat has grown oppressive, and the events of the day have left me drained and lightheaded. Additionally, and much to my dismay, I am still distracted by my lost shawl. At one point, I notice Jimmy wandering away from the group, and I wonder what's going on with him. After the meditation, as if reading my mind, Mira approaches me. "Don't worry." She smiles. "You *will* find your shawl. Just stop thinking about it."

I nod appreciatively, intrigued by her certainty. Realizing that this seems like such a petty preoccupation in the midst of our sacred work, I take Mira's advice and banish all thoughts of the shawl from my mind. I will simply buy another one when I return home.

"Hey!" Ginger runs up to me, annoyed. "I think I lost my watch. Have you seen it anywhere? I know I put it on this morning. Oh, no! It belonged to my father; he gave it to me before he died."

"Sorry, I didn't see it," I say, as Mira repeats to Ginger what she has just said to me.

Just then, Hunbatz Men announces that we have been blessed with a special treat. The Mayan priestess and her husband are going to perform a Mayan wedding ceremony for two couples and have invited us to participate. Along with a group of locals, we walk to another clearing, this one thankfully shaded by numerous trees. The priestess, always dressed in white, is donning a feathered headdress. At the center of this patch of earth lies a circular cloth bearing various offerings, including gourds, crystals, and ceramic bowls of water. I watch with delight as the bashful brides and grooms listen attentively to the priestess's blessings as she waves a crystal wand around them. Then they exchange vows and present each other with a gourd filled with water, from which they each drink. The ceremony is magical, almost childlike, and instantly refreshes me. I smile at the seeming coincidence that we would witness this unexpected earthly union of male and female energies. On our way to the bus, I ask Jimmy how he is feeling. He looks pale and fatigued.

"Today was really intense," he says. "I need to rest."

Though I'm curious to learn more about Jimmy's experience, I sense that he needs his space, so I don't press the issue.

Back on the bus, I am shocked and relieved to see my shawl stuffed down alongside one of the seats. Excited, I wave it in the air. Mira seems very pleased. "See, I told you," she laughs. I ruminate over the hidden meaning behind this little incident. What that could be, though, I'm not yet sure.

Ginger is sitting nearby. "Lucky," she says, pouting. "I'll never find that watch."

Overhearing the conversation, Jennie suddenly erupts, "This is too weird. I lost my glasses out there!" We look at each other with surprise.

"It must be the Aluxes!" someone chimes in. In Mayan folklore, Aluxes are tiny gnomes who help farmers look after their crops; they can also be pranksters. I glance at Mira, who smiles peacefully, as usual.

I'm mostly quiet during the ride to Merida, trying to process all that I have experienced. But my mind is fuzzy. I know only that I am feeling extremely centered and peaceful, and that is enough. Later that evening, I decide to go to the hotel bar for a drink before dinner. Coincidentally, Jimmy is sitting there with a beer. Of course, I am pleased to see him, believing that fate is cooperating with my wishes by bringing us together. He looks somber and a bit distracted.

"How's everything?" I ask, pulling up a seat beside him.

"Good. Everything's good." His eyes surreptitiously scan my body. "You look nice." I sense that he is happy to see me.

"Thanks." I'm wearing a sheer black silk tank top and short skirt, one of my more revealing outfits. A subconscious choice perhaps?

"Long day," he says, grabbing a fistful of peanuts. "Let me buy you a drink."

"Sure, glass of red." I scope the lobby for other group members. There is no one except for a young family waiting at the elevator. Then I realize they are the same family I saw earlier at the airport and then today at Chichen Itza in the midst of thousands! I'm surprised that we are staying at the same hotel and wave hello again. *Great*, I think, *Jimmy and I will finally have some privacy and maybe even sneak away for dinner on our own.*

We fall easily into conversation. He tells me that we are all capable of existing in several dimensions at once, and how lucid dreaming—meaning when we actually observe ourselves in a dream state—can help to facilitate this experience. Before long, we are sharing our frustrations with relationships that never seem to work out. I am pleased that we are becoming closer. A familiar tingling sensation surges through my body, as a vivid image suddenly flashes in my mind: Jimmy and I are making love in a sheltered grove near the pyramid under the moonlight! I wonder how I will be able to maintain my concentration throughout the rest of the trip, distracted as I am by my attraction. As Hunbatz Men keeps reminding us, there is so much work to do. Suddenly, I begin to feel lightheaded and hold onto the bar to steady myself.

"Why don't we . . . ," Jimmy stops short, as four other group members approach the bar and invite us to dinner. Jimmy and I glance at each other. "Great," he accepts the invitation.

"Yeah, great," I chime in, less enthusiastically. My scenario is foiled.

To my delight, we pass a wedding party in one of the plazas, which reminds me of the Mayan wedding ceremony we witnessed earlier. The message of balance and harmony is ever present. At the Hotel Caribe, we dine outside in a lovely courtyard enclosed by elegant wrought-iron balconies and overflowing with tropical foliage. I notice the two Australian men, Jack and Hugh, whom I had seen at Chichen Itza. A few others recognize them as well, and we invite them to join us. Jack, who pulls up a seat beside me, is particularly flirtatious. He's a real charmer, funny and charismatic with an athletic build and boyish good looks, though he appears considerably older than I am. Jimmy is noticeably quiet as we converse. I want to draw him into the conversation, but Jack is a bit overbearing and, it seems, territorial. I am frustrated; this is not what I had in mind. As the high-spirited evening rolls on and the alcohol and Australian jokes flow, Jack lets down his macho guard. I soon learn that he is recently divorced after twenty-eight years of marriage and is obviously in pain.

It turns out to be a fun evening, with much laughter and camaraderie. Before we start back to the hotel, Jack invites me to dinner the following night. I politely say that I already have plans. Of course, I am keeping that slot open for Jimmy, should he be so inclined. The last thing I need now is another romantic complication! We exchange good-byes, and as I turn to leave, I notice that Jimmy is already halfway down the street, chatting with another woman from our group. I shake my head with resigned disappointment. I seem to be entangled in some weird Mayan version of *A Midsummer Night's Dream*. The Aluxes must be up to their old tricks! Even so, I still sense there is more to come between Jimmy and me. I will stop being so cautious. Just because I am exploring higher states of consciousness does not mean that I cannot enjoy life at the same time. Isn't that what the Maya taught? Balance. I see myself again with Jimmy at the pyramid and fall asleep that night pondering my options.

The next morning, we gather for a final round of instruction from Hunbatz Men, this time about the famed end date of the Mayan calendar, 2012, the subject of much anticipation and speculation, academic and otherwise, not to mention media hype. I arrive at our classroom distracted, for it seems that I have lost a press kit that the local tourist authority had delivered to my room. I am planning to visit some other Mayan sites after my time with Hunbatz Men, with the intention of writing an article. Before we begin class, Jennie happily announces that she has found her eyeglasses. Another woman, who appears panic-stricken, urges everyone to please keep an eye out for her notebook, which also has gone missing!

"Hey, what's going on with everyone losing things?" Bill asks aloud, half joking.

"The Mayans believe that when you lose something you lose your spirit, which means that you temporarily lose your connection with your essence," Hunbatz Men says. "At that moment you are not your true self. When you find the object, you recover your true self."

I see how the lost objects are metaphors for what happens to us continuously throughout the day, as myriad distractions—anxieties, worries, doubts, fears—cause us to slip in and out of conscious awareness. Most of the time, we don't even realize we are on this roller coaster or how nauseating the ride can be. Remaining permanently connected to our spiritual core would make life so much more peaceful and pleasant. And yet, this task is not easily mastered. "Pay attention," I remind myself. "Pay attention!"

I soon forget about the lost press kit, as Hunbatz Men rails against the apocalyptic scenario often associated with 2012. "Contrary to what you may believe, the world is not going to come to an end in 2012!" he proclaims. "The process of transformation that the Maya foresaw in the future will not happen specifically on that date but will occur over a period of time that will include 2012." Hunbatz Men explains this process as one of purification, which necessarily involves the dissolution of destructive cultural, social, economic, scientific, and religious paradigms. Outmoded ways of thinking and behaving that no longer serve humanity's evolution will dissolve and pave the way to a higher consciousness and way of being.

Although the Maya prophesied that Mother Earth and her children will pass through a dark and challenging time, we have the opportunity to become, finally, more than we have ever dreamed possible, to create a world rooted in love, peace, harmony, and abundance for all, including Mother Earth. This shift in consciousness, then, will bring about the "end of the world as we know it." Hunbatz Men believes that more advanced beings from other areas of the universe will try to communicate with us to help us through this period. On this point, he specifically refers to the Mayan prediction that an ancient planet called *Tzoltze ek'* in Mayan (known as *Nibiru* by the ancient Sumerians) will enter Earth's orbit in the years surrounding 2012, a phenomenon that happens every 6,500 years, as mapped by the Mayan calendar. The energy produced by this event will offer a rare opportunity for both personal and collective spiritual evolution and healing, according to Hunbatz Men.

The ancient Maya viewed planet Earth as nothing less than a cosmic laboratory for the evolution of human consciousness. Numerous books, many of them published in recent years, present detailed astronomical, mythical, and metaphysical theories about the meaning of 2012. Authors and experts in Mayan cosmology, such as John Major Jenkins and Jose Arguelles, a pioneer in the field, offer compelling arguments for the profound transformation in consciousness, sometimes called the Great Shift, that the Maya predicted. The epicenter of this transformation supposedly will be marked by the exact alignment of the sun (as well as Earth and our solar system) with the center of the Milky Way Galaxy on the winter solstice, December 21, 2012. Significantly, the Maya equated the galactic center with Hunab K'u. This rare astronomical event, which occurs once every 26,000 years, signals the end of one great cycle of time and the beginning of another, according to the Mayan calendar.

Research conducted by the above authors and other experts on the Mayan calendar and hieroglyphs, and the sacred Mayan book of creation *Popol Vuh*, suggests that the years leading up to and immediately following 2012 will serve as an initiation period for humanity. The Maya viewed this initiation as a rebirth into a higher state of being that transcends dualities and the experience of separation, leading to the integration of spirit and matter, the human and divine selves. Kukulcan/Quetzalcoatl, as part bird (heaven) and part serpent (earth), represents this integration. Such self-realization, the apotheosis of the perennial wisdom "as above, so below," has long been the goal of many spiritual/mystical traditions. "Matter is spirit moving slowly enough to be seen," said the early twentieth-century Christian philosopher and mystic Pierre Teilhard de Chardin.

When we all metaphorically become Kukulcan, we will have arrived in the legendary "Age of Aquarius," when "peace will guide the planets and love will steer the stars," as the old song goes. But because we have been so long out of balance—within ourselves and with each other, Mother Earth, and the cosmos—this transformation, many believe, will be accompanied by disruptive, destructive events that will propel us into new ways of thinking and being in order to survive. These events range from the collapse of societal institutions to economic meltdowns and natural disasters triggered by global warming, resource depletion, solar flares, and a potential electromagnetic pole shift (which Earth has experienced several times in its distant past).

So what does all this mean for me, personally? Despite the challenging times that likely lie ahead, I am very excited about the current evolutionary shift and grateful to be able to participate in it. I am also grateful to the Maya, in all their genius, for preparing us. Understanding that everything we experience in our lives is a reflection of our own consciousness, and that we create our reality in tandem with Spirit, I choose to view this period as a great opportunity, not a dreaded catastrophe. A rare moment in time potentially to become more than we ever dreamed of being.

After class, I step out into the sunshine, happy at last for some time alone to wander the streets of Merida, whose pastel-toned Spanish colonial buildings, horse-drawn carriages, and unhurried pace transport me to a bygone era. On my way back to the hotel, I cross paths with Jimmy, who is on his way to the market. Naturally, I am thrilled, and we agree to meet for dinner. As I walk into the lobby, Ginger rushes up to me, breathless.

"You won't believe what happened!" Her eyes are wide. "Well, it's good news and bad news. I found my father's watch, between the bed and the nightstand!"

"Great!" I reply. "Another found object."

"But, now, you have to help me," she pleads.

"What's wrong?"

"My plane ticket. I can't find it, and we leave the day after tomorrow. The airline said it would cost two thousand dollars for a new ticket!"

"Oh, no," I pause to consider the situation. "This is all becoming very strange."

"Will you come to my room and help me look for it? I need another pair of eyes."

Before long, Ginger and I are up in her room, frantically moving furniture, stripping the beds, and turning over mattresses—an extreme measure, insisted upon by Ginger, who is becoming more panicked by the minute. "Everything was going so great till now," she mourns.

"Don't worry. We'll find it," I say, recalling Mira's advice. I'm not sure I believe this, but it worked for me.

After about fifteen minutes, we decide to give up and kick back with some white wine from Ginger's minibar. "I refuse to let this ruin my trip!" she declares, regaining her composure. "Money is only money." Ginger the eternal optimist lifts her glass in a toast, and we both erupt in laughter. I feel for her, though, knowing how agitated I would be if I were in her shoes.

Later that evening, Jimmy and I dine on lobster and burritos at a faded old Mexican restaurant opening onto the main plaza. The street musicians are out in full force, as they are each evening, serenading passersby with upbeat guitar and marimba melodies. The entire town appears to be in high spirits. Merida must be one of the few places on Earth where life is a constant celebration. Knowing that this will likely be my last opportunity on the trip to spend time alone with Jimmy, I have on a low-cut turquoise blouse that reveals my new suntan to optimal effect. Jimmy looks handsome, as usual, in a crisp white shirt and jeans. I can't help but wonder how the evening will end. Yet again, I try to reign in my fantasies, as we discuss the week's events and the many wonderful insights we've gained.

"Hunbatz says we can't keep all this knowledge to ourselves," Jimmy says, leaning in closer. His leg brushes against mine—whether this is intentional or not, I can't be sure—sending a slight tingling sensation up my back. "We're messengers."

"But, as we said earlier, a lot of people aren't open to it." I glance at my empty glass, surprised by how quickly I've consumed the sangria.

"You'll know what to say and to whom." Jimmy seems to have the right answer for everything. He casually strokes my arm.

I swiftly compute the flight time between New York and Oklahoma. It can't be more than four hours. Not so bad, as long as we both share the travel burden. The warm weather will be an extra bonus for me. He probably won't want to move to New York, so we'll keep two homes. Woooaaah, wait a minute. I recall a friend's blind date story about how she imagined the china they'd have once they were married . . . only never to see that man again.

"I'm not sure I want to leave all this," I say wistfully. "Everyday life can feel so . . ."—I search for the appropriate word— "ordinary."

"That's the hard part, the re-entry." Jimmy smiles, then gulps some beer. "People often feel a bit depressed after these soul-searching experiences. You're on this incredible high, on fire, processing all this new knowledge and then, Bam! You come crashing back to earth."

"Do you feel that way?"

"Yeah, sometimes."

"Me, too. Guess we have to learn to sustain the high, which Hunbatz Men would say is really our natural state anyway."

Jimmy gazes at the plaza, where children are shouting and couples are strolling arm in arm. It's a perfect evening. A gentle spring breeze is perfumed with chiles, jasmine, and the fried dough scent of churros from the street vendors. The sky glitters with stars. We retreat for awhile into our private reveries. Then Jimmy's expression turns serious.

"Ready to go?" he says abruptly.

"Okay . . . if you want." I would have preferred to stay longer, but I'm happy to comply.

Jimmy kindly pays for dinner, and we walk back to the hotel in what is mostly for me an uncomfortable silence. I try to make conversation, but Jimmy has drifted off, and I can't seem to reel him back. We briefly hug good night in the elevator.

"See you tomorrow," he says with a distant smile.

I am both puzzled by Jimmy's odd behavior and disappointed by the evening's fizzle.

On our last day in the Yucatan, we travel about an hour south of Merida to Oxk'intok, one of the oldest Mayan cities, where a number of pyramids, platforms, and temples have been restored. The highlight of our visit is the Temple of the Labyrinth, inside which is a labyrinth of descending and ascending steps where the Maya conducted rituals to awaken the third-eye center. This point on the forehead between the eyes, which is associated with intuition and clairvoyance, represents one of the seven levels of consciousness in Mayan cosmology and the sixth chakra in the yogic tradition. The labyrinth is an ancient symbol shared by many spiritual traditions. As a tool for meditation, prayer, and divination, it represents wholeness, unity, and a path to enlightenment.

The heart of the labyrinth symbolizes the center of the soul, which is arrived at through steps in understanding. Native Americans walked along earth-based labyrinths made of stones and other natural materials, while medieval Christian mystics walked labyrinths that were painted or inlaid on the floors of churches. *The Mayan Oracle* defines the labyrinth as "a multidimensional maze created by Divinity for the purpose of spiritual evolution. From this perspective, one's life and mind can be seen as a maze in which spiritual evolution appears to be the discovery of an 'escape route.'"

We are all relaxed and upbeat, conversing with each other joyfully, as we proceed to the temple, taking turns steering Geraldine's wheelchair. Over the past days, I feel that I have bonded in some way to everyone in our group, and I sense that the others feel the same. We have truly become the rare soul family I've been seeking. When we reach the entrance, Hunbatz Men whistles to the wind, signaling our presence.

I'm slightly uneasy as I stoop to enter the low, narrow door leading into the labyrinth. I feel my way along the cold stone walls through the suffocating darkness, walking slowly and cautiously so as not to trip on the crude steps. As I proceed inward, every so often I pass through a startling laser beam of light shining through small window-like holes.

Hunbatz Men suddenly instructs us to stop where we are standing, place our hands on the wall, and meditate in whatever way feels comfortable. A few of us begin sounding the universal OM vibration. Mira trills in a beautiful, high-pitched voice, while someone to my left chants "Om Mani Padme Hum," the Tibetan mantra of awakened consciousness that reminds me of my previous trip to Tibet.

As in earlier rituals, within minutes of our synchronized group activity, I begin to weep—as do others. I'm not sure why. I sense that I have connected to a sacred place deep within my being, penetrating layers of psyche not heretofore explored. Once again, I feel stripped to my essence, vulnerable, and ecstatic, all at the same time. And yet again, I am surprised by our overwhelming outpouring of emotion. Jimmy's sobs sound above the others; my heart wants to join with his; and I feel that it does, even though we are not physically near each other. I can't seem to stop my tears. Others are moaning and whimpering.

After a considerable amount of time, the emotional outbursts subside, and Hunbatz Men leads us back out of the labyrinth. The burst of sunlight shocks me. I'm completely spent. Everyone is silent as we each wander off on our own, trying to process this incredibly powerful experience. Jimmy collapses on the grass and begins sobbing again. His body is trembling. My first instinct is to comfort him, but I don't want to intrude. We all gather around him, paralyzed, not knowing how to react. Then, Linda, a reserved, dignified woman, kneels down and cradles him. Eventually, Jimmy calms down, and, once he is back on his feet, I embrace him without words. One by one, others do the same. And then, spontaneously, we all hug each other. Many of us have wet faces.

Again, the men and women in this group display a refreshing natural connection, untainted by gender stereotypes and expectations. I admire these men for not being afraid to express their emotions, which typically is neither encouraged nor validated by our culture. Such men, in my eyes, do not appear weak or effeminate. On the contrary, having overcome societal norms with the courage to live freely from the heart, they are models of strength for other men. This is an affirmation for me. For so long, the prospect of finding a life partner has seemed so elusive. I have often questioned my criteria. Have I been holding out for an impossible ideal? But I realize there is no need to despair. I have discovered that men with a deep capacity for relatedness do exist, and I now know, without a doubt, that I will find that special someone. Beyond that, I also understand that while we may often feel alone, we never *are* truly alone when we connect with the light and love that holds everything together in the greater whole. Hunbatz Men and my fellow travelers have helped me to see this truth.

I wonder what triggered Jimmy's sobs. Perhaps it was the pain of his divorces and other life hardships resurfacing, or the many layers of pain, grief, and loss accumulated from past lives, now requesting release. Or perhaps it was simply the liberation of surrendering to Spirit, connecting with his own divinity. Whatever it was, I suspect we all experienced something similar—likely a combination of all these factors and, ultimately, a release into unconditional love. Perhaps Jimmy was able to move more deeply into both the pain and the release.

For the rest of the afternoon everyone is mostly silent. At one point, several of us climb a pyramid to see a panoramic view of Oxk'intok and the surrounding jungle. The natural beauty is breathtaking, and we are happy to be together in what feels like a familiar, shared home. Linda and I note that we both feel lightheaded, a disorienting sensation that we have experienced repeatedly throughout the journey. We believe it is because we are crafting our light bodies and, therefore, expanding into higher frequencies of consciousness, as Hunbatz Men suggested earlier. If so, the combined presence and consciousness of everyone in the group seems to have magnified the effect.

Back at the hotel, I am pleased to find that my press kit has been delivered to my room. And for the fourth time, I cross paths with the young family I first saw at the airport. We chat for awhile. The father, a soft-spoken Jamaican man, is extremely interested in our conference. I tell him about the experience and write down the contact information for Hunbatz Men, which he graciously accepts. So my work as a messenger has already begun!

Later that evening, while enjoying a delicious farewell dinner at the hotel, we learn that the woman who lost her notebook has happily located it. Ginger is beaming, too. She tells me she found her airline ticket in the bathroom trashcan, the one place we didn't look! "So everyone's spirit is complete now," she says. I smile at the unlikely odds that all the objects lost over the course of several days were eventually retrieved. After dinner, Hunbatz Men invites us to gather in a circle outside on the patio. Candles are lit and passed around, as we give thanks for all that we've learned and experienced.

"Now that you have been initiated into Mayan cosmology, it's your job as light beings to help birth a higher consciousness, to heal each other and Mother Earth," Hunbatz Men announces. "Go out and spread the teachings!"

I'm on fire, buzzing with light. How will I be able to maintain this ecstatic state? I recall Hunbatz Men's emphasis on disciplined inner work and rituals, which keep us connected to Spirit and our higher selves, and I promise myself to be more diligent about meditating each day and practicing kundalini yoga. And I can now use the Mayan healing techniques, knowing that each moment offers an opportunity for healing myself and others. In these ways, I can continue my journey to becoming Kukulcan, the divine being that I truly am.

When the circle ritual ends, we all take turns embracing and saying good-bye, saddened that our light circle must dissolve. But I know the deep soul bond within our group will exist forever. I take more time embracing Jimmy, regretting that we are not destined for a romantic relationship. He knows this, too; he knew it all along. Our connection apparently superseded the physical. And that is fine with me.

"I love you," Jimmy whispers.

"I love you, too, Jimmy."

I see now that every event and interaction on this journey was an initiation into the knowledge of my true self as a spark of divine light, a holographic reflection of the cosmos—the experience of which delivered me continually into the infinite embrace of unconditional love. "Your chief task in life is the care of your soul," the writer Leo Tolstoy said. "You should care for your soul and work to improve it, and you can improve it only with love."

Several of us head out into the streets of Merida, which are pulsing with mariachi music, dancing, and merrymaking. It's a festival night, and we can't resist joining the celebration, kicking up our heels with unbridled joy. Ahhh, so Jimmy is a great dancer, after all. It feels good to move my body after all the intense inner work. Ginger seems to agree. At sixty, she is dancing the meanest Charleston I have ever seen. We call her "the life force," as we laugh and dance long into a night that I wish would never end.

The first peace, which is the most important, is that which comes within the souls of men when they realize their relationship, their oneness, with the universe and all its powers, and that the center of the universe is within each of us.

—Black Elk, *Black Elk Speaks*

Let me seek, then, the gift of silence, and poverty, and solitude, where everything I touch is turned into prayer: where the sky is my prayer, the birds are my prayer, the wind in the trees is my prayer, for God is all in all.

—Thomas Merton, *Thoughts in Solitude*

6

HYMN TO
NEW MEXICO

Healing

My rental car, a bright red Thunderbird, treads slowly along the rocky, unpaved road to the Monastery of Christ in the Desert, enveloped by a perpetual dust cloud. Though the road is only thirteen miles long, I feel as if I have been driving for hours. The steep cliffs and switchback curves threading through the majestic Chama River canyon require a heightened alertness. The wild beauty of the high-desert landscape—sculpted with sagebrush and stunted piñon and juniper trees, multihued mesas, and winding river rapids—keeps diverting my attention. Everything is glowing in the clear golden sunlight. The expansive turquoise sky seems close enough to touch. New Mexico is, indeed, the Land of Enchantment, as its state slogan proclaims. There are no signs, no other vehicles, no one in sight. The road becomes more difficult to navigate, and I must drive even slower, hoping that my car does not break down in the intense heat.

Storm clouds are gathering on the western horizon; I wonder whether I should turn back. I read that the road is especially dangerous when wet. My water supply is alarmingly low, and there is no cell phone reception in this remote area—no way to call for help should I get stuck. I scold myself for not being prepared for a mishap. This is the desert, after all. The fact that I am a city dweller, unfamiliar with the wilderness, compounds my trepidation. I don't even own a car and rarely drive. Perhaps I should turn around and check into a comfortable hotel in Santa Fe. What was I thinking? The accommodations here in the desert will be sparse at best.

I stop the car and roll down the window to survey the darkening sky as clouds career toward me. No, I cannot let fear take over. I can't turn back; that would be an admission of defeat. I have come to spend a week at a monastery, something I have never done before. I have spent my life chasing adventure, pushing through my edges, and I'll regret it if I let myself down now. I inch farther into the desert, accompanied only by radio static.

Nearly an hour has passed, and still not a single car. Another bout of anxiety grips me. Perhaps this road leads nowhere; perhaps the monastery is nothing more than a mirage concocted by weary desert travelers! I reign in my imagination, recalling another New Mexico journey, years ago, when I came to write about the painter Georgia O'Keeffe and her house at nearby Ghost Ranch, a sprawling former dude ranch about twenty miles down the highway just north of the tiny village of Abiquiu.

Captivated by the piercing sunlight and stark beauty of the high desert, which have long attracted artists to this region, O'Keeffe immortalized the northern New Mexico landscape in her iconic, early twentieth-century modernist paintings. She has always been one of my heroines, more for the courageous, independent life she forged as an artist than for her art itself, although I admire its bold beauty. "I believe that to create one's own world in any of the arts takes courage," she said. "Making art is like walking the edge of a knife. I'm always afraid of falling off, but I would do it all again." I have often felt the same way about writing. Driving again through the land that O'Keeffe so loved, I better understand her urgent need to capture what she called "the unexplainable thing in nature that makes me feel the world is big far beyond my understanding—to understand maybe by trying to put it into form. To find the feeling of infinity on the horizon line or just over the next hill." I realize, now, what keeps bringing me back to New Mexico, that feeling of infinity.

My magazine assignment on O'Keeffe was fraught with obstacles from the start. Not only had I been pursuing the story for four years, while the Ghost Ranch home was being renovated amid many delays, but my editor had suddenly left the magazine, and I almost lost the assignment. But after much negotiation and persistence, I prevailed, only to find myself one summer afternoon stranded in my car, lost in the desert, waiting for the tardy curator to arrive and show me O'Keeffe's home. My cell phone was dead. I simply had to wait and hope that the curator would find me. I waited several hours in the baking sun, trying to connect with O'Keeffe and her intense love of the desert, growing more agitated by the minute. The relief I felt upon my eventual "rescue" by the curator, a well-known O'Keeffe scholar, was short-lived, however, for she proved to be difficult and demanding, one of my most challenging interviews ever.

For O'Keeffe, the Ghost Ranch house represented "a kind of freedom," she said, despite the hardship of living in isolation without a telephone and with generator-supplied electricity. Her daily routine here was marked by her reverence for simple rituals and an inner clarity that allowed her to be fully present in each moment, an experience that I had hoped my visit to the monastery would deepen for me. O'Keeffe would rise early each morning and take a long walk with her dogs. After breakfast, she would venture back into the desert for a day of painting, often using her Model A Ford as a portable studio. Upon returning home, she would take an evening walk before dinner. My lasting impression of O'Keeffe's life and art, and the Ghost Ranch home that stood at its center, is that of a woman completely at ease with the natural world and with herself. Driving determinedly toward the monastery, I see how New Mexico represents for me a similar connection with the truest part of myself—a peaceful, knowing place within—a place that often succumbs to the stresses of daily life in the city. Indeed, the rocky road to the monastery is an appropriate metaphor for any spiritual path; it is long and arduous, and you must travel it alone.

By the time I wrote the O'Keeffe story, after much laborious research, I was completely spent. But I've learned that most obstacle-plagued experiences are usually accompanied, in the end, by a great gift, a reward for having endured the test. In the case of the O'Keeffe story, I was granted the rare opportunity to become part of her world on the most intimate, personal level, as a visitor in her home, which is now a research center. I experienced firsthand "her" New Mexico, as she viewed it from the large picture windows of her austere adobe house, her paintings taking shape before my eyes, the flat-topped Cerro Pedernal mountain and the dazzling red and yellow cliffs in all their shifting moods and colors.

The storm clouds continue to gather, and I cautiously pick up speed. Surely, I must be nearing the monastery; nearly an hour and forty minutes have elapsed. My impatience and anticipation grow as I cross a small bridge spanning a parched arroyo, or canal, beyond which a sign points the way to a campground along the Chama River. I smile, thinking about the final gift delivered by the O'Keeffe assignment: this morning, when I stopped by Ghost Ranch again for the first time in seven years, I was pleasantly surprised to see my O'Keeffe article, which had come so close to extinction, enlarged and prominently displayed in the window of the main office at the Presbyterian Church-run conference center that now occupies the ranch. Grateful to have played a small part in sharing O'Keeffe's inspiring life with a wider audience, I become even more excited about my stay at the monastery. What gifts, I wonder, might be waiting for me there?

Finally, the monastery's simple, rustic sign appears around the bend. In the distance, an exquisite adobe chapel with a tall bell tower, designed by the Japanese American architect George Nakashima, rises up in the mouth of the canyon like a lone sentinel, framed by towering mesas. I am entranced by its austere beauty. I park my car at the guesthouse, a hacienda-style adobe structure with a large courtyard overgrown with flowering cacti and sagebrush, and am instantly uplifted by the scent of fragrant sage and clean, fresh air.

On the cedar door opening into the courtyard, I find my name and room number posted on a list. The tiny, cell-like rooms are arranged around a U-shaped veranda, with expansive views of the mesas, cottonwood fields, and the river. The monastery—a spare, intimate complex of low-lying adobe buildings, including the chapel, a refectory, gift shop, additional guest houses, and monks' quarters, all connected by meandering dirt and stone pathways— is intentionally isolated in an untamed wilderness. The panorama is breathtaking. I walk hurriedly to the main office, situated near a small meditation garden. The entire complex is bathed in silence, which is at once comforting and unsettling. I do not see a single soul, and the office appears to be closed. In the gift shop, a handsome, rugged man greets me with a sparkling smile.

"How can I help you? I'm Dave." He inspects me intently, as one would a newly discovered, exotic object.

"Dana, New York City. I'd like to check in." I scan the many spiritual books and gift items on display, among them pretty soap bars, jars of honey, and twig crucifixes.

"Monks made those." Dave nods toward the merchandise.

"You're not a monk." He's wearing a red jersey and jeans, not the typical black monk's robe and cowl.

"True, but you're in the right place. I'm the local handyman. I look after the gift shop part-time."

"Do you have the key to my room? Where do I pay?" I reach into my purse for my wallet.

"Whoaaaaa, Miss Dana," Dave laughs. "Slow down. You're definitely a New Yorker. Not here even ten minutes and already you want to check out!"

I'm slightly embarrassed. It is clear that I have entered a unique universe, and I will need to abide by its rules. I am intrigued by Dave's obvious charm and sex appeal, qualities that seem out of place at a monastery.

"Oh, and we don't use keys here," he says with a wink.

This makes me uncomfortable, given my city-bred defense mechanisms. Then again, I'm staying at a holy place; what could be safer?

"No electricity at the guest house either," Dave continues. "Life is very simple here, as you will see. A small corner of paradise." He writes down my name and gives me a pamphlet about the monastery. "I'll tell the guest master, Father Dominic, that you're here. You're in room number five."

"I know, thank you." Already I feel the daily stresses of New York melting away.

"Let me know if you need anything, Miss Dana." Dave bows graciously, as we exchange good-byes. "And remember, take it slow."

Outside, rays of sunlight have begun to pierce through the shifting clouds. The threatening storm appears to have dissipated. I settle into my room at the guesthouse, which is about as austere as I had imagined it to be—bare cement floors and adobe walls, a twin bed and woolen blanket, a rough-hewn closet, and a simple cedar chair and desk. The battery-powered lantern has to be recharged each morning in the utility room. Surprisingly, I do not care that I must do without a hair dryer for the week. And the prospect of not having to check e-mail every day is particularly appealing. Nor do I mind the no-frills accommodations. We are so dependent on stuff—gadgets and conveniences—to get through the day that we have lost sight of what's most important, our connection to our own souls. Though I am not an excessive accumulator of material objects, I am as dependent as anyone else. I have come here not only because I have always been curious about monastic life, but because I desperately need a break from the routine, a quiet, restful retreat with no obligations or deadlines. And because I hope to gain clarity about a challenging, stagnated relationship that has weighed heavy on my heart. I have brought along a few books to read and plan to take some refreshing hikes in the surrounding desert. Beyond that, I have no expectations and am pleased that guests are not obligated to participate in the daily rituals of the monastery, although we are welcome to do so.

Since 1964, a small group of Benedictine monks have been leading a communal life here of prayer, study, and manual labor in service to God. Like the first Christian monks, or Desert Fathers, who sought refuge in the deserts of the Near East during the fourth century CE, these men have abandoned worldly preoccupations to live in silence and solitude. The famous Trappist monk Thomas Merton wrote in an essay about this monastery that the Christian monastic life is one of "hope and hardship, of risk and penance in the sense of a metanoia, a complete inner revolution." This inner revolution demands a "renunciation of ease and privilege in order to work with one's hands in the insecurity of a place remote from one's original home and even from civilization itself." Throughout Christian history, from the wanderings of Exodus to the temptations of Christ, the desert has been viewed as a place of trial and purification, where there is nothing more to rely upon than the providence of God. Stark, unforgiving and inhospitable, it is a place that forces us to look deep within and readjust our perceptions, so that we may see ourselves as we truly are.

In accordance with the ultimate goal of Christianity, the desert is, above all, a school that strips away self-centeredness and teaches us how to love, for which Merton believed an inner transformation is also necessary. "Love, in fact, *is* the spiritual life," Thomas Merton wrote in *The Wisdom of the Desert*. "We have to become in some sense the person we love. And this involves a kind of death of our own being, our own self." The Desert Fathers who went into the desert were usually part of a larger community of monks, among whom they were able to practice love in action. The fruit of this desert life of sacrifice—rooted in solitude and labor, poverty and fasting, charity and prayer—was a state of rest, "a kind of simple no-whereness and no-mindedness that had lost all preoccupation with a false or limited self," Merton wrote. In this sense, the Desert Fathers and, by extension, these Benedictine monks, have much in common with yogis and

Buddhist monks, a fact that comforts me, given my inclination to embrace diverse views of the same truth. Reflecting upon Merton's wisdom, I wonder expectantly whether I will experience a kind of inner revolution here, despite my short stay.

I finish unpacking and settle into a chair on the veranda, soaking in the gorgeous view, animated by the chirping of a bird and the soft rustling of the wind. I appear to be the first guest to have arrived. The immense silence makes me uneasy again. I wonder how I will manage here for an entire week. I read in the pamphlet that all guests must observe silence throughout their stay, just like the monks, who view it as a necessary condition for undistracted communion with God, for it is the only way to hear Him speak. At a monastery, it is considered disrespectful to interrupt this divine private conversation.

I begin to question my decision to come here, believing I have subjected myself to unbearable loneliness. It is a bizarre, self-imposed sentence for someone who values and enjoys human interaction. My initial enthusiasm about the sparse living conditions, which had seemed like a novelty, suddenly fades. Even my mother could not understand why I wanted to spend my vacation at a monastery, of all places, where there surely would be few comforts and thrills and a dearth of social contact. To her, it sounded more like hell than heaven. I silently recount my deprivations: no talking, no television, no cell phone, no wine, no snacks, no spa amenities. Then I realize how spoiled I've become and reaffirm my commitment simply to let go and relax into the unhurried flow of life here. Soon, two other women arrive and dart to their "cells," smiling tentatively at me as they pass by. I am warmed even by this modicum of acknowledgement.

For the rest of the afternoon, I stay in my room reading more about the daily rituals of the monastery, feeling somewhat disoriented, until a loud bell tolls, announcing that it is time for vespers, the evening prayer service, after which dinner will be served. Resident guests take their meals with the monks in the refectory.

How quickly I walk to the chapel, surrounded by fragrant fields of sagebrush and wildflowers. Then, recalling Dave's advice, I deliberately slow my pace. Inside the chapel, I see the monks filing in silently in their long black belted robes, some with cowls, or hoods, depending on their pecking order. A few are wearing white vestments, indicating that they are priests. The small chapel—with its adobe walls, soaring viga-and-latilla ceiling (a common architectural feature in New Mexico comprising interlaced wood crossbeams), dramatic mesa views, flagstone altar, and niches displaying rustic carved and painted santos (sculptures of saints)—is exquisitely austere, unlike the more elaborate Catholic churches of my youth. Yet the ambience, imbued with a sacred solemnity, transports me to those obligatory Sunday mornings, which, at the time, seemed like such a nuisance.

Now, more than thirty years later, having long ago rejected the Catholic religion in favor of a more expansive spirituality anchored in the teachings of diverse traditions—Eastern, Western, and indigenous—I am slightly bewildered to find myself genuflecting toward the large wood crucifix behind the altar. The monks, seated in two separate groups on each side of the chapel, begin reciting the Psalms in a call-and-response Gregorian chant devoid of harmony. It is a spare, monophonic melody that sounds both alien and captivating. Monks sing this official liturgical chant of the Roman Catholic Church seven times a day, seven days a week, from sunrise to sunset. Chanting together this way, in one voice, they proclaim their solidarity with each other and with Jesus. A form of prayer or meditation, chanting is supposed to help keep the mind focused on God. The pace is slow, like breathing. I follow along clumsily, using the prayer book as my guide. I am put off by the ancient couplets of the Psalms, which are often ruthless and damning in their exhortations of punishment for misdeeds. Other prayers are interspersed between the Psalms, accompanied by a precisely timed sequence of kneeling, bowing, sitting, and standing that requires effort and concentration to perform correctly. Observing the proper timing of these gestures, while meditating on the meaning of the prayers, apparently also helps to keep one's mind focused. I had thought the service would be more relaxing; there seems to be so much to do!

Surveying the other guests, who appear to be following the service with ease and familiarity, I feel frustrated and out of place. I will opt out of further prayer services. Praying like this even once a day, let alone seven, seems like a punishment. I do not consider myself religious anyway; spiritual, yes, but religious, definitely not! This *is* supposed to be a vacation.

My long-held resistance to Catholicism resurfaces with a vengeance, as I recall one of the most traumatic events of my childhood. In the confessional box one Saturday, as I knelt and confessed my sins to our parish priest (then again, how many sins could a child of eight possibly have?), I suddenly froze, unable to remember how many times I had fought with my brothers. Impatient with my reticence, the priest, a formidable presence, accused me of not being a good Catholic, of "making fun of God." Making fun of God?! "Get out of my confessional!" he bellowed. I ran to my mother crying, devastated because I thought God didn't love me anymore. My parents were, of course, furious that I had been treated so cruelly. From that point onward, we gradually stopped going to Sunday mass. I am sure that this episode played a major role in my lifetime pursuit of an alternative spirituality outside the Catholic Church. And here I sit at vespers, immersed in an even more ritualized version of that same religion. It is the first religious prayer service I have attended in decades. Revisiting my painful memory, I am confused. Why, really, have I come here?

After the service, the monks return to their quarters as the guests silently leave the chapel and proceed to dinner in the adjacent adobe building, where pleasant conversation promptly erupts. Socializing is allowed in the vestibule outside the refectory and in the gift shop, which I soon discover is a lively gathering place for guests and monks alike. A tall, kindly man approaches me and introduces himself as James. He is a former Trappist monk who spends summers here helping where needed, whether landscaping or oiling the cedar doors.

"Welcome," James says. His smile is warm and comforting. We converse for awhile about life at the monastery.

"I'm not sure how much I want to take part in these services," I confess sheepishly, secretly hoping for an absolution of guilt. "I really just came to read and rest."

"Oh, no pressure. You're free to do whatever you want here." He waves at a few of the other guests. "But for the monks, life is centered around prayer. It's the main work of the monastery. They will leave a task unfinished so they can pray."

"For most of us, it's just the opposite." I ponder the seemingly immense sacrifice of a life devoted to prayer. "We're often too busy working to find time to pray."

I reexamine my resistance to this beautiful ritual. Just because I happen to be at a Benedictine monastery does not mean I have to become a Catholic again to pray in my own way.

"I'm here if you need me." James pats me on the back and begins directing us into the refectory, a cavernous room with high-beamed ceilings, a colorful folk mural of the Holy Trinity, and a beautiful stained-glass window through which an abundance of light shines.

Rows of long, sturdy hardwood tables face each other on either side of the room, guests on one side, monks on the other. All is silent as everyone takes a seat. We recite a blessing before two monks begin serving food. Tonight, the meal consists of pasta with tomato sauce, red beans, and boiled vegetables, plain but simple fare that characterizes the mostly vegetarian cooking here. I learn later that meat and fish are served on rare occasions. I smile at James, who is seated at my left, and then at the attractive, middle-aged woman to my right. Briefly forgetting the strict law of silence, I introduce myself to her, and we begin chatting. It is a natural reflex for me, being the product of an Italian heritage where eating and conversing are intimately intertwined. I learn that Catherine is a professor who lives about an hour away.

I feel a tap on my shoulder. "Shhhhh," James says, raising his finger to his mouth. I nod apologetically. Catherine and I instantly shut up.

In between forkfuls, I try to make eye contact with a few monks sitting across the room, who are eating with slow-motion deliberation. Not one cracks a smile; they don't even acknowledge me. I feel even more isolated by this lack of simple eye contact. I had thought that a stress-free life of divine contemplation would produce a consistent feeling of inner peace and joy. And if so, shouldn't these monks be noticeably happier—like the Dalai Lama, for example, who wears a perpetual smile and always appears to be laughing? Whoops, I am making a judgment. How could I possibly know how the monks feel inside? Perhaps they really are joyful. "We don't even know our own souls, let alone those of others," the writer Virginia Woolf said.

I finish my meal, noticing with some embarrassment that everyone else is still eating. With nothing left to do but sit and wait, I vow to slow down my eating at future meals—something of a challenge. Back home, in the midst of my busy life, I have come to view meals simply as obligatory fortification. Sometimes, eating seems like a waste of time. I think about how eating slowly and silently is similar to deep listening. And I realize how the overuse of words can become a hindrance to hearing our inner voice and cultivating a peaceful state of being. Even when we do speak, a lot of what we say seems superfluous. I make a pledge to say only what is necessary, truthful, and loving.

I gather that the ultimate aim of all this silence and slowness is to help us pay attention, to be more present in the moment. I recall Jung's self-proclaimed need for silence and solitude, particularly as he grew older. As Claire Dunne quotes him in *Carl Jung: Wounded Healer of the Soul*: "Solitude is for me a fount of healing which makes my life worth living. Talking is often a torment for me, and I need many days of silence to recover from the futility of words. . . . This realization becomes clearer every day as the need for communication dwindles."

At what seems like an appropriate moment, I carry my dirty dishes to the clean-up cart and proceed out of the refectory. Catherine soon joins me, and we take a seat outside on the bench, watching the fiery sun sink behind a distant mesa.

"I don't know how I'm going to make it through the week," Catherine says. She is perky and quick-witted, with bright eyes and cropped blonde hair.

"I know what you mean," I laugh. "I don't like too many rules and regulations, adapting to an imposed structure."

"So you're a nonconformist?" she asks knowingly.

"I guess you could say that."

"Me, too. And I'm not exactly the religious type, either. Had too much of it growing up. I got sick of going to church all the time. You?"

"Lapsed Catholic."

"I see," she says, gazing at the sunset. "Well, I came here to get away from my boyfriend and get some work done in peace and quiet. I doubt that I'll be attending any of the services."

"I felt the same way tonight at vespers. I was resisting all the ritual and rigidity. But I've been thinking . . . why not just attend the services as my own personal meditation? I meditate anyway. It couldn't hurt, right?" I look to her for solidarity.

Catherine reflects for a moment. "You know, you're right. How about we do it together?"

"I'm thinking sext, the prayer service just before lunch, and vespers just before dinner. That's twice a day."

"And convenient, too," she says. "Since we have to eat anyway. Okay, it's a deal!"

"Good. I think vigils would be pushing it at 4 a.m.!" We laugh and head back to our rooms. I am heartened to have found a friend, even though I know that communication will be limited here.

The following morning I awake at 6 a.m., which is unusual for me, as I rarely see the crack of dawn. I am one of those late-night creatures often made to feel guilty by early risers. The first rays of sunlight flood my room through a single small window, framing a patch of brilliant turquoise sky. I am instantly uplifted and filled with expectation. I shower in the public bathroom, dress, and settle into the guest lodge, a communal living area with a fireplace and rustic log chairs, a long oak table, a small kitchen, and shelves of books on nature, spiritual topics, and New Mexico. It is chilly outside at this early hour, so I make myself a cup of tea and find a spot to read that offers a maximal view of the surrounding landscape, whose pristine beauty sends me into near rapture. As a lifetime city dweller, I cannot imagine living in such unspoiled wilderness, immersed every second in the bounty of nature. And what a gift to anticipate the entire day before me, uncluttered with deadlines, e-mails, appointments, and expectations, simply unfolding in rhythm with the momentary stirrings of my soul.

This becomes my morning routine, rising early to watch the sunrise, sipping tea, and reading, while admiring the stunning, high-desert view. Oddly, not one other guest disturbs this cozy space while I'm here, further guaranteeing my solitude. I have always required a fair amount of solitude as a writer. Still, I had not been sure what to expect, having subjected myself to such an extreme version of it. And yet, by the second day, I begin to adjust to the pace of slowness and silence, while expanding into it. Surprisingly, I find myself wishing to stay longer. Each day takes on a particular, albeit loose, structure. After breakfast, I wander down to the river to a private spot just beyond a small shed, where a makeshift wood seat has been built into a tall, shady cottonwood. Here, I sit for several hours, sometimes reading, but mostly just observing and experiencing the natural beauty of the site as it metamorphoses from moment to moment in the shifting light, something I rarely do back home.

One morning, I watch as bright sunbeams caress the softly flowing river, creating tiny dancing points of light on its surface that appear to me as transient divine sparks and ignite a sense of my own eternal connection to all that is. I gaze at the river's wavelets reflecting off the backs of tree leaves. I listen to the syncopated whisper and howl of the wind and the silences in between, a flock of screeching crows soaring overhead, and the incessant incantation of an endless variety of insects. Grasshoppers cavort in the tall grasses along the riverbank, while an ant hoarding a food crumb slowly climbs the tree trunk upon which I am leaning. I observe the ant in all its struggles, falling back, turning around, trying again, like the mythological Sisyphus continually pushing a stone up a mountain, only to find himself sliding back down again. Of course, I can identify, having many times felt the frustration of encountering obstacles and delays to my well-intentioned efforts, from the novel I have wanted to publish to the film I have been trying to make for years. But this diminutive creature will not relent until it reaches its destination, wherever that may be. I am impressed by its fortitude, persistence, and patience, the latter not being one of my virtues. Eventually, the ant makes it to the top of the tree. I take this as an affirmation that perseverance pays off eventually, no matter how long the climb. If only I can remain patient.

I notice that my thoughts, momentarily stilled by the quiet majesty of nature, have returned again to worldly concerns— financial obligations, work pressures, my stagnated relationship. My intermittent anxiety about the future creeps back, causing me to doubt my ability to sustain a true and lasting inner peace. Suddenly, I hear the chapel bell. It is a pleasant yet disruptive sound, ringing seven times each day, signaling that it is time to abandon all tasks in order to pray. I check my watch; it is nearly 1 p.m. I feel disappointingly interrupted from my riverbank idyll. But I remember my promise to myself (not to mention my pact with Catherine) and begin walking toward the chapel, a quatrain from Leonard Cohen's song "Anthem" resounding in my mind: "Ring the bells that still can ring / Forget your perfect offering / There is a crack in everything / That's how the light gets in."

Okay, I will try not to be so harsh on myself when I start worrying unnecessarily. I am only human. Nevertheless, I will continue to make a sincere effort to worry less and trust more, knowing intuitively that whatever shows up in my life, however great the test, must be molding and polishing me into an even better version of myself—just like a chunk of coal buried deep within the earth endures eons of pressure eventually to become a diamond. I take a deep breath. Then Dave crosses my path.

"Are you going to pray?" he inquires, walking beside me.

"Yes, I'm going to . . ." For some reason, I cannot remember the name of the afternoon service.

"Sext . . ." He pauses. "As in sex." He winks at me with a devilish smile.

"Right, odd name for a prayer service."

"Okay, see you around, Miss Dana." He bows and scampers off.

Inside the chapel, I try to release all thoughts and focus on the Psalms, which is less challenging during the ten-minute sext. Although I must admit that the tantalizing thought of a brief tryst with Dave shockingly and surreptitiously enters my mind. But I banish it . . . along with persistent thoughts about what I might be eating for lunch today.

Soon, we make our way to the refectory. I notice Catherine up ahead. After lunch, she motions with her hand that she has decided not to speak at all, having decided that she enjoys the silence. I'm somewhat surprised, lamenting the apparent loss of one of my few opportunities for conversation. She seems to be adapting better than I had expected! I return to my room for a nap.

Hiking has become a pleasant ritual that I undertake each day, despite the scorching sun. During these sublime walks along the dirt road curling through the canyon and then into the surrounding desert—through clumps of sagebrush, spinifex, prickly pear cactus, and piñon and juniper trees—I feel very much at peace, so connected to the land and to myself. Some days, I venture out in the early evening, when the striated, multihued mesas shift from their fiery midday brilliance to a diaphanous luster in the golden-pink twilight. Ironically, in this seemingly empty, barren place, I feel full, filled with gratitude for simply being able to walk the earth in such serene silence, along with wild rabbits, lizards, and the occasional snake, reminding me that the desert is, indeed, alive. I read that this wilderness is ancient Pueblo land and, therefore, imbued with the deep wisdom and generosity of spirit embodied by the Native Americans. No wonder the Benedictines chose this site for their monastery. Here, alone in nature, I do, indeed, feel a sense of all-encompassing oneness—that rare, mystical state aspired to by both the monks and Native Americans. I often recite a prayer as I hike, the same prayer spoken by the princess who brought the holy pipe to the Lakota Sioux, as related by the great Lakota visionary and healer Nicholas Black Elk in *Black Elk Speaks*. "With visible breath I am walking. A voice I am sending as I walk. In a sacred manner I am walking. With visible tracks I am walking. In a sacred manner I walk." This prayer, like the chanting of the Psalms, focuses my mind into a laser-like awareness. I notice that with each passing day this awareness seems to grow deeper, becoming less and less diluted by random wandering thoughts.

During one afternoon hike, I pick a few sprigs of sage for my room, inhaling its wonderful clean scent, while offering my gratitude. I am keenly aware now of the sacred consciousness flowing through all living things, how we are all interconnected in and through *Wakan Tanka*, the Lakota word for "Great Spirit."

Sage has been used by the Native Americans for millennia for its healing properties. It can be smoked or taken as a tea to relieve congestion or applied to the body as a poultice to treat colds, fevers, swelling, and migraines. It is also used in the smudging ceremony, a sacred Native American ritual that cleanses and purifies the energy fields that surround all living things, objects, and their environments.

On my way back to the monastery, I pick up a bleached twig and two sparkling white stones, intending to create, along with the sage, an altar on my modest windowsill. I am so grateful for the many rejuvenating gifts of nature, long revered and worshipped by the Native Americans. "There were no temples or shrines among us save those of nature. . . . The Indian . . . would deem it sacrilege to build a house for Him who may be met face to face . . . upon dizzy spires and pinnacles of naked rock, and yonder in the jeweled vault of the night sky!" wrote Charles A. Eastman in *The Soul of the Indian*. "He who enrobes himself on filmy veils of cloud, there on the rim of the visible world where our Great Grandfather Sun kindles his evening campfire . . . He needs no lesser cathedral!" Part of the unique, soulful allure of New Mexico is that both its ancient Native American and centuries-old Christian heritages are peacefully interwoven, culminating most dramatically for me at this monastery. Here, prayer claims no specific culture or peoples, but rather, like the rain, nourishes the sacred land they all share. On this leg of my hike, I say the words "Lord have mercy" silently with each step. This contemplative prayer, which has been practiced by monks since the time of the Desert Fathers, is meant to be repeated hundreds of times a day until it becomes as spontaneous as breathing, according to Thomas Merton in *The Wisdom of the Desert*.

Each evening at sunset, after vespers and dinner, I meditate sitting on a huge tree stump at another spot along the river, hidden by tall grasses and a grove of trees. The weather can change quickly at this hour when storm clouds roll in, often unleashing a spectacular sound and light show accompanied by a brief, sudden downpour, which I have come to view as a daily cleansing of sorts. Before leaving this secret spot, which no one else seems to have discovered, I stand on the stump and give thanks to Mother Nature, bowing to each of the four directions held sacred by the Native Americans.

Doing so, I recall my last visit to Taos Pueblo, where I met Peter, a Native American who makes drums and sculpts small clay animals. I walked into his shop, and we quickly developed a rapport. When I asked if he would share some Native American teachings, he took me to the back of the shop and smudged me with a sage and cedar stick. "Honor Mother Earth and thank her for her blessings while standing in each of the four directions," he said, fanning the smoke around my entire body. "You and the earth can heal each other. The earth will transmute your pain, sorrow, and grief. You can purify yourself by smudging, while offering thanks." He hugged me hard, his eyes filled with kindness and generosity. "In our ceremonies, we don't just pray for ourselves. We pray for the earth and all its creatures, which we are destroying. We are all related. It is only in our minds that we are separate from the whole." We hugged again. I felt an unexpected surge of emotion. Neither of us wanted to let go, strangers to each other just moments ago. "It is a gift that we met," he said softly. "Thank you. Our hearts will always be connected."

Now, as I complete my offering here on the stump, I give special thanks for Peter and his wisdom. Dwarfed by this infinite Earth canvas, I am humbled by my seemingly insignificant place in the universe yet, at the same time, more conscious of my connection to it. Gazing upward, as the sun dips behind a distant mesa, I feel that I have begun to merge with the landscape, and I see myself like a pillar, a conduit between the earth and the heavens. Everything— the river, the mesas, the sky, and the desert brush—appears like a dream at times, as though it is on the verge of disappearing. I begin to understand what Black Elk meant when he said, referring to the unseen realm of Spirit, "The real world is behind this one, and everything we see here is something like a shadow from that world."

As more days pass, defined by my self-imposed routine of praying, eating, hiking, and meditating, I notice that I become more fully attuned and present in each moment, having surrendered to the natural ebb and flow of life here. I relish the all-pervading silence and solitude, which no longer seems punishing, because I am aware that I am in constant communion with something greater than myself. Eventually, I lose track of time, which is punctuated only by the ringing of the chapel bell. One afternoon, while praying at sext, I smile upon seeing the words "Weekdays in Ordinary Time" on the prayer book cover. I suppose that the monks are distinguishing ordinary time from divine time. How brilliant! I am chagrined to learn later, however, that this is an official liturgical phrase denoting the span of time between holidays and special feast days. I liked my interpretation better.

As I become more deeply immersed in the otherworldly atmosphere of the monastery, I also notice that my thoughts— when I allow them into that increasingly pleasurable "no-mind-ness" that I have diligently cultivated—appear to manifest instantly, much as they did at the end of my stay in Cairo. For example, at dinner one evening, I feel drawn to one of the two sisters seated across from me. Though the monastery was created for men, I have learned that these sisters are staying here temporarily while their convent is being rebuilt. I think how interesting it might be to have a conversation with this particular sister, although I am not sure how to approach her. After lunch the next day, I stop by the gift shop, whereupon I find Catherine and that very sister pleasantly conversing. Catherine waves me over.

"I thought you weren't talking," I say, mildly surprised.

"Oh, that's over now," Catherine laughs, introducing me to Sister Solari, who appears to be in her fifties, though she radiates a youthful vibrancy.

"Thank you for coming," Sister says warmly, offering her hand. She has smooth, olive-toned skin and intense brown eyes. "Catherine has asked me to tell her about my life here. Why don't you join us?"

"Yes, I'd love to, thank you." I am pleased that my small wish has been granted.

We proceed to a conference room across from the gift shop and sit down at a table.

Over the next half hour, we listen attentively to Sister Solari's life story, delivered with down-to-earth humor and openness. She was a Carmelite nun as a young woman, but left the convent to get married and have children. She later divorced and took her vows again after several stays at this monastery twelve years ago. How refreshing. I had automatically supposed that everyone here was, for the most part, a stranger to the outside world, and I could not understand why one would choose such an austere and solitary path devoid of the many comforts and pleasures that most of us take for granted. I knew I could never make that choice. I had even wondered whether clerics, in general, were simply unable to cope with the stresses of daily life in what I viewed as the "real world." But I see how faulty and limiting such judgments can be. Who is to say which world is more real?

As if reading my thoughts, Sister Solari says, "This life feels comfortable to me, like an old shoe. It's a step-by-step process of letting go of worldly things." She glances at her watch, apparently eager to get back to work. Like the monks, the sisters engage in labor for part of each day. Sister Solari oversees the daily operations of the gift shop.

"You know," she says, leaning forward and peering at us intently. "In the end, it's all about love and service. This life, any life." There is a reverent silence.

"I can't think of anything more important," I say.

"I've been thinking, Sister," Catherine interjects. "What would it take to become part of a community like this?"

I nearly fall off my chair. Does Catherine realize the import of what she has just said? She has been here just a few days, a confirmed non-religious, non-churchgoing soul, and now she wants to be a nun?!

"Well, now . . . well," Sister Solari hesitates. Even she seems surprised by the question. "You would have to go through a very challenging training, and you would have to leave behind everything you know and take a vow . . ."

"Oh, it was just a thought," Catherine says. "I'll be in touch."

"Thank you, ladies. I have to run." Sister smiles graciously, rising to shake our hands before scurrying off, her black robe and habit billowing behind her.

I turn to Catherine, still shocked by her unexpected question. "Do you really want to be a nun? What about your boyfriend and your teaching that you enjoy so much?"

"I don't know," Catherine reflects. "I guess I'm feeling like it's time to devote myself to something bigger. Nothing lasts forever."

"No, I guess not," I reluctantly agree.

"Well, if I don't see you before I leave tomorrow . . ." She gives me a big hug. "Don't forget to keep in touch."

The following day, I decide to participate in chores, which I had been stealthily avoiding. After breakfast, one of the monks calls out assignments on the porch. I get gift shop duty, which consists, I am told, of simply keeping an eye on the shop while sitting in a chair and directing paying customers either to leave their money in a box or fill out a credit card form. The shop is not exactly overflowing with customers, given this isolated location. I could just sit and read, as I have seen Dave doing on a number of occasions. I congratulate myself on my good fortune. But just as I sit down and crack open my book, Sister Solari rushes out of the back room.

"I'm so happy to see you again!" she beams. "Today we have a lot to do. Would you mind going around to all the shelves and tables and counting the books?" She gives me a thick stack of papers. "You can note how many are left, and then I'll order more, if necessary."

"Sure, okay . . ." This is not what I had in mind. There goes my reading time.

"Then I want you to help me with some other things," she says with the boundless energy of the never idle and always productive. "Thank you, dear!"

Once I finish the book inventory, no small task, as the shop is abundantly stocked, Sister asks my advice on the Christmas display, even though Christmas is months away. "You look like you have a good sense of design," she says.

I suggest that perhaps a few sprigs of sage would look prettier than the sparkly purple cotton cloth suffocating the Nativity scene. Sister embraces this idea wholeheartedly, sending me outside with a long apron and scissors and a plastic bag to cut the sage. An apron? I am happy for the chance to be outdoors, having realized that I may be held captive in the gift shop longer than I had expected. I now wish that I had been asked to weed the garden.

It takes several hours to finish my morning assignment, after which Sister Solari expresses her heartfelt gratitude. I gladly return the apron, which made me look disturbingly like an extra on the old television series *Little House on the Prairie*, and I sigh with relief that the job is over.

The next day, when I report for work, I am again assigned to the gift shop. Well, maybe since I completed my tasks yesterday, I can have a morning of quiet reading while supposedly tending shop. But wait; here comes Sister Solari! She could not be happier to see me again.

"What do you think about the way the tables and shelves are arranged?" she says breathlessly. "And how about all those clay santos and icons and incense sticks?" It is obvious that little attention has been paid to the aesthetics of the shop, not to mention the energy flow.

"Sister . . ." I pause, not wanting to insult her. "I have to say that this shop . . . does not have good feng shui."

"Fung what?" She looks puzzled.

"The ancient Chinese art of harmonizing the energy flow of the environment with the people in it," I explain. I have just begun studying feng shui in New York and try to simplify the explanation. "You know, *chi*. The energy is called chi."

"Brilliant!" She throws up her hands. "Go ahead, you have my permission to rearrange the whole shop! Whatever you can do to make it better."

Why must I always open my big mouth?! For the next few hours, Sister and I lift heavy tables and carts and shelving units and place them in what I deem to be more optimal locations, both aesthetically and energetically, and then offer some blessings and meditations. I also rearrange the placement of all objects. By the time I am finished, Sister Solari is my new fan. I am drained.

"Beautiful," she proclaims, her hands clasped in a prayer gesture at her chest. "Just beautiful!"

"Thanks," I say. What a surprise. I am truly happy to have been of service. Not having expected anything in return has made the experience surprisingly that much more pleasant, liberating even. My labor here did not even seem like labor. And my compensation was simply the moment-to-moment joy of helping someone else.

"You can put me on your resumé!" Sister says with enthusiasm. "I can't wait to show the brothers. Fung, what was that again? Oh, never mind."

With my work completed and Catherine gone, I am eager for more company, despite having grown accustomed to spending so many enjoyable hours alone here. Soon, this desire is answered, too. When I stop by the gift shop the following afternoon to inspect my finished product, I meet a young monk, who is leaning against a bookcase, his arms folded across his chest, as if he were expecting me. I cannot believe my luck. There had seemed to be little opportunity to engage any of the monks, who are always busy praying, reading, or working, even though a few of them have, over the course of several days, smiled and said hello as they rushed in and out of the gift shop. We introduce ourselves, after which I learn that Brother Ernesto, who is from a small town in Mexico, has been living at the monastery for the past ten years. He is forty years old, tall and balding, with a slight beard. His round face is almost cherubic, his eyes filled with sweetness. I feel an impulse to hug him, in a sisterly way. But this would be inappropriate.

"Everyone must ask you why you decided to become a monk," I say, half apologetically, for that is the burning question on my mind. And I had not been completely satisfied with Sister Solari's oblique response earlier in the conference room.

"When I was outside, in the world, I prayed a lot," Brother Ernesto says, smiling peacefully, his voice bordering on a whisper. "Even as a young man, I was not satisfied with fleeting pleasures— alcohol, drugs, women. And the more I prayed and felt close to God the less I needed them. When you feel the love of God, nothing else compares."

I marvel at his faith and courage, not to mention his discipline. "And you don't miss anything from the outside?"

"This is not an easy process, letting go," he continues, as though revealing a heavily guarded secret. "It happens in stages, until you find your heart gradually opening up, releasing judgments, having compassion even for those who offend you. Soon, every act becomes a prayer, every thought pure and loving."

"I admire you," I say, humbled by his presence. How is it that a man of his age could be so unbelievably wise and loving? He is obviously a rare, enlightened soul.

He lowers his head, visibly embarrassed by my comment. "Don't admire me," he says, his eyes moistening. "We all have an important role to play. Just because we are not in the world does not mean that we reject it. We also have compassion for it. You see, being spiritual is not about living at a monastery, or how often you go to church, or even how many good deeds you do, necessarily. It's about where your attention is. When your attention becomes increasingly focused on God, from minute to minute, then you are living a spiritual life."

He wants to know more about me, and is especially interested in my travels. "What was that like?" he repeats with childlike curiosity, as I relate my life in a nutshell. "We monks don't get out much," he jokes. "Then again, there is astral travel, but you have to leave your body to do that." We burst into laughter.

"Thank you so much for your time and generosity, Brother Ernesto," I say, and as I prepare to leave, a priest walks into the gift shop.

"Ah, Father Jonathan Michael, I want you to meet Dana." Brother Ernesto winks at me. "Father lived in Pittsburgh, too. Why don't you two sit down here." He pulls up another chair. "I'll bring you some tea."

"Lovely to meet you," Father says. He is very attractive, with sculpted Mediterranean features, salt-and-pepper hair, and a distinguished bearing.

"My pleasure, Father. But you don't have to drink tea with me. I'm sure you're very busy." Not only do I not want to inconvenience him, but I feel a bit nervous chatting with this important man, particularly given my reservations about Catholicism.

"Not at all, I'll take black tea with honey," Father says, nodding to Brother Ernesto.

"Me, too." I take a seat beside Father, who begins telling me about his work at the sister monastery in South Africa, the years he spent in Haiti, and, of course, Pittsburgh, where I grew up. I am pleased to discover our common love of travel. My thoughts drift to my father, who passed away four years ago. He had attended a Benedictine college. Like my father, Father Jonathan Michael also happens to be Italian. My father had been a best friend and my biggest cheerleader. For a moment, I feel his loss again, that familiar emptiness and grief, which, even after several years, unexpectedly resurfaces now and then. The gap left by his death was enormous. Brother Ernesto returns with our tea, along with some peanut butter sandwiches, and then politely excuses himself.

Having been very careful not to reveal my alienation from the Catholic Church, I nevertheless cannot resist asking a particularly intriguing question. "Father," I hesitate, knowing that I am treading on slippery ground, "I have read that Jesus very likely spent a number of years during his youth in India, Tibet, and Egypt, gaining much of his mystical training from the holy men there. What do you think?"

His eyes widen with what appears to be a mix of curiosity and disbelief. I instantly regret the question. "In all my years as a priest, I have never read anything like that," he declares authoritatively, adjusting his vestments. "No, I don't believe so." He looks away. I am humiliated.

Then Father turns to me again, his mouth easing into a delicate smile. "But then again, you never know." What a relief. I suppose I will not be kicked off the premises. "You know, we are also affiliated with a Buddhist monastery in Tibet, where life for the monks is much like ours here. There are a lot more similarities between religions than it seems." I am both surprised by and appreciative of his open-mindedness.

"Thank you, Father, for the opportunity to talk to you. I have one last question."

"Yes?" his eyebrows arch with expectancy.

"What is the most important requirement for a spiritual life?" I did not want to end such a rare conversation without garnering one last gem of wisdom.

"A constant daily practice, like prayer or meditation, and being consistent with it," he replies with conviction. "Not always easy."

"No, but I see what you mean." I take another sip of my tea, before thanking Father again and slipping out of the gift shop, happy for this unexpected connection.

I think of my father again and of how I came to New Mexico several years ago, shortly after his passing, instinctively knowing that the Land of Enchantment would offer solace and healing. Its wild and holy beauty and bright magical mornings soothed my soul. As I walk slowly back to my room, along a meandering stone path marked at each bend with cedar crosses presiding over shaded meditation grottoes, I see my father again, waiting patiently for me at the airport as he did for so many years on so many holidays. There is the quick flash of his smile and the firm grip of his hand, which made me feel like I was always standing on solid ground. I stop for a moment, picturing him before me, strong and sturdy in both body and mind, with the build of a linebacker and the soul of a sea captain who has weathered all variety of storms. I sense his unswerving faith in me and hear our rich conversations and then the telephone ringing in the middle of the night, my brother's voice hushed and quivering. "Dad passed away. A few hours ago, in his sleep. Heart attack." I feel the knife pierce my chest again, then relive the moment that the loss became real. My father was not waiting for me at the airport when I arrived back home in Pittsburgh. The chapel bell announcing none, the afternoon prayer service, breaks my reverie.

Kicking up the stones again, I notice that I feel different than usual after communing with my father. My heart is much lighter, as though a weight has been lifted. Is the healing finally complete? Does one ever heal from such a loss, even over time, after the unbearable grief has transformed into anger and then indifference and stubborn resignation? Perhaps not completely, but I find comfort now in knowing that it was only by gradually surrendering to sorrow at its deepest level that I have been able to move beyond it. I am more certain now than ever that my father is not really gone. He is right here in my heartbeat, as always.

Before I leave the monastery, I decide to dive in completely and participate in every official prayer service, in effect becoming a transient, secular monk. The night before vigils, I can barely sleep, knowing that I must soon awaken for the 4 a.m. service. Uuuggghhh. It is such an uncivilized hour. I dress without bothering to shower. The desert night chills me to the core as I walk to the chapel in the moonlight (picking up my diligently practiced slow gait just a tiny bit), my elongated shadow leading the way. The landscape is particularly breathtaking, enveloped by an opalescent penumbra. And the chapel is aglow with candlelight, emanating a striking mystical beauty in the early morning darkness. I am surprised to see the guest pews filled. Apparently vigils is the place to be. The ancient Christian custom of praying at night allows Jesus Christ's servants to keep vigil along with him against the powers of darkness.

After the hour-long service, during which I struggled to stay awake yet nevertheless felt comfortably at peace, I walk silently with the other guests to the vestibule at the refectory, where we help ourselves to tea and coffee. I am grateful for the warming shot of caffeine. At 6 a.m., I return to the chapel for lauds, one of the two main daily prayer services, along with vespers in the evening. Most of the other guests have gone back to their rooms, presumably to take a nap. Lauds is morning praise traditionally sung when the world comes out of darkness into light, symbolizing Christ's resurrection. A morning mass follows lauds on weekdays, but because this is Sunday I attend the more formal mass or Eucharist at 9:15 a.m. That is, after I eat breakfast and put in my time at terce at 8:45 a.m., the prayer of the third hour marking the time of the Crucifixion, which lasts about ten minutes. Eucharist, on the other hand, takes more than an hour.

Given the grueling schedule, I consider skipping the Eucharist. After all, I attended so many Sunday masses as a child. Surely one of them could stand in for this particular mass. But I reject the thought, knowing that I will be disappointed in myself for such a childish lack of discipline. As I stand offering hymns of praise and reciting the Lord's Prayer, I am happy with my decision. I marvel at the beauty of this elaborate mass, the incense burning in silver censers, the priest sprinkling holy water on everyone with a silver staff, the sparkling gold goblets used for the wine and wafers distributed at communion. It is as if I were attending mass for the first time. I don't remember it ever being so exquisitely and gracefully served. Such ritualistic beauty obviously was lost on my youth. During a brief refreshment period after Eucharist, I meet Jill, a Protestant psychotherapist, and Leslie, a psychologist who has converted from Judaism to Catholicism. They are both impressed by the Benedictine way of worship and are avid fans of the monastery. I smile at the irony, wondering what I might have been missing all these years, having left Catholicism behind.

No sooner do I return to my room than the bell begins ringing again. It's 11:30 a.m., time for sext, the midday prayer marking

Christ's suffering on the cross, which I have been attending at 1 p.m. on weekdays. Oh, no, not again! I quickly refresh myself and walk back to the chapel, regretting my decision to live like a monk, particularly because it is an exceptionally bright and sunny day. As usual, sext is followed by a light lunch, after which I rejoice at the prospect of an uninterrupted afternoon hike. That hike, of course, proves to be short-lived, for at 4.p.m. the bell calls me back to none, the prayer of the ninth hour when Christ died on the cross. I begin to feel like I have made too great a sacrifice, given my short time at the monastery and all the reading and hiking I have left to do. I was benefiting from my stay here anyway, before this experiment. It is typical of me to make things more complicated than they need to be. But again, I dismiss the complaint, acknowledging Christ's own monumental sacrifice, not to mention the greater depth of stillness and heart-centered awareness that each day here cultivates in me. It is the least I can do for myself.

Before I know it, I am singing the Psalms again at vespers, teetering on exhaustion, for my early morning start has caught up with me. Though physically compromised, I am pleased to find that I am still remarkably focused. By the time compline rolls around at 7:30 p.m., I am barely hanging on, as I listen to the monks chant the Psalms in Latin to close the day, another day soon to begin again at the bright and early hour of 4 a.m. Finally, back at my room, I collapse onto my bed. Praying all day like the monks is much harder work than I realized! Had it been a weekday, I would have had to squeeze in a few hours of manual labor as well. But I am pleased to notice how peaceful and centered I feel, how completely still my mind has become, even more than on the preceding days. All my worries and anxieties have officially dropped away. I admire the monks, who have become so accustomed to their rigid prayer schedule that they do not seem physically affected by it, despite the fact that they are also praying, studying, reading scripture, and working in between the services. I do not recall any one of them appearing the least bit fatigued. I suppose being a monk takes practice, like everything else.

I have one last thing to do, and that is to say good-bye to Sister Solari. I awake on the final day of my stay with this intention, knowing that finding private time with Sister will be a challenge, as she barely appears from behind closed doors. By the time dinner ends, I begin to regret that I've probably missed the opportunity. And yet, just as I step outside the main building, there she is, sitting on a bench, quietly admiring the sunset. I've not seen her enjoying a few moments to herself like this in public. It's as if she heard my thoughts and is waiting for me.

"Sister, I'm so glad to see you," I say, sitting down beside her. "I didn't want to leave without saying good-bye."

Her face brightens with appreciation. "I'm so happy to see you again, too, my dear." She grasps my hand. "You did such a wonderful job in the gift shop. Thank you again."

"Oh, I enjoyed it." I look out across the mesas and the peach and pink dappled sky, saddened to be leaving such dazzling beauty, not to mention my new friends at the monastery.

"Sister, the most interesting thing has happened to me here," I continue. "It seems that every time I have a thought it manifests instantly. I have been thinking all day how much I wanted to talk to you, and now here you are. Or whenever I have a question in mind, someone like Brother Ernesto or Father Jonathan Michael shows up to answer it. Then there's the *New Yorker* magazine article that I brought along to read." My voice brims with excitement. "Miraculously, on the back of the last page is the beginning of an article about the Psalms! I discovered it when I began reading the article here."

Sister lets out a delightful giggle. "Dear, you are living in the moment, from your soul. God wanted you to have this rest. Now, he will send you many other gifts. Take them with thanks, but know that they won't last. Just be grateful."

"I definitely will." I hug her good-bye, knowing that I have received an affirmation of sorts. Perhaps I have begun to see some of the fruits of my inner labors, compounded over the years, surely, but brought to a heightened awareness at this special place.

Walking through the guesthouse courtyard, anchored by a carved and painted Christ on a cross surveying his earthly kingdom, I brace myself for going back "outside" into the world, recalling Jesus's exhortation in *The Gospel of Thomas* to "be a passerby." That means trying not to get too distracted by worldly concerns and desires, because they are so fleeting and inconsequential compared to the lasting peace and contentment cultivated by our constant connection to Spirit. That's what Sister Solari meant, too. Easier said than done, of course.

The following morning, I pack my few belongings, return the gas lantern to the utility room, and start out again on the rocky road in my red Thunderbird, feeling as though the past week has been a wonderful dream. An eagle soars overhead, as the dust swirls around me. My heart expands with gratitude and a deeply contented, nourishing feeling that I can only describe as love. Love for this land and all its creatures, for the sun and the wind and the trees and the sky, for all the people at the monastery, most of them still perfect strangers to me, though I had felt welcomed into their gracious community. Love for the time that I have spent here reviving my soul. Love for myself.

And deeper love, surprisingly, for the man in my life that I have so often wanted to stop loving. Love even for that harsh priest long ago, wherever he is now, who threw me out of the confessional. I see how much richer my life has been because of that painful incident and how forgiveness teaches us how to love. And I realize that I don't have to reject Catholicism anymore. I can embrace it without judgment as a worthy spiritual path, acknowledging its own unique beauty, even though I do not choose to practice it, let alone become a convert to monastic life. My mission, like that of many others, I believe, is to integrate Spirit in the world, to reconcile the conflicting forces of self and other in a less extreme environment. Perhaps I have experienced my own metanoia here at this monastery, in the way that Thomas Merton defined it. From this moment onward, I sense that I will be able to trust more in the divine flow of events, knowing that I must continue to walk the fine line between doing and being that will allow me to accept whatever shows up in the moment. The dull pain weighing down my heart when I arrived seems to have lifted. I am renewed. New Mexico has once again worked its healing magic.

To be enlightened is to be aware, always of total reality in its immanent otherness—to be aware of it and yet to remain in a condition to survive as an animal, to think and feel as a human being, to resort whenever expedient to systematic reasoning. Our goal is to discover that we have always been where we ought to be. . . . But the man [woman] who comes back through the Door in the Wall will never be quite the same as the man [woman] who went out.

—Aldous Huxley, *The Doors of Perception*

7

PERUVIAN MAGICAL
MYSTERY TOUR

Activation

B e in this world but not of it," the enigmatic imperative of
mystics throughout the ages, resounds in my mind as I sit
crosslegged in a thatched-roofed hut deep in the Amazon
jungle of northern Peru, quivering with fear. The dancing light from
kerosene torches and the menthol scent of copal incense infuse
the thick, autumnal darkness with an otherworldly aura. Here, in
this simple ceremonial space, eight of us have assembled to walk
through a door in the wall, the wall of our everyday consciousness.
I glance at my travel companions, fellow castaways from the other
America; their faces are somber and contemplative, their bodies
stiff with foreboding expectation.

Over the years, I believed I had gained some understanding
of what mystics have meant about striving to transcend the
world, the consensus reality of planet Earth, while simultaneously
participating in it. This rarefied ability, once achieved, frees us
from all suffering and elevates us to a state of infinite joy and peace,
according to the perennial wisdom. I have sincerely tried, albeit
inconsistently and with frustratingly fleeting success, to meet that

challenge. But now, thousands of miles from civilization, in trying once more I am about to receive a kick in the pants, so to speak, a nudge from the mysterious beyond embodied in a viscous bitter, green-brown hallucinogenic drink called ayahuasca.

Made by slowly boiling pieces of the ayahuasca vine with chacruna leaves, both native plants of the Upper Amazon Basin, this potent brew has been used for millennia by indigenous peoples of the region as a sacred medicine for healing the body, mind, and soul. Typically administered by shamans, or curanderos, known as *ayahuasqueros*, ayahuasca is sometimes simply called the Medicine or even more simply yet deceptively, tea. It acts as an emetic to induce vomiting, which in shamanic ayahuasca lore is known as *la purga*, or "the purge." This uncomfortable, often violent effect supposedly produces both a physiological and spiritual cleansing, a rare case in which vomiting becomes a good thing. But ayahuasca is perhaps best known for its hallucinatory properties, purported to transport the user to supernatural realms offering visionary insights.

Fittingly, the word *ayahuasca* means "vine of the soul" in Quechua, an indigenous Peruvian language. In the Upper Amazon, the vine and drink are also referred to as *yage*, a term made famous by the counterculture icons writer William Burroughs and poet Allen Ginsburg. My mounting trepidation, as I wait in the open-air hut to ingest ayahuasca for the first time, is not unfounded. "This is the most powerful drug I have ever experienced. . . . That is, it produced the most complete derangement of the senses," Burroughs wrote in *The Yage Letters Redux*. "This loss of control can be completely terrifying. . . . Take the boiled preparation in standard dose and you experience paranoid delusions and hallucinations, horrible nausea, chills and a complete loss of coordination. I am sure that this dose would kill anyone in poor condition."

I now regret that the extent of my experience with drugs over four decades has consisted of nothing more than a few puffs of marijuana. I was just a child in the 1960s, when the counterculture erupted; my sole meager attempt at political activism was wearing for two years a P.O.W. bracelet engraved with the name Colonel Roger Metzger. Not only that, but I am a city girl unschooled in the everyday life-and-death dramas of the jungle, let alone hallucinogenic plant medicines. What if I'm not physically fit enough—a death sentence, according to Burroughs. What if I go so deep into the experience, become so transported, that I am unable to return to ordinary consciousness? Yet the prospect of instantly achieving an altered state with its accompanying extrasensory features was too enticing to reject.

I'm startled from my dark musings by Jose, the young, extremely handsome resident shaman of our primitive yet scenic jungle camp in a small, remote river village. The central camp comprises three thatched-roof huts on stilts—one with mosquito-netted hammocks and hardwood platforms for beds, another used for ceremonies and celebrations, and the third our open-hearth kitchen. Two tiny shacks serve as outhouses. Jose sits down on a bamboo rocker in front of us and begins singing blessings in Spanish, while puffing purifying tobacco smoke over a plastic container of daylong-boiled ayahuasca.

I recall our early morning excursion along the mighty, undulating Amazon and its narrow twisting tributaries in search of the fabled ayahuasca vine. Two crude dugout canoes, with obligatory machetes and rifles on board, are our sole mode of transportation in the jungle. The water was high and clear—reflecting the brilliant green vines, trees, and tropical plants that strangle the riverbanks and seem, now and then, to take the shape of animals and people—as we glided by in the slow-boiling heat. Once ashore, we hiked deeper into the jungle, where Greg, one of the Peruvian men assisting us, climbed a towering tree to cut the ayahuasca vine. Many of the trees are so tall—up to two hundred feet, with massive, sprawling roots—and the rainforest canopy so thick and vast, that I felt engulfed by a strange primordial presence, pulsating with mysterious, even dangerous possibilities.

From the moment we boarded the worn-out, triple-decker riverboat, a chaotic mix of gringos, locals, and supplies for a fourteen-hour overnight cruise from Iquitos—the lawless frontier town and faded Spanish colonial gateway to the Peruvian Amazon—danger became a constant companion. That is, thanks in no small part to the rhapsodies of our magnetic trip leader, Peter Gorman, a rugged, chain-smoking, lovable Irish bear of a man. Peter, whose body is covered with scars and "war wounds" from a lifetime of cheating death in the jungle, warned us repeatedly not to lean too far over the canoe, for we could easily capsize and instantly be devoured by a black caiman (the local crocodile) or an eighteen-foot anaconda! They are among the three most feared jungle beasts, the jaguar being the third.

On the riverboat, where we sampled magic mushrooms (under whose influence I felt little effect but for a lingering nausea), Peter had issued another stern warning: "If any of you guys lean over that railing while you're on mushrooms to get a better look at the sunset or whatever, then you run a real risk of falling overboard and getting sucked in by that boat propeller! I'm serious; pay attention. Because I'm not jumping in after you!" And one day, as we ventured out to explore an oppressive swamp carpeted with a blanket of chartreuse vegetation, swarms of insects, and giant lily pads, Peter again tried to ensure our safety. "Listen up! We are going to be canoeing through a maze of vines and trees covered with poisonous spikes," he bellowed. "Touch one, and that's it. You could die! And please, please don't fall out of the canoe; you do that, you're gone. There's quicksand in that swamp!"

Before long, our anxiety exploded in laughter, and we decided to write a group book called *101 Ways to Die on the Amazon*, to which we added fictitious entries daily. Not surprisingly, we were similarly prepped for the ayahuasca ceremony, as Peter explained that we likely would be falling all over the place, perhaps "flying off" the platform, vomiting profusely, and running to the outhouse to otherwise relieve ourselves. All this would be done while he and his crew stood by with "eighty-two rolls of toilet paper," ready to comfort us.

Peter is, of course, seriously concerned for our welfare, and he is probably right to scare the hell out of us, even though he waxes dramatic. In the jungle, which can be alternately hostile and hospitable, the contrast between teeming life and instant death is strikingly apparent—from lush vegetation and the abundance of fruits and vegetables, like the yucca and plantains that villagers gather daily, to the threat of hidden predators, or something as eerily natural as a mother spider devouring her young. Although I basically feel safe here, more protected than threatened, I am deeply aware of the fragile balance that underpins our survival, both individually and collectively, and of our need to respect and honor Earth, whose most remote frontiers, steeped in beauty, have more to teach us than we can imagine. Along with its constant reminders of transience, the jungle also presents evidence of continual rebirth, whether it's a boa constrictor shedding its skin or a caterpillar that shapeshifts into a gorgeous cobalt-blue-winged butterfly. Throughout my Amazon journey, I keep thinking that a similar drama needs to take place in our consciousness. We must be willing to become the butterfly, emerge from the darkness of a cocoon that no longer serves us and become a new breed of human, connected at the deepest level to our hearts, Earth, and all living things. That is how we will survive the self-destructive nightmare we have perpetrated on the planet and create a more enlightened way of being.

Once we found and cut the ayahuasca vine, we each took turns silently carrying a piece of it through the jungle back to our canoes. By doing so, we introduced ourselves to mother ayahuasca, mingled our energy with hers, and asked for her guidance and whatever teachings we were supposed to receive. Ayahuasca is said to be a plant with an abundance of feminine energy, and I had felt something of this nurturing quality as I carried the vine in my arms. "Trust me, it's like nothing you've ever experienced," Peter said, prepping us at breakfast for the ceremony that evening. I was intrigued despite my anxiety. There was no turning back.

We ate little all day, because it is not advisable to take ayahuasca on a full stomach, and lolled about in the oppressive heat, waiting for what seemed like an eternity for the evening ceremony to begin. Everyone became increasingly silent as daylight faded into a velvety darkness, the infinite night sky illuminated with billions of stars and milky galactic swirls. There were the Southern Cross, Orion's belt, the planet Venus, seemingly close enough to touch. I had never seen such a brilliant heavenly tableau, nor felt so humbled by my own relative insignificance. My travel companions and I exchanged polite glances but few words. I assumed they were either overcome with similar awe at the glories of nature or fighting off encroaching ayahuasca fears, as was I, though no one would admit it.

Now, sitting in the ceremonial hut and reflecting on these events, I ask myself repeatedly what I am doing here, walking the edge in the middle of nowhere, risking physical and mental torture? Should something happen to any of us, there will be no doctors or hospitals for thousands of miles. It will literally be the end of the road. Then Jose approaches me with a tin cup of the dreaded brew. He has measured out specific doses for each of us. First, though, he pours agua florida into my cupped hands, and I pat it on my body. This floral-scented water is used in ayahuasca ceremonies and other local shamanic rituals for purification and to keep away negative spirits. Then I sniff a bottle of essences and dab some sweet-smelling perfume on my wrists and face—another purification—before swallowing the ayahuasca, which tastes so awful I can barely get it down. Jose gives me a Halls Mentho-Lyptus® drop to soothe the bitter taste, finishes administering to the other initiates, and returns to his rocker, whereupon he begins singing again in a melancholy, rhythmic voice, blessing and praising the plant medicine, while shaking a shacapa leaf rattle as accompaniment. This hypnotic chant continues all night.

After about thirty minutes, I feel as though I'm rocking back and forth, like I'm on a canoe. My fingers and toes tingle, and then waves of nausea slowly coil through me. My eyes are closed. Strange fluorescent spinning shapes flash in my mind like patterns in a kaleidoscope. Before long, a host of anonymous people—a snarling man smoking a cigar, a rough blonde woman driving a pick-up truck—appear and fade away. They are bizarrely haunting, and I have the sensation of being lost in a carnival funhouse. It seems as though mother ayahuasca is taunting me. I am more disappointed than amused. I open my eyes for reassurance of my physical presence, something I do periodically throughout the ritual in an effort to ground myself. I now understand the reason for Jose's continual chanting; it is a solid real-world comfort, as I launch into more visions, acutely aware that I am inhabiting two worlds at once. A huge, slithering anaconda appears, then the fierce faces of a jaguar and a tiger, which startle me, as I have never felt a particular connection to these animals. As I scan the forest beyond the hut, I see an Egyptian temple; three phantom-like women of varying ages stand inside, holding offering cups.

Of course, I am determined to prevent myself from purging, foolishly thinking that I can defy this powerful plant medicine. I watch as some of my fellow travelers rise, one by one, and clumsily walk out into the forest to vomit their guts out. It is neither a pleasant sound nor sight, hazy as it is in my altered state. Finally, after about an hour, I succumb to the nausea that has completely overtaken me. I can barely walk; my limbs are soft and unresponsive, as though disconnected from my brain. I am frightened. This is much worse than an alcoholic stupor. Selma, a lovely young Peruvian woman who has been assigned to look after the women, takes my hand as I stumble off the platform. It is pitch black, and I can barely see in front of me. Peter holds me up as I purge. My first physical reaction to the plant is violent, and why wouldn't it be? I am cogent enough to realize that I have just ingested poison, and my poor body wants to eject it.

"When is this going to end?" I groan.

"Don't worry," Peter says, chanting over me. "It will pass." Back at my seat, feeling slightly better, I continue journeying through space-time, now lying down to stem the nausea.

A photograph of my mother as a young woman appears, followed by the word *LOVE*. My eyes tear. I see the letter *W* in calligraphic script, wondering what it means as I hear the words "waiting, waiting, waiting"—an appropriate description for the state in which I find myself at this particular point in midlife, waiting for some dreams to take shape. The hero in Henry James's story *The Beast in the Jungle* waited his entire life for something monumental to happen, only to be disappointed that not only did the "beast" never appear, but he had missed so much along the way, waiting. Then I hear "Get it down, get it down!" which I interpret to mean that I must record this experience so that I don't forget it. Mother ayahuasca is definitely speaking to me. After some odd, frustrating visions of furniture, the Egyptian temple appears again, and then an image of myself kneeling at an altar, where a priestess leans over and drapes me with a garland. I feel humbled by her acknowledgment, but of what I do not yet know.

Twice more I purge during the four-hour ceremony, after which I unsteadily grope my way back to my bed, assisted by Selma and a flashlight. But I cannot sleep, as I am still racked with nausea. My roommate, Paula, a compassionate, nature-loving soul, watches over me, as I sit doubled over on the porch for a few more hours before I can lie down.

The next morning, I awake weak and exhausted, grateful that the unsettling ayahuasca effects have largely worn off. I am alarmed to discover that Doug suffered severe dehydration from purging and was in so much pain that he believed he almost died.

After dunking ourselves in the river to seal off our crowns to keep spirits from reentering, we walk about in a slow-motion haze. Nobody has much of an appetite for breakfast, though our jungle meals, ranging from spiced vegetable, bean, and rice dishes to freshly grilled caiman and chicken, have been consistently delicious. My physical experience of ayahuasca was undeniably harsh and disturbing, as Burroughs had promised. But unlike Burroughs, I am not particularly astounded by the visions I received or the scant knowledge they imparted. I want more. Nevertheless, Peter assures me at breakfast, as I force down some papaya, that I've had a very productive first session with ayahuasca. "You will need more time with her," he says. "You're just getting to know each other."

I am, however, more clear about one thing. Under the influence of that trickster plant medicine, I had little control of my mind and body. Ayahuasca reminded me that, in our mere humanness, we are not in complete control of anything. This prophetic message actually came to me much earlier—before our journey even began. The company that had organized the trip informed us at the last minute that it would have to be postponed due to financial difficulties. Would the trip ever launch? Would we ever see our money again? We had no way of knowing. I was shocked. It was easy to succumb to anger and judgment—my initial reaction. But I soon realized and accepted that if I were meant to take this journey, everything would fall into place. I would have to trust a higher intelligence. What a test.

How appropriate that we would be confronted at the trip's outset with such uncertainty and lack of control—an ongoing theme in the life-and-death drama of the jungle. As if to emphasize our condition, before venturing here Peter took us to the local prison in Iquitos, where we stood outside the high barbed-wire and brick walls so that we could feel the pain of the prisoners. That odd excursion didn't make sense to me then, but it does now. I see more clearly how we can become our own worst enemies, creating our own prisons from our assumptions, expectations, and self-limiting consciousness. For this reminder, despite all its attendant agony, I am grateful to mother ayahuasca. Sometimes we must be clubbed over the head with the truth, or suffer a violent purge, before we finally get it.

The need to relax into and accept what turns up in my experience is further reinforced when I discover that someone has stolen two hundred dollars from my backpack. I left it unattended on my bed in the jungle hut for about an hour, while I was taking photographs of the beautiful children from the village who were always wandering around our camp. Though Peter kindly offers to replace the money, that small violation tweaks my equanimity . . . as do the routine last-minute schedule changes, delays, and unclear communications that inevitably accompany any long journey, particularly in the third world.

Perhaps the biggest challenge to my peace of mind is daily life in a jungle camp: Amenities and creature comforts are expectedly scant. No electricity, hot water, bathrooms, or showers. We must bathe in the murky brown river, which is teeming with piranhas and eels, and perhaps a rare anaconda, while negotiating banks of shin-deep mud.

Bathing proves challenging for me, as Felina, a beautiful thirty-something Peruvian woman with an infectious laugh who is part of the camp crew, can confirm. I often catch her standing behind a tree laughing as I exit the outhouse disgusted, carelessly tossing away the bucket of water that we use to flush the crude toilet. "You are so funny," she says, giggling and hugging me. "I love you." One afternoon, she takes me out on a canoe to bathe at a sequestered bend in the river, where she often goes herself and where we can have privacy. How on earth did Katharine Hepburn ever manage to stay so elegant sailing downriver through the jungle in *The African Queen*? Felina uses a torn plastic container to drench herself with river water after she lathers up.

"Don't you ever go into the river?" I ask, surprised.

"Oh, no, never. Too many creatures in there!" she says, laughing.

I decide that if she, a Peruvian, does not swim in her native river, then I surely will not. But attempting to stay on the canoe while washing proves disastrous. I keep sliding off the canoe boards, hurt my back, and, unthinkingly, allow our canoe to drift away from a spindly tree, whose branch I have been holding to anchor us.

"Throw me the oar!" Felina screams, half naked. We laugh loudly as she paddles back to our spot, out of view from camp. I try to help her row but give up, as both the oar and canoe are very long and heavy.

"How did you do that?!" I say, admiring her dexterity. I am embarrassed by my inadequacy, certain that I could not survive even a few days here on my own. She giggles again, then finishes bathing, while I cling to the tree.

"I'm sorry," she says graciously, rowing us back to shore.

"No need to apologize, Felina!" I am warmed by her heart-felt sensitivity to my discomfort.

As much as I try to hit my comfort stride in the jungle, it is no use. The torments keep accumulating. The canoe is a literal "pain in the butt," particularly because I often find myself sitting on the lowest and narrowest plank above a perpetual puddle of water when we embark on our river expeditions. The mosquitoes are out in full force, immune to all varieties of repellent—including Bounce fabric softener—and some of them undoubtedly carry malaria. Then there is the threat of yellow fever and venomous snakes. Mud accumulates everywhere, on the floorboards, our luggage, clothes, and shoes. "I can't live this way!" even easy-going Paula shouts, as she keeps repacking her clothes. I endure a string of sleepless nights, kept awake by a combination of the hard board at my back; the endless chatter of insects, croaking frogs, and screeching bats; my roommate's habit of rising at 6 a.m.; and my own partially delirious mental state. Add to that the suffocating heat and wretched physical effects of ayahuasca, and I am officially exhausted much of the time.

But complaining is useless. I have pushed my body to its physical limits as never before, connected with my elemental self, taken a walk on the proverbial wild side where I have undergone a thorough—and I'm sure essential—dry cleaning. Having gone days without make-up, a blow dryer, or even a shower, I finally simply don't care. How I might appear to others does not concern me. I feel liberated and simply remain present in my wretchedness. At times, I feel like pure consciousness itself, capable of taking flight at any moment. And that sensation, though strangely unsettling, makes me giddy.

No sooner have we almost recovered from our first ayahuasca experience than Peter announces that we are going to sample two more sacred Amazonian medicines—nu-nu, a snuff, and sapo, frog sweat—that are used by the local Matses Indians (a semi-nomadic tribe who tattoo and paint their faces to resemble jaguars) to thrive in the nearly uninhabitable deep jungle. Peter, a writer and expert in Amazonian medicines, explains that sapo is a secretion of the phyllomedusa bicolor tree frog. It both sharpens the senses and builds stamina for long hunts and treks; it also cures ailments ranging from malaria to chronic fatigue and the grippe. Research has shown that sapo has many other medical benefits, including potential use as a painkiller and blood pressure regulator. Nu-nu is a psychoactive bright green snuff made by mixing the dried powdered leaves of jungle tobacco, called mapacho, with the powdered inner bark of the Macambo tree. The Matses use nu-nu to receive visions of where to hunt or new areas in the jungle where plant medicines can be found. Like most indigenous Amazonian peoples, the Matses view plants in the same way they view animals, as sentient beings with whom they can communicate and receive teachings, including extensive medicinal knowledge.

But how can I put myself through what surely will be more torture on such short notice? I still feel weak and rubbery and slightly dazed from the ayahuasca. Peter calls us to gather around, as Pedro, a Matses Indian, uses a thin stick to scrape milky white sweat from the body of a lime green frog whose legs have been splayed and tied to four upstanding twigs. Playing with the frog's toes, he stimulates it to produce more of the secretion, which protects the frog from predators. I gasp at the sight of the poor frog, who Pedro assures us has not been harmed and will soon be released back into the jungle. He places the tiny, glue-like balls of sweat in a row on a piece of split bamboo, each one representing one dose of sapo. I pray that I will not have to ingest them. My wishes are answered, for sapo is administered beneath the skin, so that it will directly enter the bloodstream! How appealing. Another experience that I will never forget. (And I still have the scar to prove it.)

"What am I doing? I must be crazy," I say to myself repeatedly. When it's my turn to take sapo, I sit down on the floor of the ceremonial hut. Pedro burns a small circle into my arm with a sharp hot ember and rubs off the skin. I shake my head "no" when he tries to singe me again. I am not a fan of body mutilation. He then spits on a ball of sapo and dabs it over the open wound, which burns slightly. This does not seem sanitary.

Within minutes my heart nearly pounds out of my chest, and my head is on fire. Then I get the chills. I do not have to purge like some of the others in the group who have taken larger doses. The experience is manageable, nowhere near as frightening as ayahuasca. For the remainder of the day, I am pleased to notice that I experience a sense of well-being. I feel stronger, more awake, and grounded in my body.

And now for the nu-nu. Pedro squats in front of me with a long, hollow reed, places a pinch of the snuff inside and blows it three times up each of my nostrils, smiling ebulliently. My head jerks backward with each of his forceful blows, and I cough up green phlegm. Once again questioning my sanity, I await the effects.

I do not receive any visions. But the haze of my ayahuasca hangover disappears instantly, and everything appears brighter and more colorful, as though I am really seeing for the first time. I am calm and slightly intoxicated. So I have passed another test, for what reason I cannot say. Once again, I've pushed myself to the edge, beyond my fears, which in itself is physically and spiritually empowering. Of course, peer pressure did play a small part.

Dr. Steve suffers the most of anyone in our group. He is doubled over in pain on the platform, gagging and moaning. I am grateful for having been spared that agony.

"The nu-nu must have gone directly to his brain," I say to Paula, fully aware that my own brain is now suspect. I cannot even remember what day of the week it is, or, worse, how long I have gone without washing my hair. And I do not care what time it is. Yet I do notice that I am serenely present in each passing moment. Like a child, my thoughts rarely drift beyond our immediate experience; nothing else seems important. Then again, time is elusive in the jungle, even when you're not taking sacred plant medicines (or what some, including my aghast mother, would narrowly call drugs). It is as if time does not even exist, as though we have checked out of everyday reality into an eternal green present.

Doug, a fit, attractive man in his early fifties, and I speak of this and other philosophical puzzles under the bright new moon and stars, having opted out of the second ayahuasca ceremony to sit on rocking chairs on the front porch of our hut.

"We both know that we don't need drugs to achieve an altered state," Doug declares, defending our choice to defect.

"Of course not," I say, rocking emphatically.

Spending long periods simply passing "time," with nothing particular to do and nowhere particular to go, just waiting (as my ayahuasca vision had indicated), which sometimes feels claustrophobic, has become another theme of our Amazon journey. It has taken me several days to surrender to the slow jungle rhythm. Against the sonorous background of Jose's distant chanting and our travel companions' purging, Doug and I also talk of our mutual quest for "a big revelation" and how we are so far disappointed that it has not yet revealed itself. Why come to a place like Peru anyway? Waiting for this revelation, my own "beast in the jungle," I notice that my impatience is growing. I should know better than to have such expectations, yet I do anyway. I remind myself that it is enough to "be here now," as the mystic Ram Dass has famously urged, to be simply and fully present.

"It's funny," I joke. "We came here to evolve, but I feel like I have actually *de*volved, taking drugs, wading through mud in tall unfeminine rubber boots, using an outhouse, not showering."

"I know what you mean," Doug laughs. We fall silent. After a few moments, he turns to me intently, as though he has just retrieved an important thought. "You know, everything always boils down to self-worth. So much pain and suffering comes from believing you're not good enough in some way. The only answer to every situation is unconditional love toward yourself and others."

"Yes, I guess so," I say, pausing to consider this unexpected yet profound wisdom. I think about how the Peruvians, who are so visibly affectionate, seem to be particularly skilled at giving and receiving love, whether to each other or to complete strangers. I have been moved to tears by their declarations of love, and I continually feel my heart expanding. Whether it is Felina and Selma, who are constantly embracing me; the little village girls who like to sit on my lap on the porch and play with my hair while teaching me Spanish; or the boy from Iquitos who constantly roams the streets hustling his mother's handcrafted jewelry. I purchased a few Amazonian seed bracelets from him at the outset of the trip. One evening, he came back to find me at an outdoor café, hugged me, and whispered, "I love you." Though most Peruvians have little in the way of material wealth and comforts, they are always smiling and joyful.

"It's getting late. Good night." Doug smiles and retires inside the hut.

We have struck up an ambiguous friendship, Doug and I, often finding ourselves together on the canoe or a hike, talking passionately about a variety of subjects that interest us—literature, healing, metaphysics. Although a mutual respect and warm familiarity have developed between us, I am not interested in him romantically, so when he confided that he was attracted to me, I politely told him that I was seeing someone. Though he said he understood, I am always slightly guarded around him.

Our group is small, and we spend every waking minute together over the course of three weeks. Doug is particularly intense and cannot let go of the attraction or the idea that we may be destined for each other. I enjoy his company but do not want to cross the proverbial line. At times, I feel overwhelmed by his attention, which he senses, asking me to understand his vulnerability in being eager to find his soul mate.

Then there is Peter. Although he means well, he is so sensitive that he sometimes perceives our comments as criticisms of the trip and his efforts. At times, I feel as though I am walking on eggshells, afraid to say anything at all. As I reflect on my reactions to interpersonal challenges, I fortuitously retrieve an e-mail in Iquitos from my Australian friend, Trish, that includes the following quote: "Always be kinder than necessary, for everyone you meet is fighting a battle of some sort." When I hug Peter one afternoon at lunch, saying how much I appreciate all that he is doing for us, his entire body softens, and his face lights up. If only we could remember to do that more often, to show our appreciation.

Our last night at the jungle camp, we celebrate with a fiesta. We drink a delicious milk and cane alcohol drink and dance in the ceremonial hut, decorated with swathes of toilet paper and flowers, to live bongo music with the camp crew and neighboring villagers and their children. Juan, Jose's adorable two-year-old son, nearly wears me out. It is a joyful experience for all, of holding hands and kicking up our heels in mutual recognition and appreciation.

But before we leave the Upper Amazon, we have one last opportunity to take ayahuasca, this time at a lovely shamanic retreat outside Iquitos. Having relaxed for several days after the first ayahuasca ceremony, I conquer my fears and force myself to participate. Peter says that each ayahuasca ceremony is unique, due to the different curanderos who perform it and the different ratios of ingredients with which the ayahuasca is prepared. I am still holding out for my big revelation and know that I will regret missing this opportunity.

It is dusk by the time we reach Sachamama. To get here, we traveled two hours in a van from Iquitos, then did a long muddy climb uphill through the forest. This beautiful rustic compound has thatched-roof huts, a botanical garden, and a large art gallery displaying folk paintings of surreal ayahuasca visions. Roberto, the resident curandero and ayahuascero, also works with healing perfumes. He is a slender, warm-hearted middle-aged man with a boyish demeanor. After we check into our rooms, outfitted with mosquito-netted platform beds and blankets, we hike deeper into the forest to a pond, where Roberto cleanses each one of us with cool rose-petal water. Once we arrive at the ceremonial hut, with its convenient built-in benches and mats, we take turns sitting on a tree stump while Roberto pats our bodies with a palm frond soaked with a pleasant cedar-scented perfume. I have been suffering from a terrible headache all day, but it magically disappears after these refreshing rituals. We take our seats on the benches, as Roberto and his younger assistant, Maria, sit behind a tree-carved altar, singing to and blessing their ayahuasca preparation. I wonder how the woman's presence might impact my experience. Again, my heart pounds with anxiety and expectation, and I glance at each of my travel mates, who seem to have slipped into their own expectant reveries.

My body trembles when Roberto calls me forward and presents me with a small gourd filled with the brew. Again, the taste is so bitter I can barely swallow. After about thirty minutes, I am surprised and relieved to find that I do not feel the same harsh physical sensations that I had the first time. I have more control of my motor skills and purge only once. Eventually, I slip into a calm, extremely relaxed state, enveloped by what seems to be a vast emptiness. This black emptiness takes on the appearance of outer space, illuminated by infinite tiny points of light, which I interpret to be stars and planets. It is the same miraculous sky I have seen at the jungle camp, only this time I am observing it from the inside, far beyond Earth. I am floating in the cosmos and feel myself expand to merge with it. I hear the words "we are all one," and see faces of the people I know and love. It doesn't make sense that they have individual bodies, which now seem more like boundaries separating us, because I know that we are all the same. As if to confirm this truth, a stream of liquid begins to pour out of the sky into a single glimmering crystal goblet; it seems to be the essence that unites us all. Lulled by the shamans' melodious singing and the rustle of their shacapas, I see a large pyramid and a tunnel of light, along with myriad giant plants and trees.

Then a frightening jaguar face appears, as it did during my first ayahuasca ceremony. I acknowledge that the jaguar is an animal of great power and ask her why she keeps coming to me. "Don't be afraid of your own power," she replies.

I repeat those words as I walk back through the darkness to my hut after the ceremony, grateful that mother ayahuasca had been so gentle with me this time. I am also grateful for her profound teaching.

The sense of unity consciousness stays with me as we leave the Upper Amazon for higher ground in the Andes. The jungle has pushed me beyond doubts and fears to the threshold of what I know myself to be. And there is nowhere to go but through the door.

We fly from Iquitos to the scenic city of Cusco, the ancient capital of the Inca Empire nestled high in the Andes Mountains at around eleven thousand feet. From the moment I step off the plane, I am enveloped by a warm, piercingly bright light, which I have rarely seen anywhere other than New Mexico. Unique for its stunning clarity, this light casts a golden glow upon everything it touches: the vibrant, geometric weavings and silver jewelry sold by indigenous Andean women and girls who wander the streets in native dress—colorful, embroidered jackets and shawls, skirts with petticoats, and bowler hats; the steep narrow cobblestone streets and red-tile roofs of old stone buildings, many of which still retain their original, seamless Inca walls; and the elegant fountain and profusion of flowers in the large central square, Plaza de Armas, which is flanked by three churches and a baroque cathedral constructed by the Spanish on sites once graced by sumptuous Inca palaces filled with gold. And over all tower the awesome, snow-capped mountains that hug the city, standing witness to centuries of grandeur and turmoil during the meteoric rise and fall of the Inca civilization from 1438 to 1533, when Spanish conquistadors invaded Cusco and destroyed much of the ancient culture.

Descendents of the Inca and other ancient cultures of the Andes believe that their mountains are the home of spirits or light beings called Apus, who must be revered and honored with ceremonies and accompanying offerings, or *despachos*, to ensure continued harmony between the spirit and human worlds. Indeed, all of nature is sacred, including the wind, rocks, trees, water, and sun and moon, as well as Mother Earth herself, whom they call Pachamama, the protector and sustainer of life. And their spirits must be honored in the same way, in an act of respect and reciprocity. In Andean cosmology, there is no separation between matter and spirit. Local shamans regularly "slip between 'cracks' in earth-time to enter this separate reality," where spirit beings dwell, explains author J. E. Williams in *The Andean Codex: Adventures and Initiations among the Peruvian Shamans.*

Cusco, which means "the navel of the world" in the local Quechua language, is shaped like a puma, an Andean totem animal symbolizing the power of the Inca Empire. Designed as a solar city, Cusco is activated by the solstices and equinoxes. For example, each year at the winter solstice, which in the southern hemisphere is on June 21, the rising sun ignites the energy of the city by lighting each street and sacred site within the puma's body, an important ceremonial event that the Inca once celebrated royally in the central square.

Along with Pachamama, Inti, or Father Sun, is central to the Andean spiritual tradition, which considers all human beings Children of the Sun. "Every day we enjoy the light and warmth of the physical Father Sun," wrote the Inca spiritual teacher Jorge Luis Delgado in *Andean Awakening: An Inca Guide to Mystical Peru.* "Behind our Father Sun we also have the 'Sun behind the sun,' or the Divine Presence, Who sends the life force energy through the Father Sun to Mother Earth for all people and all of nature. We receive this spiritual light energy in our spiritual body, from which it then flows to our physical body. In the spiritual body we can find the essence of the authentic self, for each of us is a unique ray from the same Sun."

One of the unfortunate byproducts of a stay in Cusco is altitude sickness, which can cause belabored breathing, nausea, vomiting, insomnia, and loss of appetite. Fortunately, I suffer only a headache and mild dizziness during our three-day stay. Locals combat altitude sickness by chewing coca leaves, a sacred plant that is native to the Andes. Coca, which increases the oxygen content in the blood, enhances energy and stamina and promotes a sense of well-being. It is also used as an offering of friendship and hospitality and in ceremonies to expand one's consciousness. Sean, our guide on this portion of the trip, gives each of us a stash of the pale green leaves, which I fold in half and place in the corner of my mouth, along with a small pinch of black bark paste that activates coca's healing properties. After about forty-five minutes of chewing, my headache and dizziness happily subside.

Wandering through Cusco's winding streets, I am rejuvenated by the pure mountain air and brilliant sunlight. As I relax on a bench in the Plaza de Armas, I lift my chest upward, allowing my heart to absorb this magnificent light—the simple healing technique that I learned on my journey to the sacred Mayan sites of the Yucatan. My eyes settle on the large white statue of Jesus with open arms that overlooks the city from a distant hilltop. I smile as the Beatles's song "All You Need Is Love" plays in a nearby café.

An old woman with a knot of gray hair and a sun-weathered face sits down beside me. She has a satchel of handcrafted jewelry, and she shows me her beautiful silver earrings and serpentine stone Inca crosses. But realizing that I am not interested, she quickly puts them away. She tells me her name is Esperanza, and she inquires about my travels, listening intently to my answers. Then she tells me about her family. After some minutes, she touches my arm with a warm smile and says, "Thank you for talking to me, my friend. I hope we meet again."

My heart expands, as I remember the spontaneous affection with which the Peruvians have greeted me over the past weeks. I have been in an ongoing state of *munay*, or love—the first of the three ancient Inca laws, which, when practiced, help us to live in harmony with the joy and abundance of the cosmos, Delgado explains in *Andean Awakening*. Showing love, respect, and gratitude toward all things connects us to our divinity.

Although Cusco has become a tourist mecca, home to an overflow of restaurants, cafés, and gift shops, the old way of life is still evident in the grassy, wooded highlands surrounding the city. Here, indigenous peoples, a few of whom can be seen from the roadside, grow potatoes and corn and herd sheep, llamas, and alpacas (of Peruvian sweater fame). One evening at sunset, we climb several hundred feet above the city to Sacsayhuamán, a sprawling Inca hilltop fortress and ceremonial center distinguished by massive zigzag walls of expertly joined boulders, stairways leading nowhere, and trapezoidal doorways. I am captivated by the magical quality of the site, especially the doorways, which seem to suggest an opening into other dimensions. I believe they are symbolic of the new gateways into my consciousness that I have been entering while in Peru.

My internal barriers increasingly seem to fall away, as we continue our voyage by van through the majestic Sacred Valley of the Incas, descending to warmer, lower altitudes and following the course of the Urubamba River, which eventually winds through the jungle to the Upper Amazon. In Andean cosmology, the Urubamba is a sacred river that mirrors the Milky Way, the sacred river in the sky. Sacred sites or power places within the Sacred Valley, built in alignment with solar and lunar events, represent particular constellations in the Milky Way, reaffirming the interrelationship between the earth and the heavens and the temporal and the Divine, according to a belief shared by the Maya and other ancient cultures. The Sacred Valley is breathtakingly beautiful, fringed by craggy, snow-capped mountain peaks and red granite cliffs, carpeted with lush green terraces and patchwork fields planted with fruits, vegetables, and grains, and studded with quaint villages and the remains of ancient palaces, temples, and fortresses. Our destination is Ollantaytambo, reportedly the best-preserved living Inca village in Peru, beyond which lies Machu Picchu, the legendary "lost city of the Incas." Throughout our journey, Machu Picchu has dangled in the far reaches of my imagination like a bright crystal, holding out the promise of another grand revelation. I grow excited as we approach what I believe will be the climax of my Peruvian adventure.

The temple-fortress town of Ollantaytambo greets us with golden, late-afternoon sunlight and the laughter of children, who run playfully around the central square and fountain and along the dusty narrow streets and canals, framed by pyramid-like mountains carved in terraces. High atop one of the terraces at cliff's edge sits the pre-Inca Temple of the Wind, built of huge boulders that seem to defy earthly engineering skills. The entire town, viewed from here, has the shape of a llama, another totem or power animal in the Andes, in addition to the puma, serpent, condor, hummingbird, and eagle. The llama, according to *Andean Awakening*, represents service to mankind in the Kay Pacha, the Middle World or earthly domain, symbolized by the puma. Uku Pacha is the Underground World, a mysterious realm symbolized by the snake to which we can release heavy energies—such as fear, pain, grief, and guilt—via Pachamama. Hanan Pacha, symbolized by the condor, represents the Upper World of divinity and light beings. These worlds comprise the three levels of the ancient Andean cross, or *chacana*, and are often represented by stone step-like carvings and patterns at ruins throughout the Sacred Valley.

One of the highlights of our stay in Ollantaytambo is a healing ceremony with another master teacher plant, San Pedro—a cactus found mainly in the Andes that contains the psycho-active alkaloid mescaline (like the peyote cactus of North America). San Pedro, slices of which are boiled for hours then cooled as a liquid, has been used and administered by shamans in Peru for millennia for healing and hallucinogenic purposes. Before we left the Amazon jungle, Peter explained that this sacred medicine develops the power of perception as well as the telepathic ability to transmit oneself across time and space. He also assured us that it would be less physically debilitating than ayahuasca—news that makes me sigh with relief. Nevertheless, I still have reservations about venturing into this new psychic territory, unsure how my body and mind might react.

As our group sits waiting on the patio of our small lodge in Ollantaytambo for Julio the shaman, I feel a rush of expectation. And I'm excited that there will be a full moon tonight, which should bring even more energy to our healing ceremony. Julio is nearly two hours late, and we grow impatient. But just as we begin to plan our own full-moon celebration, he shows up, a short stocky man with long black hair and a radiant smile. A woven medicine bag hangs over his shoulder. Julio explains the San Pedro ceremony via his translator, Gabriel, a soft-spoken young man, announcing that we will have a special feature in honor of the full moon: a sweat lodge. I am pleasantly surprised. I have long wanted to experience a sweat lodge, knowing it to be a sacred ritual of the Native Americans.

"There is only one hitch," Julio says. "We will all be naked in the sweat lodge." Naked?! I feel the color draining from my face. I know that not all sweat lodges have this requirement. We glance at each other, eyebrows raised.

"In the sweat lodge, we die a symbolic death in the womb of Mother Earth and are reborn as new beings. We do not come into the world with clothes on, do we?" Julio proclaims.

"Does anyone feel uncomfortable with this?" Sean, our guide, asks.

"I'm not thrilled about it," I volunteer. Everyone else remains quiet.

"Heck, you'll probably never see these people again," Sean says.

"Oh, who cares." I recall how much we have already been through together, but still I feel uneasy about the idea, given that most members of our group are men.

We head back to our rooms to retrieve towels and water bottles, before hopping into taxis that take us to a forest retreat center about twenty minutes away. Ignacio, a serene, white-bearded man and owner of the retreat, greets us warmly. He speaks eloquently of the great shift to higher consciousness that is occurring on the planet at this time, and how we must purify ourselves to be of service to humanity. I listen intently as we huddle around him, enveloped in mist, the full moon shining brilliantly behind a mountain peak, streaked by drifting clouds. We then proceed to a large, teepee-like wood-framed temple, where a red cloth covering the center of the floor serves as an altar, holding numerous rocks, crystals, and amulets. I sit down on one of the cushions forming a circle around the altar, aware that my heart is racing once again with both anticipation and trepidation. Julio kneels and begins singing and praying for our healing. He then explains that before we drink the first cup of San Pedro, we must ask forgiveness for all the hurts we've caused and received from others. The second and third cups will help us to heal ourselves of any imbalances, whether physical, spiritual, or emotional, and better manage the stresses of daily life; these last two doses are optional.

We cleanse ourselves with agua florida, the same way we did during the ayahuasca ceremony. Then Julio walks around our circle, offering each of us a gourd filled with the cactus potion. As I try to swallow the bitter drink, which is not as foul tasting as ayahuasca, Julio makes cross-like motions with his hands around my head. I am startled by this gesture, for I am the only one to receive it. I want to ask him what he is doing, but I know that would be hugely inappropriate in the middle of a silent ceremony. During the twenty-minute intervals between drinks, Julio and Gabriel prepare an offering, or *despacho*. While chanting, they fold and fill numerous small sheets of paper with dried grains and seeds and place them on the altar cloth, along with multi-colored confetti, cookie crumbs, candies, and a huge quartz crystal, which they arrange as a symbolic representation of the three-tiered Andean cosmos. I bravely choose to receive both the second and third drinks. After we finish the ceremony, Julio asks us to undress for the sweat lodge. So here we go. I wait anxiously for the San Pedro to take effect.

Wrapped in towels, we walk silently through the forest to a clearing dominated by a tiny mound-like structure covered with a plastic tarpaulin. One by one, we crawl inside naked and squat next to each other on the dirt floor. A young couple from Tenerife and a nurse from South Africa have joined our group, and we are packed like sardines. It is dark and warm inside. My friends' faces are barely visible. Julio and Ignacio begin shoveling hot coals into the central fire pit; our feet press precariously against its edges. They then dowse the coals with several buckets of water, producing clouds of steam that make me choke. The temperature rises, and the lodge becomes unbearably hot, almost suffocating. I sweat profusely, a symbolic purification. Scanning the lodge for a tiny rip in the tarpaulin, I wonder how long this will last. But, alas, there are no air pockets. I struggle to breathe, as Ignacio chants about the need for compassion and service and about how we must erase our old ego-centered ways and help those in need, particularly in the third world. He bemoans the tragedy of first-world decadence, referring particularly to the United States: "Life is not just about Coca Cola, cigarettes, and material gain!" I am initially moved by the power of his words. But as he repeats them, they begin to sound like an angry condemnation, and I realize that this "guru" has some issues. I know I am quick to judge him, and not wanting to feed negativity, I consciously return to neutrality.

Throughout the sweat lodge ceremony, I am challenged to rise above such judgments, not to mention the physical strain on my body. When will I experience the full effects of San Pedro—which at this point has left me feeling only mildly lightheaded? Mercifully, I feel no nausea.

Eventually, we pass around a gourd rattle and introduce ourselves, stating where we live and why we have come here. "I'm from New York, and I have come to be of service," I say, shaking the rattle. After the last person finishes, Julio lifts the small door flap. I am grateful for the gust of fresh air and wonder, hopefully, whether the ceremony has ended. Uuugggghhh, not yet. He unloads more hot coals, then another bucket of water, some of which sprinkles over us like rain. The steam thickens, and the lodge becomes even hotter. I feel like I am going to die. It is apparently time for round two. Everyone sighs. I become anxious, fearing that I may not be able to withstand the heat. My legs seem locked in place, and the dirt floor chafes my skin. I hear my heart pounding as Ignacio begins chanting again.

"Okay, we get it, we get it! Let's move this along, now," the South African nurse blurts. Everyone laughs. Someone starts singing "Row, Row, Row Your Boat," and we all join in with joyful silliness. Then we pass the rattle around again, thanking Mother Earth for her many blessings. Julio reminds us of our responsibility as bridges to a new age of consciousness, which the Inca called PachaKuti—the return to the essence of the cosmos. The Inca believed that there is a one thousand-year cosmic cycle, half of which represents daytime and half nighttime, according to *Andean Awakening*. We are now emerging from a period of darkness and beginning a new daytime cycle, or sunrise, which will awaken us to our divine essence and connection to the cosmos. I hear his words as if from a distance. I am still having trouble breathing, and my entire body is soaked. I have never sweated so profusely. Again, the men shovel hot coals into the pit, again the water and the suffocating burst of steam. For several moments, I sense that my body has dissolved, and we are only voices, one voice, in the darkness. It is a disorienting yet liberating sensation. I no longer care about how much time has elapsed, or even when the sweat lodge will end. Finally, Ignacio announces that we have been purified and reborn into a higher consciousness. It is another initiation, and I am grateful to have survived it.

We leave the lodge one by one, kissing Mother Earth at the threshold. As luck would have it, I am one of the first to crawl out, alarmingly aware that everyone has had a good view of my behind! It is misty and cool outside, the moon casting a surreal, opalescent glow from behind the distant mountain peaks. By now, I feel high from the San Pedro, as though I'm floating, yet I'm still able to keep my balance. Oh, oh. Everyone is hugging each other! Here we go again. I am careful not to let my eyes wander below each person's neck, as I stand comfortably at a distance while politely leaning over to pat their backs. As I pick up my towel, I notice a fully clothed man sitting on a log nearby. But it is too dark and I am too woozy to discern his face. I decide that it is probably one of the workers at the retreat. Yet I find it strange that someone would be observing all this.

"You're doing really well, really," Paula keeps saying as we head back to our rooms, as if in disbelief that I, the city girl from New York, has survived another challenging adventure intact.

The entire night I struggle to breathe through clogged sinuses. It is frightfully uncomfortable, and I wonder if I have had an allergic reaction to the cactus. The following day, exhausted and still recovering from my sinus condition, I am shocked to discover that the man who was sitting on the log at the sweat lodge, watching us cavort around naked, was Doug! He had decided, for health reasons, not to participate. I knew he was not in the sweat lodge with us but thought he had remained in the temple. Ha! For the whole trip, I'd tried so civilly to diffuse any potential sexual energy, only to find myself unknowingly parading naked in front of him! Thank you, San Pedro, for materializing my fear and expanding my perception. For showing me, metaphorically, that in order to become completely transparent to the light of our own best selves, our divine power, we must neither hide nor withhold anything.

Early the next morning, we depart for Machu Picchu, the crown jewel of our journey. The train from Ollantaytambo takes us through a deep gorge that descends into the jungle, threaded by the rushing, boulder-strewn Urubamba River, until we reach Aguas Calientes, the small ramshackle town at the foot of Machu Picchu that is named for its hot springs. I grow more excited as we quickly check into our hotel and hop onto a local bus that transports us up a series of switchbacks to the fabled Lost City of the Incas, majestically perched high atop a mountain surrounded by lush jungle. Having lain forgotten for centuries until the American archaeologist Hiram Bingham discovered it in 1911, Machu Picchu dazzles the eye with cascading emerald green terraces and the remains of ancient stone temples, houses, staircases, and trapezoidal doorways and windows, all of which are perfectly integrated with the breathtaking landscape.

Enveloped by clouds and mist and tree-carpeted mountain peaks that evoke a fantastical primeval world, the city is even more mystical and dramatic than the many images I've seen of it. Said to mean both "old peak/mountain" and "old bird" in the indigenous Quechua language, Machu Picchu at various vantage points takes on the shapes of both a lizard and condor in flight. The conical mountain framing it, called Huayna Picchu, or "young peak/ mountain," can be viewed as a crouching puma. These animals represent the Pacha, the three spiritually interconnected worlds of the Andean cosmos. Theories abound as to Machu Picchu's original purpose. Some archaeologists believe it could have served either as an exclusive religious complex, a coca plantation, or a royal Inca retreat.

I become anxious as we explore the sun-drenched ruins, stopping with our guide at such sacred sites as the Temple of the Condor (marked by a giant rock slab shaped like a condor's head), the Sun Temple, and the Hitching Post of the Sun (both once used as solar observatories). Unfortunately, the crowds are diminishing the power and intensity of this sanctuary, which feels very much alive to me. I wish I could spend time alone here.

Later that afternoon, after most of the tourists have left, Anna and her husband, Barry, and Doug and I stay behind to meditate in a grassy clearing near a cave along one of the ridges. We find our own places, leaning against the ancient rocks. Barry plays a Native American flute that he brought along. As I drift deeper into a meditative state, lulled by the enchanting flute music and the soft, nurturing energy that seems to permeate the entire city, a jaguar face emerges in my consciousness. At first I am taken aback, not expecting to meet this Amazonian beast again, especially in the mountains. I thought I had left her with my ayahuasca visions.

Then I hear the familiar words: "Don't be afraid of your power." Sitting here in this magnificent power place, I understand that this message may now contain another layer of meaning. So I ask the jaguar for her teaching. "You must use what you have learned," the voice continues. "Share your knowledge; heal others as you are healing yourself."

I repeat the words, overcome with gratitude, sensing that I have been welcomed into yet another level of consciousness, knowing intuitively that such initiations never end. I am now in my late forties. How deeply I desire to serve something greater than myself. I've received the appropriate message at the appropriate time, as I have recently studied and begun to practice a form of energy healing, a radical departure from my work as a journalist. I vow to stay open to new and more fulfilling directions on my life's path, as I contemplate the second Inca law, *llancay*, the law of service through meaningful work and the creative expression of one's individual gifts.

I become even more captivated by the message from my meditation, when Anna tells me that she has an intuition that Machu Picchu was likely used as a metaphysical school for training women priestesses and healers. I am stunned to find Anna's theory confirmed in *The Andean Codex*, which states that while Machu Picchu apparently served as a powerful ritual center, given the number of shrines used to observe the sun, its "primary purpose . . . was as a sanctuary for *akllas* (divine virgins of the sun) and *mamakunas* (wise women). It was the residence of the most powerful *layqas* (female sorcerers and healers) in the Incan empire."

That evening, back in Aguas Calientes, I have an opportunity to put my power to the test. We are sitting outdoors at a Mexican restaurant, having just finished dinner, when Sean, our guide, who has been drinking all day, unexpectedly decides to pick a fight with me. I have been talking casually to the others, still wrestling with my sinus discomfort from the San Pedro ceremony and sniffling profusely. Doug offers me a container of tiny herbal antihistamine pills, and I promptly take a few of them.

"Do you know what you're putting in your mouth!" Sean explodes. I turn to him, alarmed. "What are you putting into your mouth?!" he rants. "I didn't give you permission to do that. You should have asked my permission!"

We all exchange puzzled glances. No one says a word. Sean has fallen into a drunken rage. "I don't have to ask your permission for anything, Sean," I say. "I know exactly what I'm doing. I have traveled the world alone without your help for many years." My words are polite but fiery. Sean glares at me, surprised by my comeback. I stare him down and then continue my conversation with the others as he falls silent. Anna smiles at me with sisterly approval.

Later that evening, walking the streets of Aguas Calientes, we unexpectedly cross paths with Julio, the shaman who had directed our San Pedro ceremony in Ollantaytambo just days earlier. He decided at the last minute to come here with his friend, the South African nurse, who had not yet seen the site. I had wanted to ask Julio about the ceremony and his curious blessing for me, and now here he is, presenting just that opportunity. I am thrilled that my intention has materialized.

"Julio, why did you make those hand motions around my head before you offered me the San Pedro?" I ask, after we've posed for a group photograph.

"I saw some blocked energy around your sinuses and cleared it so you can breathe better," he says, smiling. "It's working its way out now, which is why you probably feel some discomfort."

I am astounded. Julio had identified the chronic sinusitis that has been plaguing me for years. "That is exactly what's happening. My sinuses are still clogged, and now it seems like I may be getting a cold." I sniffle into a Kleenex.

He gently touches my shoulder. "You will feel better soon."

"Thank you very much, Julio," I hug him. We happily pose for another group picture before he darts off with his friend.

The following day, Anna and I trek up to Machu Picchu for one last visit. Thankfully, there are fewer crowds this time, allowing us to explore the site with little distraction. We lean against some of the massive boulders to feel their ancient energy. My pulse races, and my fingers tingle. Then my entire body begins to buzz. It feels as if I have just plugged myself into an electrical current. I recall my similar experiences in the Outback, Egypt, and the Yucatan. The local guide yesterday said that there is a lot of quartz crystal in the boulders, thus the energy blast. As we climb along the crumbling rocks, weaving in and out of various chambers, we are greeted by a host of creatures. Tiny rabbits and lizards scurry in and out of caves and crevasses. A chinchilla eyes us curiously, while llamas graze the grassy terraces. Standing in a chamber, engaged in an intense conversation about love, faith, and trusting our inner guidance, we notice that a large spider has suddenly stopped in its tracks on a nearby rock, seemingly eavesdropping. Surprisingly, it does not stir when a group of tourists nearly trample it to death. Time seems to have stopped, for we find that we have passed nearly an hour at this spot, though it feels like minutes.

Once again, I am drawn to the trapezoidal doorways framing the misty mountains like works of land art. I stand cautiously inside one of them, peering out over the edge of a cliff. One more step would send me on a free fall nearly one thousand feet into the stunning, river-carved valley below. I gaze into the mist. The lush, cloud-ringed mountains appear insubstantial, as if I am viewing them through waves of air or energy pockets, suggesting other dimensional realities. My body becomes lighter with each breath. I feel like I'm floating. It is the same disorienting yet liberating sensation I had in the sweat lodge, as though I'm dematerializing. I feel as if I have slipped into a dimension in which I have connected deeply with Spirit and my own divine essence. And I realize that Machu Picchu itself is such a doorway, a portal of transcendence that offers us the opportunity to dive even further within. Peering into the abyss below, I consider the third Inca law, *yachay*, the law of wisdom that allows us to access our authentic selves and live in harmony and unity with the cosmos. By consistently practicing munay, llancay and yachay, we can continue to evolve spiritually, according to the Inca.

I slowly step back from the doorway, filled with gratitude for what Machu Picchu has taught me. In Peru, I have crossed intoxicating thresholds of new growth and expansion. My life seems more mythic and magical. And I more fully embrace my own power, trusting that I can manifest everything I desire, in service to a higher purpose. "You are given the gifts of the gods to create your reality according to your beliefs," wrote Jane Roberts in *The Nature of Personal Reality*. "Yours is the creative energy that makes your world. There are no limitations to the self except those you believe in."

AFTERWORD

Reflecting on each of these soul journeys, I realize that I cannot adequately describe their impact on my day-to-day life now without revisiting the early groundwork that made them possible. In the years prior to my Outback adventure, in my mid-twenties, I began freelancing with considerable ambition, single-minded focus, and a high tolerance for risk. My first assignments came while I was living in Paris, indulging a long-held, bohemian writer's dream. From the Left Bank to Manhattan, typewriter to laptop, the *International Herald Tribune* to the *New York Times*, the articles piled up, rewarding me with a sense of professional accomplishment, which, naturally, came with its share of struggles. Along the way, I was privileged to meet and interview many noted figures, including His Highness the Aga Khan, writers Toni Morrison and Erica Jong, choreographer Twyla Tharp, architect Richard Meier, and artists Kiki Smith and Louise Bourgeois.

When friends ask how I launched myself as a journalist, I tell them about the time I waited in a magazine office for several hours, refusing to leave until I saw the editor. Little did I know in my brazen youth that all my hard work was not necessarily about worldly achievement and success. For by the time I had traveled a good part of the globe, it became clear that the real reward was not outside of me, but rather inside, through the seemingly inadvertent yet divinely guided journey into my own soul. After each of these soul journeys, I returned home transformed, with a deeper understanding of the laws of the universe and of myself, knowing that inner transformation is never-ending, as long as I remain open and willing to confront and cross my growth edges, no matter how uncomfortable the process.

Each soul journey left its own particular imprint on my consciousness, igniting some enriching shifts in my life. For example, the sensual, earth-based teachings of the Outback inspired me to find more pleasure simply being in my body, which led me to the Latin and Egyptian dances that continue to fill me with their own uplifting magic. Whenever I feel out of sorts, using the Mayan mantra "In Lak'ech, A Lak'en" (I am you, you are me), and recalling the deep feeling it stirred within, helps me to forgive others and myself more easily. The excessive noise and frenzied chaos of the city's streets extracts less of a toll on my psyche when I meditate on the words "Lord Have Mercy" with each step, which instantly transports me to the sacred wild beauty of New Mexico. Adopting the Tibetans' uncompromising faith helps me to trust that a higher guiding force is compassionately conspiring on my behalf. When doubts, worries, and fears threaten my equanimity, the ancient Egyptian mysteries remind me to step out of my own way into the universal flow of abundance. The increased frequency and speed with which synchronicities and manifestations are transpiring suggest that I am getting better at this. When my heart weighs heavy with sorrow and grief, I merge with the all-seeing bodhisattvas of Angkor to find my way back to center. And the multidimensional consciousness that I tapped into in Peru continues to help me meet each challenge with renewed courage and self-empowerment.

But perhaps the most powerful cumulative effect of these soul journeys is that I am better able to balance and activate the chakras they stimulated, which allows me greater access to my fullest potential. As a result, my desire and ability to be of service to others continues to deepen and expand.

Of course, I have found that my inward journey does not always require an outward journey to a far-flung corner of the world (though I admit to being a bit of an "adventure" addict). For it has continued through retreats and workshops closer to home and with my renewed commitment to daily practices like meditation, guided visualizations, and prayer. The wisdom and greater self-knowledge that I gained from my soul journeys have inspired me to investigate a number of other spiritual disciplines with many well-known teachers. In addition to the Vipassana meditation and kundalini yoga I practiced early on, these have included Sufi rituals, transcendental meditation, feng shui, a residency at Nine Gates Mystery School, shamanic healing, and several other healing modalities.

Although friends have often teased that I seem to be taking too many "retreats" from everyday life, I have in fact found that frequent retreats into my deepest self have had just the opposite effect. They have allowed me to engage more fully in my daily activities with greater presence and heart-centered awareness. This mostly expresses itself not in grand dramatic moments but in quotidian events, gestures, and interactions that I once overlooked or failed to appreciate. For example, I have found myself moving more slowly and thoughtfully through my days (not an easy task for a New Yorker!), which means that I don't race to catch the subway train or beat the changing stoplight. I don't overload myself with too many tasks in a single day, having struck a better balance between being and doing. This inner spaciousness has helped me to feel more centered, peaceful, and receptive. I take more time to chat with my neighbors, the doormen, and the kids in the elevator, and I try to acknowledge the efforts of others. I find that I am smiling more and worrying less (a tough one), listening more attentively and consciously indulging my senses—whether it's noticing a beautiful architectural detail, enjoying the crisp, fresh scent of autumn leaves, or savoring a delicious meal. I use more discernment before taking action, and I am more aware in the moment of my own energy dynamic as well as that of others. Even in a city like New York, I have developed more tolerance, whether for the surly waiter, the lost taxi driver, or the disgruntled salesperson. I notice that I'm not as likely to be unhinged by events beyond my control. And I am able to "see" with my heart, my true compass, with more clarity and compassion.

Like every other human, I am not *always* blissful and free of discord. But as a result of the many wonderful insights and teachings I received on these soul journeys, and the ongoing expansion they have fueled, I find that I am able to sustain states of joy, love, and gratitude over longer periods of time. It's not about "acting as if" anymore but about fully embracing my power and aligning my will with divine Will in service to Spirit and all that emanates from it. It's about truly walking the walk. Indeed, I would not want my epitaph to read like the one I saw in a funny *New Yorker* cartoon: "Here lies [Dana]. She talked the talk but didn't walk the walk."

As we grow in our collective spiritual evolution, we are being challenged to be all that we are and have always been—mystics, magicians, lovers, and ambassadors of light—knowing that at the eye of the earthly storm raging around us lies an immense inner peace, where every thought, word, and breath becomes a prayer when we are truly present. Each day brings new remembrances of our divinity, the divine Presence in all beings, and our eternal connection to each other. I am so grateful to be here *NOW* . . . with you.

BIBLIOGRAPHY

Arguelles, Jose. *The Mayan Factor: Path beyond Technology*. Santa Fe, NM: Bear & Company, 1996.

Babbitt, Irving, trans. The Dhammapada. New York: New Directions, 1965.

Barks, Coleman, trans. *The Essential Rumi*. San Francisco: Harper San Francisco, 1996.

Batchelor, Stephen. *The Tibet Guide*. Boston: Wisdom, 1998.

Black Elk, Nicholas, and John G. Neihardt. *Black Elk Speaks*. Lincoln, NE: University of Nebraska Press, 2000.

Blavatsky, H. P. *Isis Unveiled*. Pasadena, CA: Theosophical University Press, 1976.

Bryan, Betsy M., and Erik Hornung, eds. *The Quest for Immortality: Treasures of Ancient Egypt*. Washington, D.C.: National Gallery of Art and Prestel, 2002.

Burroughs, William, and Allen Ginsberg. *The Yage Letters Redux*. San Francisco: City Lights, 2006.

Campbell, Joseph. *The Hero with a Thousand Faces*. Princeton: Princeton University Press, 1973.

Chatwin, Bruce. *The Songlines*. New York: Penguin, 1988.

Craig, Mary. *Tears of Blood: A Cry for Tibet*. Washington, D.C.: Counterpoint, 1999.

Davies, Stevan, trans. *The Gospel of Thomas*. Woodstock, VT: Skylight Paths, 2004.

Delgado, Jorge Luis. *Andean Awakening: An Inca Guide to Mystical Peru*. San Francisco: Council Oak, 2006.

Dostoyevsky, Fyodor. *The Brothers Karamazov*. New York: The Modern Library, Random House, 1996.

Dunne, Claire. *Carl Jung: Wounded Healer of the Soul*. New York: Parabola, 2000.

Eastman, Charles A. *The Soul of the Indian*. Lincoln, NE: University of Nebraska Press, 1911.

Eliot, T. S. *Four Quartets*. New York: Harcourt Brace Jovanovich, 1971.
_____. *Selected Poems*. New York: Harcourt Brace Jovanovich, 1964.

Flaubert, Gustav. *Flaubert in Egypt*. Translated and edited by Frances Steegmuller. New York: Penguin, 1996.

Foundation for Inner Peace. *A Course in Miracles*. Mill Valley, CA: Foundation for Inner Peace, 1992.

Fremantle, Francesca, and Chogyam Trungpa, trans. *The Tibetan Book of the Dead*. Boston: Shambhala, 1987.

Grof, Stanislav. *Books of the Dead: Manuals for Living and Dying*. New York: Thames and Hudson, 1994.

Guenther, Herbert V., trans. *The Jewel Ornament of Liberation by sGam. po.pa*. Boston: Shambhala, 1986.

Hamilton, R. *Ancient Egypt: Kingdom of the Pharaohs*. Bath, UK: Paragon, 2005.

Hanh, Thich Nhat. *The Miracle of Mindfulness*. Boston: Beacon, 1987.

Harrer, Heinrich. *Seven Years in Tibet*. New York: Jeremy P. Tarcher/ Putnam, 1997.

H. H. the Dalai Lama. *The Meaning of Life from a Buddhist Perspective*. Translated and edited by Jeffrey Hopkins. Boston: Wisdom, 1992.

Hornung, Erik. *Conceptions of God in Ancient Egypt*. Ithaca, NY: Cornell University Press, 1982.

Huxley, Aldous. *The Doors of Perception and Heaven and Hell*. New York: HarperCollins, 2004.

James, Henry. *The Beast in the Jungle*. Mineola, NY: Dover, 1993.

Jenkins, John Major. *Maya Cosmogenesis 2012*. Santa Fe, NM: Bear & Company, 1998.

Judith, Anodea. *Wheels of Life: A User's Guide to the Chakra System*. Woodbury, MN: Llewellyn, 1987.

Jung, C. G. *Alchemical Studies*. Vol. 13 of *The Collected Works of C. G. Jung*. Princeton: Princeton University Press, 1976.

_____. *Memories, Dreams, Reflections*. New York: Vintage, 1989.

Kerouac, Jack. *On the Road*. New York: Viking, 1957.

Lamy, Lucie. *Egyptian Mysteries: New Light on Ancient Knowledge*. New York: Thames and Hudson, 1981.

Lawlor, Robert. *Voices of the First Day: Awakening in the Aboriginal Dreamtime*. Rochester, VT: Inner Traditions, 1991.

Leadbeater, C. W. *The Chakras*. Wheaton, IL: Quest Books, 1972.

Mahfouz, Naguib. *Palace Walk*. Vol. 1 of *The Cairo Trilogy*. New York: Anchor, Doubleday, 1990.

Men, Hunbatz. *Secrets of Mayan Science / Religion*. Santa Fe, NM: Bear & Company, 1990.

Merton, Thomas: *Thoughts in Solitude*. New York: Farrar, Straus and Giroux, 1999.

_____. *The Wisdom of the Desert*. New York: New Directions, 1970.

Mitchell, Stephen, trans. Bhagavad Gita. New York: Three Rivers, 2000.

_____. *The Selected Poetry of Rainer Maria Rilke*. New York: Vintage, 1982.

Mouhot, Henri. *Henri Mouhot's Diary: Travels in the Central Parts of Siam, Cambodia, and Laos during the Years 1858–61*. New York: Oxford University Press, 1966.

Neruda, Pablo, *The Sea and the Bells*. Translated by William O'Daly. Port Townsend, WA: Copper Canyon, 2002.

Parker, K. Langloh, and Johanna Lambert. *Wise Women of the Dreamtime*. Rochester, VT: Inner Traditions International, 1993.

Roberts, Jane. *The Nature of Personal Reality*. San Rafael, CA: Amber-Allen and New World Library, 1994.

Spilsbury, Ariel, and Michael Bryner. *The Mayan Oracle: Return Path to the Stars*. Santa Fe, NM: Bear & Company, 1992.

Talbot, Michael. *The Holographic Universe*. New York: HarperCollins, 1991.

Tedlock, Dennis, trans. *Popol Vuh: The Definitive Edition of the Mayan Book of the Dawn of Life and the Glories of Gods and Kings*. New York: Simon & Shuster, 1996.

Watts, Alan W. *The Wisdom of Insecurity*. New York: Pantheon, 1951.

Williams, J. E. *The Andean Codex: Adventures and Initiations Among the Peruvian Shamans*. Charlottesville, VA: Hampton Roads, 2005.

Wolf, Fred Alan. *Taking the Quantum Leap: The New Physics for Non-Scientists*. New York: Harper & Row, 1989.

INDEX

About the Author

Dana Micucci is a journalist who specializes in culture, art, and travel as well as social and spiritual issues. Over the past twenty-five years, she has written for the *International Herald Tribune,* the *New York Times,* the *Chicago Tribune, Architectural Digest, Veranda, House Beautiful, Harper's Bazaar, Town & Country,* and *Art & Antiques,* among other publications, having served as a contributing editor at several of them. She is the author of *Artists in Residence: A Guide to the Homes and Studios of Eight 19th-Century Painters in and around Paris; Best Bids: The Insider's Guide to Buying at Auction;* and *Collector's Journal.* Ms. Micucci was formerly a senior publicist at Christie's, the international art auction house. She holds a B.A. and an M.A. in English from Northwestern University and a certificate from Columbia University's Creative Writing Program, where she was a senior writing fellow. She divides her time between New Mexico and New York City.

Quest Books

encourages open-minded inquiry into
world religions, philosophy, science, and the arts
in order to understand the wisdom of the ages,
respect the unity of all life, and help people explore
individual spiritual self-transformation.

Its publications are generously supported by
The Kern Foundation,
a trust committed to Theosophical education.

Quest Books is the imprint of
the Theosophical Publishing House,
a division of the Theosophical Society in America.
For information about programs, literature,
on-line study, membership benefits, and international centers,
see www.theosophical.org
or call 800-669-1571 or (outside the U.S.) 630-668-1571.

To order books or a complete Quest catalog,
call 800-669-9425 or (outside the U.S.) 630-665-0130.

Related Quest Titles

Dreams of Isis, A Woman's Spiritual Sojourn, by Normandi Ellis
The Feminine Face of Buddhism, by Gill Farrer-Halls
In Search of the Sacred, by Rick Jarow
Pilgrimage, by David Souden
Sacred Space, Sacred Sound, by Susan Elizabeth Hale
The Shaman and the Medicine Wheel, by Evelyn Eaton
Shamanism, edited by Shirley J. Nicholson
The Traveler's Key to Ancient Egypt, by John Anthony West
The World of the Dalai Lama, by Gill Farrer-Halls

To order books or a complete Quest catalog,
call 800-669-9425 or (outside the U.S.) 630-665-0130.